Monetary Union and Fiscal Stability

Contributions to Economics

Christoph M. Schneider
Research and Development Management: From the Soviet Union to Russia
1994. ISBN 3-7908-0757-5

Lars Olof Persson/Ulf Wiberg
Microregional Fragmentation
1995. ISBN 3-7908-0855-5

Ernesto Felli/Furio C. Rosati/Giovanni Tria (Eds.)
The Service Sector: Productivity and Growth
1995. ISBN 3-7908-0875-X

Giovanni Galizzi/Luciano Venturini (Eds.)
Economics of Innovation: The Case of Food Industry
1996. ISBN 3-7908-0911-X

David T. Johnson
Poverty, Inequality and Social Welfare in Australia
1996. ISBN 3-7908-0942-X

Rongxing Guo
Border-Regional Economics
1996. ISBN 3-7908-0943-8

Oliver Fratzscher
The Political Economy of Trade Integration
1996. ISBN 3-7908-0945-4

Ulrich Landwehr
Industrial Mobility and Public Policy
1996. ISBN 3-7908-0949-7

Arnold Picot/Ekkehard Schlicht (Eds.)
Firms, Markets, and Contracts
1996. Corr. 2nd printing 1997
ISBN 3-7908-0947-0

Thorsten Wichmann
Agricultural Technical Progress and the Development of a Dual Economy
1997. ISBN 3-7908-0960-8

Ulrich Woitek
Business Cycles
1997. ISBN 3-7908-0997-7

Michael Carlberg
International Economic Growth
1997. ISBN 3-7908-0995-0

Massimo Filippini
Elements of the Swiss Market for Electricity
1997. ISBN 3-7908-0996-9

Frank Hoster/Heinz Welsch/Christoph Böhringer
CO_2 Abatement and Economic Structural Change in the European Internal Market
1997. ISBN 3-7908-1020-7

Christian M. Hafner
Nonlinear Time Series Analysis with Applications to Foreign Exchange Rate Volatility
1997. ISBN 3-7908-1041-X

Sardar M.N. Islam
Mathematical Economics of Multi-Level Optimisation
1998. ISBN 3-7908-1050-9

Sven-Morten Mentzel
Real Exchange Rate Movements
1998. ISBN 3-7908-1081-9

Lei Delsen/Eelke de Jong (Eds.)
The German and Dutch Economies
1998. ISBN 3-7908-1064-9

Mark Weder
Business Cycle Models with Indeterminacy
1998. ISBN 3-7908-1078-9

Tor Rødseth (Ed.)
Models for Multispecies Management
1998. ISBN 3-7908-1001-0

Michael Carlberg
Intertemporal Macroeconomics
1998. ISBN 3-7908-1096-7

continued on page 226

Frank Bohn

Monetary Union and Fiscal Stability

A New Approach

With 17 Figures
and 5 Tables

Physica-Verlag
A Springer-Verlag Company

Series Editors
Werner A. Müller
Martina Bihn

Author
Dr. Frank Bohn
Alfred Weber-Institut (AWI)
University of Heidelberg
Grabengasse 14
69117 Heidelberg
Germany
email: Frank.Bohn@mail.awi.uni-heidelberg.de
Internet: http://www.uni-heidelberg.de/institute/fak18/institut/awi/ls_siebke/home_bohn.html

Europäisches Institut für Internationale
Wirtschaftsbeziehungen (EIIW)
University of Potsdam
August-Bebel-Straße 89
14482 Potsdam
Germany
email: bohn@rz.uni-potsdam.de
Internet: http://www.euroeiiw.de/eiiwlink/bohn.html

ISBN 3-7908-1266-8 Physica-Verlag Heidelberg New York

Cataloging-in-Publication Data applied for
Die Deutsche Bibliothek – CIP-Einheitsaufnahme
Bohn, Frank: Monetary union and fiscal stability: a new approach / Frank Bohn. – Heidelberg: Physica-Verl., 2000
ISBN 3-7908-1266-8

Softcover-Design: Erich Kirchner, Heidelberg

SPIN 10750398 88/2202-5 4 3 2 1 0 – Printed on acid-free paper

Foreword by Andrew Hughes Hallett

Monetary Union in Europe began, for 11 countries, on 1 January 1999. Others will no doubt join later. However, from a strictly economic perspective, discussions on the design of monetary unions, and the desirability of joining one, have been most conspicuous by their absence. Descriptive material, usually emphasising either the benefits or the costs in general terms, we have in great quantities. But serious assessments based on quantitative evaluations of the costs, benefits and likely consequences of monetary union in general - and of the policies associated with it - are few and far between. There may be many reasons for that; but among the most important must be the fact that the analysis seldom leads to clear cut answers. There is always an element of compromise, and of balancing costs against benefits. The assessment will vary country by country and across different policy scenarios. That makes a quantitative study both inevitable and indispensable - not only because we have to determine whether the net impact of all these changes will be big or small, positive or negative; but more importantly because we have to identify the essential trade-offs which joining countries must meet and resolve.

Frank Bohn's book does just that, which is a valuable step forward. But it does more than that. By examining what might have happened with a hypothetical monetary union some ten years earlier and thereby explicitly including the transition phase, he is able to explain a number of outcomes which have now become apparent in the actual EMU. For example, the early weakness of the Euro; the conditions necessary for a lasting fiscal consolidation; the trade-off between interest and exchange rate changes and their consequences for the real side of the economy; the implicit asymmetries which, given different positions on these crucial trade-offs, explain the differences observed in the success of the "periphery" countries but the lack of success in the "core" countries. Not only do these results give new insights into how a monetary union actually works and what we can expect from it. The fact that these results can explain many of the events on the real side and in the financial markets that were not predicted before, is a powerful tribute to the value and importance of this type of research.

October 1999

Andrew Hughes Hallett
University of Strathclyde
Glasgow

Preface

The European Monetary Union (EMU) was established on 1 January 1999. Advanced economies voluntarily gave up their national control over monetary policies to form a monetary union. This is a historically unique event. However, it may only be the start of a series of similar moves: consider recent suggestions for monetary unions in South East Asia and Latin America as well as the Argentinean proposal for a unilateral monetary union with the US. At the same time, other European countries are trying to join the EMU.

Since the decision to form the EMU was taken, three sets of issues have been discussed: (i) the institutional set-up of the EMU; (ii) the medium and long term impact of the EMU; and (iii) the macroeconomic implications of the transition to the EMU. The third set of issues contains two big themes: effects produced by fiscal policies to comply with the Maastricht Criteria; and the impact of interest and exchange rate adjustments (caused by any monetary union) on the real economy of individual countries. The literature has focused on the former issue while largely ignoring the latter one.

However, a monetary union typically produces (considerable) changes of interest and exchange rates in prospective member countries. In this treatise it is shown that these impulses and their joint real effects are not always obvious. Furthermore, it is argued that the impact of fiscal consolidation policies can only be understood against the background of specific interest and exchange rate impulses caused by joining a monetary union.

More specific results go beyond the assessment of the impact of monetary unions in general. For instance, macroeconomic effects can be inferred for newly joining members, especially for Eastern Central European EMU candidates like Hungary, Poland, Slovenia, or the Czech Republic. Moreover, it is argued that fiscal consolidation policies may lead to a weak Euro if the European Central Bank sticks to a prespecified monetary target. This may be an additional explanation (besides the boom in the US and the Kosova crisis) for the depreciation of the Euro in the first half of 1999.

To study the implications of interest and exchange rate impulses it is necessary to account for the transition to a monetary union explicitly. Notwithstanding the Lucas Critique, it is shown that such a structural break can be modeled within the framework of a standard dynamic multi-country simulation model, as long as results are interpreted qualitatively, not quantitatively. To do this, a new approach involving innovations in the solution methodology had to be developed. The trick here is to endogenously generate a steady state solution which is consistent with the short term dynamics produced by the model. This approach may also be applied to structural breaks in other contexts, such as allowing for realignments in a pegged exchange rate system.

The idea for this thesis was born, and some preliminary work mainly on the simulation model done, during an 18 month visit to Princeton University. The development of the treatise in terms of contents and methodology was stimulated by Andrew Hughes Hallett and Peter Kenen. I am indebted to them for their longlasting support.

The thesis was, however, submitted at the Economics Department of Heidelberg University under the title "Monetary Union and the Trade-off between Interest and Exchange Rate Impulses". For his general support, for providing office space, and for discussions in the early stages of my thesis, I would like to thank very much my thesis adviser, Jürgen Siebke. For helpful discussions and comments, I am also very grateful to Arno Bäcker, Ralph Bryant, Switgard Feuerstein, Jürgen von Hagen, Stefan Lutz, Yue Ma, Paul Masson, Marcus Miller, Christoph Schmidt, Steve Symansky, Karl-Heinz Tödter, and Paul Welfens. Technical assistance was provided by Gary Burns and Dirk Jennerjahn.

For their continuing moral support I am very thankful to Arno Bäcker, Wolfgang Eichhorn, Malte Faber, Andy Hughes Hallett, Peter Kenen, and Paul Welfens. This so-called human competence is sometimes even more significant than any material help. Of course, I am much obliged to my wife who made my work possible. Above all, I am indebted to my son Frederik without whom the thesis would have been written in half the time. He did, however, provide me with the everyday joy and distractions necessary for recharging my batteries.

Financial support by Princeton University, the International Finance Section (Princeton), the Deutscher Akademischer Austauschdienst, the Landesgraduiertenförderung, and the BMW Stiftung is gratefully acknowledged.

September 1999 Frank Bohn

Table of Contents

1 Introduction

Forming or joining a monetary union requires acceptance of a common currency and a common central bank irrespective of cross-country differences in initial conditions. This is sometimes called the "one-size-fits-all" problem. From the perspective of an individual country, the common monetary policy induces *interest rate impulses* relative to interest rates obtained under national monetary autonomy, because short term nominal interest rates are equalized across the union. At the same time, national currencies are irrevocably fixed to the common currency at certain conversion rates. Compared to exchange rates that would have obtained without monetary union, there are *exchange rate impulses* which depend on the procedure for fixing conversion rates – as shown in this treatise. Both nominal impulses exhibit macroeconomic effects in a monetary union.

Despite these known facts, the discussion on the European Monetary Union (EMU) largely focused on political issues, in particular on which countries were likely to qualify under the so-called Maastricht Criteria[1]. The Economist (11 April 1998a) even com-

---

[1] The Maastricht Convergence Criteria are specified in the Treaty on the European Union (EU, 1992, article 109 j (1)) as well as attached protocols (cf. ÖNB, 1995, 107-111). They were reference points for judging the degree of convergence as required for the EMU. The idea was twofold: to make the formation of the EMU a smooth process, and to ensure its sustainability. Each country's macroeconomic performance was to be scrutinized in terms of inflation rate (not more than 1.5 % above the rate of the - three - countries with the best price stability record), average long term nominal interest rate (not more than 2 % above the one of those same - three - countries), government budget deficit (not primary deficit; deficit-GDP-ratio of not more than 3 %), national debt (debt-GDP-ratio of not more than 60 %), and exchange rate (inside normal band of the Exchange Rate Mechanism (ERM) of the European Monetary System (EMS), i.e. not more than $\pm 2\frac{1}{4}$ % fluctuations

plains that the "debate about its potential effects has been notable for its absence".[2] This is not entirely true, but some aspects, especially the aforementioned interest and exchange rate impulses, seem to have been ignored in contributions by economists.

Interest and exchange rate impulses can only be captured if the transition to the EMU *and* the period after its actual start are included in the same model. In a multi-country setting, this is virtually impossible within the framework of a small theoretical model.[3] Therefore, this treatise resorts to a comparative simulation analysis based on various specifications of a counterfactual European Monetary Union as of the 1980s (henceforth hypothetical EMU). This approach was chosen despite general problems with large econometric models and arduous specific adjustments which had to be made for the purpose of this study.

In the literature, costs and benefits of the EMU have already been assessed by comparing results accounting for aspects of the EMU to outcomes under alternative conditions. This is done in simulation analyses using calibrated or estimated models. In a first strand of papers, Hughes Hallett and McAdam (1998a and

---

of exchange rates around a central parity, and no unilateral depreciations).

[2] In his review article on EMU history, issues and literature, Wyplosz (1997) goes one step further. He regrets that "we [as economists] are unable to compute them [the costs and benefits of monetary union] with any precision." Some attempts to assess costs and benefits are, however, mentioned further down in this introduction.

[3] Clausen (1998), for instance, comes close to tackling interest and exchange rate impulses by discussing the "inappropriate choice of the conversion rates" (relating to the exchange rate impulse) and the "uncertainty with respect to the future stance of monetary policy" (relating to the interest rate impulse). But his small theoretical model does not allow him to capture interest rate impulses for individual countries caused by the *transition* to a common monetary policy. Nor does he evaluate the *joint* effect of interest and exchange rate impulses.

b) and von Hagen and Lutz (1996) investigate the macroeconomic repercussions of attempts to implement the fiscal convergence criteria of the Maastricht Treaty. In particular, their results point to inconsistencies between nominal and fiscal criteria. They use full scale macroeconomic models (MULTIMOD – also employed here – and the Taylor (1993a) model, respectively) to analyze fiscal adjustments prior to the start of the EMU (cf. further discussion in subsection 8.1). They do not, however, model the EMU itself.

Other papers simulate the EMU after its start, but do not capture effects caused by its formation. Hughes Hallett and Ma (1996) examine the implications of fiscal consolidations by using a calibrated Dornbusch model with two small countries to form a monetary union. Based on the same model, Hughes Hallett and Vines (1993) advocate fiscal flexibility by analyzing the effects of asymmetric shocks. Masson and Melitz (1991) arrive at similar conclusions. Based on a three-country-version of MULTIMOD, they analyze the response to symmetric shocks when national preferences differ. In the former two papers, bilateral conversion rates result from solving a joint optimization problem for the two countries of the monetary union. In the latter, market exchange rates of the reference model are imposed as conversion rates.

This treatise differs from the existing literature in several respects. First and most importantly, the structural break resulting from the transition to a monetary union is modeled explicitly to capture the aforementioned interest and exchange rate impulses. Relative to a situation without monetary union, these nominal impulses occur year after year. The main finding of this treatise is that, each year, there is a potential trade-off between these two impulses. They affect the macroeconomic outcome of any monetary union year after year – relative to a situation without monetary union. In fact, joining a monetary union can be interpreted as a *permanent* asymmetric shock originating in structural changes to monetary policy. Modeling the transition explicitly also allows to capture anticipation effects in the run-up to the monetary union.

Second, various procedures for fixing conversion rates are discussed (henceforth conversion procedures). By doing so, results can not only be applied to the real world EMU as of 1999, but also to future members of the real world EMU or any other monetary union (based on a different conversion procedure). Other potential changes caused by a monetary union are abstracted from, for instance, a shift in the monetary stability orientation of the European Central Bank, further asymmetric shocks, potential efficiency gains, or various conceivable adjustments of agents' behavior. Fiscal convergence criteria à la Maastricht are only introduced as an extension in the final part.

This treatise is organized in three parts. Part I (sections 2 to 4) covers the major aspects of the economic and methodical background of the analysis. Section 2 discusses the model and the simulation strategy. Section 3 accounts for model changes to capture the features of a hypothetical EMU as defined in this treatise. Section 4 examines some methodical specifications and limitations of the simulation analysis focusing on sensitivity analyses and changes to the solution algorithm.

Part II (sections 5 to 7) is based on previously published papers.[4] Simulation results are presented and related to the real world EMU as of 1999 in three steps. Section 5 offers quantitative simulation results for the hypothetical EMU. In section 6,

---

[4] Bohn, 1997, 1998a and b. They also cover aspects of part I and appendix A.

the causes for nominal impulses are identified and their transmission on the real side is analyzed. The aforementioned potential trade-off between interest and exchange rate impulses is substantiated. In section 7, qualitative findings are applied to the real world EMU. Furthermore, some indications for economic limitations and possible extensions of the analysis are provided.

In part III (sections 8 and 9), one of these extensions is taken up and analyzed in detail – to emphasize the relevance of interest and exchange rate impulses for the current political debate on fiscal stability. In a case study for Italy, fiscal consolidations are examined in a situation without monetary union (section 8) and under the conditions of the hypothetical EMU (section 9). In addition to the potential interest-exchange trade-off revealed in section 6, there are interdependencies between the fiscal consolidation program in Italy and interest and exchange rate impulses as well as effects caused by the hypothetical EMU. Policy implications for monetary unions and limitations of the analysis in part III are also discussed.

In concluding section 10, approach and findings are critically reviewed and some policy recommendations for joining monetary unions in general are offered.

PART I

Model and Methodical Background

2 Simulation Framework

Within the framework of part II (sections 2, 3, and 4), this section outlines the methodical basis for this treatise. In subsection 2.1, the approach and core elements of the underlying model are summarized. In subsection 2.2, the strategy used for conducting comparative simulation exercises is discussed. Finally, subsection 2.3 sets out to justify the strategy of constructing counterfactuals in an ex post analysis based on historical data.

2.1 General Approach and Underlying Model

It is not straightforward to capture the aforementioned interest and exchange rate impulses in a model, because the structural break resulting from the transition to a monetary union must be modeled explicitly. In principle, two approaches are available: (small theoretical) analytically tractable models and (large econometric) simulation models. On the one hand, the explanatory power of small theoretical models[5] is limited in a dynamic multi-country world, even if the structural break is not included.[6] Hughes Hallett (1986) captures the problem more precisely:
"... There are three spillover channels to consider (via income, monetary, and terms of trade linkages) and we need to evaluate

---

[5] There is a large number of analytically tractable two or three-country models. Feuerstein and Siebke (1990), for instance, present a comparative-static analysis of a Keynesian model. Examples of dynamic models including a supply side are Aoki (1981) and Clausen (1998).

[6] In the preface of Allen and Kenen (1980), the conceptual difficulties for constructing an analytical multi-country model are summarized extensively.

net spillover effects when all three channels are operating. No theoretical model has yet managed to treat all three channels simultaneously. ..." (In subsection 6.4, it is shown that these three channels do, in fact, determine the outcome of simulation results presented in this treatise.)

On the other hand, the use of a large econometric model – in this treatise – proved to be technically and methodically arduous and time-consuming. To account for effects caused by the structural break implied by any monetary union, the analysis involves three stages: first, counterfactual simulations for a historical time period (methodical background in part I, quantitative results in section 5, part II); second, qualitative interpretations of simulation results (section 6, part II); third, application of findings to the real world European Monetary Union or any other monetary union (section 7, part II). Similarly, these three stages must be repeated for the fiscal policy analysis in part III.

In this treatise, economic implications are derived from simulation results, not from deductions extracted from small theoretical models. Nolens volens, this treatise may be seen as part of a "revolutionary shift in the economic paradigm" towards "simulations along with provocative experiments and empirical papers" (Kreps, 1997; similarly in Hahn, 1994).

The simulation analysis presented in this treatise is based on a 1991 variant of MULTIMOD (cf. IMF, 1991), an annual econometric multi-country model. It was developed by the International Monetary Fund (IMF) and is widely used for international policy analysis.[7] 470 equations depict ten countries and regional

---

[7] For instance: on the EMU cf. Hughes Hallett and McAdam (1998a and b), Masson and Symansky (1992), Masson and Melitz (1991), the European

blocs: the seven G7 countries, the rest of the OECD, the oil exporters, and the rest of the developing world. MULTIMOD incorporates rational expectations (in financial markets and the decision-making by firms and households) and complete information. This means it is a perfect foresight model requiring perfect credibility of policy decisions (e.g. on the start and membership of a monetary union).[8]

MULTIMOD follows "the prevailing paradigm in which a broadly neoclassical view of macroeconomic equilibrium coexists with a new Keynesian view of short-to-medium term adjustment" (Mitchell, Sault, Smith and Wallis, 1995). It is a modified (dynamic) Mundell-Fleming model combining short run demand determination and IS-LM structure with long run steady state properties determined by capital accumulation and aggregate supply. Inflation dynamics depend on capacity utilization (a Phillips curve type relationship), imported inflation effects, sticky prices and a forward-looking component. However, for the long run, nominal neutrality obtains, because short run nominal rigidities are smoothed out over time. MULTIMOD accounts for stocks of debt, money, and net foreign assets as well as for international trade and financial flows. An overview of the structure of the standard industrial country submodel is presented in appendix A.1.[9]

Commission (1990); on the German unification cf. Hughes Hallett and Ma (1994); on policy rules cf. Frenkel, Goldstein, and Masson (1989); on monetary policy in Switzerland cf. Zurlinden (1992); and on imperfect credibility of policy regimes cf. Masson and Symansky (1993).

[8] The standard model needs to be changed in order to allow for incomplete credibility. In Masson and Symansky (1993), for instance, the degree of credibility is explicitly measured by an additional parameter. – Probability proxies for the formation of EMU could, for instance, be obtained from forward interest rate spreads as persuasively suggested by Weidmann (1996).

[9] Depicting eleven equations, the key features of MULTIMOD are cap-

The data set in MULTIMOD consists of historical data from 1972 to 1988 as presented in the *International Financial Statistics* (IMF, 1990a) and of projected data for the model future (1989 to 2045) as published in the IMF's (1990b) *World Economic Outlook*. MULTIMOD is *not* designed to generate forecasts. Instead, forecasts for the model future are taken from other research conducted at the IMF. As components of the model, forecasts are treated exactly like historical data.

2.2 Comparative Simulation Strategy

This treatise is based on a comparative simulation analysis. The overall strategy is to contrast the historical outcome (henceforth called baseline or baseline scenario[10]) with counterfactual developments that would have occurred, if the EMU had been introduced in 1983 (henceforth called hypothetical EMU scenarios). A number of choices determine the nature of the counterfactuals – as detailed below as well as in the next section.

---

tured in a stylized core model in Bohn (1997). A more complete description of the model including its theoretical underpinnings and estimation details (univariate, multivariate, pooled estimations; error correction models; calibrations) can be found in Masson, Symansky, and Meredith (1990). These authors and Mitchell, Sault, Smith and Wallis (1995), and – on previous versions of MULTIMOD – Masson, Symansky, Haas, and Dooley (1988), and Helliwell, Meredith, Durand, and Bagnoli (1990), provide standard simulation exercises illustrating the properties of the model. They also present examples for using MULTIMOD in policy analyses. Furthermore, Mitchell, Sault, Smith and Wallis (1995) and Bryant, Hooper and Mann (1993) compare MULTIMOD with other multi-country models. See also question 1 in section 4 on the model properties.

[10] A scenario is a sequence of events (real world or constructed) to study causal connections involved in a particular (macroeconomic) question. The concept of a ***baseline*** originates in physical science and is used in comparative simulation analyses to describe a benchmark.

MULTIMOD contains G=470 endogenous, H=81 expectational, and K=132 exogenous variables covering T=74 periods. Since the model includes 4 lags and 5 leads, the first four periods are necessary to provide initial values for lagged endogenous variables, and the last five periods serve as terminal conditions (cf. question 4 in section 4). Hence solution values can only be produced for a maximum of 65 periods (cf. question 6 in section 4).

MULTIMOD's *baseline scenario* can be defined by the following non-linear system of equations (cf. Fair, 1994, p.4):

$$f_i(Y, Y^e, X, \gamma_i) + u_i = 0, \qquad i = 1, \ldots, G \tag{1}$$

where Y is a [TxG] dimensional matrix of endogenous data, Y^e is [TxH] (expectational data), X is [TxK] (exogenous data), γ_i is the vector of coefficients, and vector u_i contains so-called residuals (see further down). Y (and Y^e)[11] and X represent the (historical and forecast) baseline data set (cf. previous subsection). The f_i describe the structural specification of the baseline model (consisting of G equations), and the γ_i are the corresponding baseline parameter values. Since parameters cannot be estimated jointly for the entire system, the IMF derived most parameter estimates from multivariate or univariate subsystems based on historical data. Some components of γ_i are also calibrations.

For equation 1 to be fulfilled in the baseline, an (additive) residual u_{it} is fitted for each equation i in each period t. This is standard practice (Fair, 1994, pp. 262-263, 273, 371 (footnote), 325). For historical periods, these residuals correspond to the

[11] By virtue of rational expectations (and perfect foresight) the values of expectational variables must equal those of corresponding endogenous variables (in future periods).

error terms of the estimated subsystems, not to those of the entire system though. "Once the residuals are added to the equations, they are never changed. The same set of values is used for all experiments" (Fair, 1984, p. 303).

Hypothetical EMU scenarios analyzed in part II and part III contain a structural break. For modeling the common monetary policy, the structural specification f_i is replaced by f_i' for several i in equation 1. A switch of the policy regime (structural change) also requires a modification of the f_i. Examples are: a change from exchange rate to money supply targeting by national central banks in the announcement period prior to the start of the hypothetical EMU (cf. section 3); or an alteration of the government tax rate reaction function to account for a fiscal retrenchment (cf. section 8).[12] Modifications to other components of the model play a minor or no role in this treatise. First, individual parameters are modified (γ_i' instead of γ_i) to account for private agents' behavioral changes. In question 2 of section 7, the influence of aggregate European instead of national inflation rates on wage setting in the EMU is discussed. Second, the effect of residuals u_i is analyzed in question 3 of section 4. Third, changes to exogenous variables X (exogenous shock analysis) are not considered in this treatise.

A solution[13] for a particular hypothetical EMU scenario is obtained by an iterative solution algorithm based on f_i', and γ_i' (and u_i' if changed) as well as unchanged values for X and u_i while taking the baseline values of Y (and Y^e) as start values. To account

---

[12] The formation of expectations is also part of the structural specification which could be (but is not) changed to introduce an explicit functional format for Y^e (cf. footnote 11).

[13] The word 'solution' usually refers to technical aspects or results of a 'simulation' run.

for expectational variables Y^e, a standard Gauss-Seidl algorithm is combined with a Fair-Taylor procedure.[14] An equilibrium solution is said to be achieved when for each endogenous and for each expectational variable the change in value from the previous iteration is smaller than preset so-called *technical* convergence criteria, say 0.1 % and 0.2 %, respectively.[15]

It is also possible to obtain a solution for the baseline scenario. By construction of the residuals, the endogenous values of the original (baseline) data set also represent a consistent *solution*. Baseline data (used as start values) are reproduced as a "'perfect tracking' solution" (Fair, 1984, p. 303). This means that the economic history is also part of a particular model solution.

2.3 Ex-Post Analysis

Comparative simulation analyses are mostly conducted as ex ante simulations which are based on the model future (hence forecast baseline data). For instance, all simulation studies mentioned in the introduction are ex ante analyses. However, comparative simulation analyses can just as well be conducted as ex post simulations based on a historical time period – and historical baseline data (Wallis, 1988, p. 226). Each approach is suitable for different purposes and has implications for simulation results and their

---

[14] In the Gauss-Seidl algorithm, Y^e is treated as exogenous. But after each complete Gauss-Seidl solution loop, expectational values are set equal to the values obtained for endogenous variables Y. See footnote 11. Cf. Fisher and Hughes Hallett (1988) and appendix A.2.

[15] On technical convergence criteria, cf. question 5 in section 4. For more references and some more detail on the solution technique, its properties (existence, uniqueness, and stability), and sensitivity analyses, confer other questions in section 4, and appendix A.2.

interpretation. For the purpose of this treatise, ex post simulations for the 1980s are used instead of the seemingly more realistic (ex ante) scenario for the EMU starting in 1999, and instead of any other (ex post) historical scenario for another time period. In the following, it is argued that effects caused by the EMU cannot be analyzed in an ex ante analysis (for technical reasons), and that the period from 1983 offers ideal economic conditions (in the baseline) for such an analysis.

The decisive (technical) drawback of ex ante simulations is that interest and exchange rate impulses caused by a monetary union would be obscured or even completely concealed. In econometric multi-country models, forecasts for the immediate future typically represent an adjustment path to a steady state equilibrium. In this version of MULTIMOD (IMF, 1991),[16] the steady state is already reached before the start of the real world EMU in 1999. Exchange rates are constant, and interest rates are constant and equal across countries from 1997 onwards.[17]

Thus introducing the hypothetical EMU would not make a difference any more, and the essential effects would not appear in an ex ante analysis. First, the introduction of a monetary union could not have an interest equalization effect. Second, underlying appreciations and depreciations in the historical baseline would not feature in a steady state baseline. Hence, there could not

[16] Reasons for using this version of MULTIMOD are given in the last paragraph of this subsection.

[17] Even if the steady state started a few years after 1999, the arguments presented in the next paragraph remain relevant because effects caused by an alternative hypothetical EMU as of 1999 would still be reduced and possibly blurred. This is so because the model typically reverts to the steady state very quickly. Thus, the dynamic adjustment to the steady state may dominate effects caused by the transition to the monetary union.

be any effects caused by changes in exchange rate expectations caused by the hypothetical EMU. Third, conversion rates could be fixed exogenously at non-steady state values, but there would be no effects under endogenously determined market conversion rates (because the steady state would prevail). Furthermore, it could not be demonstrated that these three effects may be countervailing.

Another disadvantage of an ex ante perspective may be seen in the fact that an additional error enters the analysis, because its baseline data must be forecast. Furthermore, it is true that a projected trend baseline (used for ex ante simulations) incorporates zero residuals, whereas historical baseline residuals are non-zero. However, neither approach is methodologically superior. A trend baseline represents one specific realization of a given model, just as the historical baseline is but a very particular realization (of the same or another model).[18]

As to the economic justification, it is argued for choosing a particular historical time period, i.e. the 1980s (from 1983) instead of the 1990s, for introducing a hypothetical EMU. After 1983, the European Monetary System (EMS) was fairly stable in comparison to the previous period, and there was no realignment between 1987 and 1992. In contrast, monetary turmoil with the break-up of the Exchange Rate Mechanism and ensuing exchange rate instability, especially for the Lira, could be observed in 1992. Moreover, from 1983, GDP growth rates were positive and very close in the large real world EMU member countries

---

[18] To study the effects of other draws of the error terms on simulation results, (additional) deterministic shock analyses or stochastic simulations are required. Cf. inter alia Bryant, Hooper, and Mann (1993). According to Fair (1994), pp. (262 and) 273, this is "not likely to be necessary", if one is "interested in the mean path of variables", not in their variability.

Italy, France, and Germany (baseline data is shown in appendix B.1; in Britain, business cycles followed a somewhat different pattern). Hence, possible recession or overheating effects caused by a hypothetical EMU in these three countries cannot be blamed on divergent underlying business cycles of the historical baseline.

Nonetheless, by choosing the historical conditions of the 1980s as the point of reference, considerable nominal disparities among European countries (much larger than in the 1990s) are incorporated in the analysis. Due to large interest rate differentials (spreads) between prospective member countries of the hypothetical EMU and exchange rates far away from purchasing power parity (Hill, 1986), large adjustments are likely to be induced by the introduction of a hypothetical EMU. There are two consequences: first, simulation results will exaggerate effects compared to those expected for the real world EMU starting in 1999; and second, quantitative outcomes are less ambiguous, thus facilitating qualitative interpretations.

Given that the smaller European countries are not modeled individually in this version of MULTIMOD (IMF, 1991), the choice of Italy, France and Germany as members of the hypothetical EMU is validated in retrospect. The decision on which country to include in the hypothetical EMU is, however, not primarily based on the desire to honor the Italian attempts and the British reluctance to participate in the real world EMU. Instead, it is rather motivated by the macroeconomic constellation as of 1983 and by the economic importance of these countries. Large nominal disparities and coinciding business cycles seem to be the perfect conditions for analyzing transmission mechanisms of macroeconomic effects that are caused by the EMU (or monetary unions in general).

There are also more recent versions of MULTIMOD containing historical data for the 1990s. However, unresolved technical problems resulted from inconsistencies and teething troubles caused by changes to the model (e.g. including labor markets explicitly, treating Germany as united - even in the period before unification). In contrast, the 1991 version of MULTIMOD used here (IMF, 1991) was updated several times and produces reliable results (cf. question 1 in section 4 on the model properties).

3 Baseline and Hypothetical EMU Scenarios

In this section, the (three) hypothetical EMU scenarios referred to in this treatise are outlined in four subsections. This is done with reference to the baseline scenario which is defined by the model specifications in MULTIMOD to capture the historical real world situation. To allow for anticipation effects in the hypothetical EMU, an announcement phase is specified (in subsection 3.1). The hypothetical EMU itself rests on assumptions concerning (i) Euro exchange and conversion rates (subsection 3.2), (ii) European money demand (subsection 3.3), and (iii) European monetary policy (subsection 3.4). Except for a distinction of various procedures for fixing conversion rates in subsection 3.2, all features are common to all scenarios.

3.1 Announcement Period

Based on the general discussion of ex post simulations in subsection 2.3, the hypothetical EMU – consisting of Germany, France, and Italy – is modeled to be announced (unexpectedly) at the beginning of 1982 to start at the beginning of 1983. With the announcement, the Exchange Rate Mechanism (ERM) of the EMS (as specified in subsection 3.4) is to be abandoned (whereas in the baseline, the ERM applies in 1982 as well as in subsequent years). In the following, the one year announcement period and the choice of flexible exchange rates for the last year prior to the start of the hypothetical EMU will be justified.

On 2 May 1998, the European Council Meeting in Brussels decided inter alia on the final go-ahead for the real world EMU, its member countries and bilateral conversion rates. This was less than a year before the actual start of the prospective EMU, but the aforementioned decisions were already expected several months in advance. Moreover, the participation of individual countries in the real world EMU was anticipated with varying probabilities since the Maastricht Treaty in 1992 (Weidmann, 1996). (Similarly, future applications for membership will probably be known at least two years in advance.)

However, since MULTIMOD requires perfect credibility and full information (cf. subsection 2.1), it seems reasonable to limit the announcement period to one (or two) years. In this analysis, private agents will anticipate correctly in 1982 (but not before) nominal interest rate equalization and fixed exchange/conversion rates between EMU member countries as of 1983. Obviously, real world anticipation effects may be exaggerated by simulation results, because (rational) expectations switch abruptly from one annual period (1981) to the next (1982) and all adjustments are squeezed into one period (1982) only.

There are two reasons for assuming flexible exchange rates in the announcement period of all hypothetical EMU scenarios: first, due to several realignments in the beginning of the EMS (from 1979) the real world history resembles – in terms of annual data – a floating exchange rate regime; and second, the modeling strategy (in this treatise) intends to show market and policy responses, but without government interventions in foreign exchange markets. This objective contradicts the exchange rate criterion of the Maastricht Treaty (EU, 1992), i.e. keeping exchange rates within a $\pm 2\frac{1}{4}$ % band around the central parities of the European Exchange Rate Mechanism (ERM) prior to the start of the EMU.

But it more or less reflects the real world situation of the ERM with extended band width (±15 % since the 1992 shake-up).

So far, assuming an announcement period and flexible exchange rates were merely justified by an attempt to reconcile objectives of this treatise and limitations of the underlying model with economic and political real world conditions. However, there is no choice for modeling the EMU differently. With (narrow) ERM bands in place in 1982 or without an announcement period, simulations would simply not converge (cf. question 1 in section 4, and scenarios V.1 on page 213).

It is not clear, if the non-convergence is caused merely by the solution algorithm, or if such a *modified* hypothetical EMU scenario is theoretically non-sustainable, i.e. that such a setting is inconsistent with the perfect credibility assumption. One of the reasons may be that prices are not flexible enough to adjust to the structural shock. Irrespective of the underlying reason, it reveals the force of the adjustment process required at the start of the EMU. It is possible, but cannot necessarily be concluded from these results that the narrow band exchange rate criterion of the Maastricht Treaty is incompatible with the transition to the EMU. (In a similar vein, inconsistencies between fiscal and nominal criteria (including exchange rates) were found by Hughes Hallett and McAdam (1998a and b) and von Hagen and Lutz (1996) – as mentioned in the introduction.)

3.2 Exchange Rates and Bilateral Conversion Rates

In MULTIMOD, exchange rates are determined by the uncovered (open) interest parity condition:

$$e^k = \frac{\left(1+\frac{i^{US}}{100}\right) * Ee^k_{+1}}{\left(1+\frac{i^k}{100}\right)} \tag{2}$$

Country k's exchange rate vis-à-vis the US-$ depends on the interest differential $i^k - i^{US}$ and the expected exchange rate for next period Ee^k_{+1} (E is the expectation operator). In the baseline, there are separate exchange rate equations for France, Germany, and Italy.

For the hypothetical EMU scenarios, individual exchange rates for member countries are replaced by a single Euro-$ rate (and conversion rates are used to fix each national currency to the Euro). The exchange rate of the (hypothetical) Euro vis-à-vis the US-$ again depends on two components: the expected Euro-$ exchange rate for next period Ee^U_{+1}; and the union-wide short term interest rate i^U relative to its corresponding US rate i^{US}. For hypothetical EMU scenarios, i^U is determined by the reaction function of the hypothetical European Central Bank specified in subsection 3.4. The European (open interest parity) exchange rate equation is given by:

$$e^U = \frac{\left(1+\frac{i^{US}}{100}\right) * Ee^U_{+1}}{\left(1+\frac{i^U}{100}\right)} \tag{3}$$

For fixing conversion rates, three alternative procedures are used in this treatise: "market conversion" procedure **CUR** (stands for current rate), "central parities" procedure **CP**, and "purchasing power parity" procedure **PPP**. To stay within the logic of an annual model, exchange and conversion rates in MULTIMOD must be yearly averages. Therefore, none of the three conversion procedures corresponds to the one chosen for the actual EMU at the EU Summit in May 1998 (EU, 1998). However, CP and CUR procedures together capture all important features of the actual conversion procedure to be used in the real world EMU. (As an additional reference, the PPP procedure is used for "better" representing real economic conditions in each of the member countries.[19]) Procedures will be presented first, then it will be argued that the real world procedure can be considered an intermediate case of CP and CUR.

Normalizing the Euro at 1 DM as of 1983, the start of the hypothetical EMU, reduces the number of conversion rates needed. Then, the French exchange rate to the US-\$ (e^F), for instance, equals the Euro-\$ rate e^U (which is identical to the DM-\$ rate e^G) times the respective conversion rate to the Euro $\left[\frac{FF}{Euro}\right]$ (identical to $\left[\frac{FF}{DM}\right]$). With France as an example, the three procedures for conversion rates (specified as Franc-DM rate from 1983, $e^{F,G}_{t\geq 1983}$) can be defined as follows:

$$\textbf{CUR:} \quad e^{F,G}_{t\geq 1983}\left[\frac{FF}{Euro}\right] = e^{F,G}_{1982} \tag{4}$$

$$\textbf{PPP:} \quad e^{F,G}_{t\geq 1983}\left[\frac{FF}{Euro}\right] = \frac{ppp^F_{1980}}{ppp^G_{1980}} * \frac{P^F_{1982}}{P^G_{1982}} \tag{5}$$

$$\textbf{CP:} \quad e^{F,G}_{t\geq 1983}\left[\frac{FF}{Euro}\right] = cp^F_{1982} \tag{6}$$

---

19 In fact, it turns out that CUR produces similar results to PPP (cf. section 6).

Under **CUR**, conversion rates as of 1983 are set to their corresponding *simulated* bilateral exchange rates as of 1982, the year before the start of the hypothetical EMU. An equivalent conversion procedure in the real world would be the fixing at (annually) averaged market rates (i.e. *not* at the last exchange rate quotations of the day before the start of the monetary union as envisaged for the real world EMU). Hence, CUR must be interpreted as an averaging procedure suggested by Lamfalussy, the first president of the former European Monetary Institute. It consists of calculating conversion rates as the mean of past exchange rates.[20] In terms of model simulations, CUR conversion rates are entirely endogenous, because simulated rates as of 1982 are used, not baseline rates. CUR is referred to as market conversion (procedure).

PPP and CP are labeled exogenous conversion procedures. Under **PPP**, the purchasing power of 1 Euro is equalized across countries. The PPP procedure uses exogenously determined 1980 estimates for the purchasing power parity (ppp^k_{1980}) of, say France (F) and Germany (G) relative to the US.[21] They are updated by 1982 prices (P^k_{1982}) which are endogenously obtained in the respective simulation run. P is the non-oil GNP deflator, the central price variable in MULTIMOD. According to **CP**, conversion rates correspond to the annual averages of central parities cp^k of the

[20] De Grauwe, Dewachter, and Veestraeten, 1998, offer a formal distinction and treatment of conversion rates set at last quotations versus the Lamfalussy Rule as they call it. – In a theoretical context, the Lamfalussy Rule is a possible solution to the so-called indeterminacy problem, i.e. the possibility of self-fulfilling prophecies (on exchange rates), which arises, if the last quotations of market rates before the start of a monetary union are to be used as conversion rates (de Grauwe, 1997; Obstfeld, 1998).

[21] Hill, 1986, p. 140, table 3, bottom line.

European Exchange Rate Mechanism (ERM). These are entirely exogenous to the model.

The Maastricht Treaty[22] stipulates that the external value of the European Currency Unit ECU (which is to be replaced by the Euro) is not to be affected by the conversion of national currencies into Euro. Despite changes to the exchange rate dynamics, this allows, theoretically, for various kinds of conversion rate procedures, both exogenous and endogenous (de Grauwe, Dewachter, and Veestraeten, 1998). The conversion procedure chosen at the EU Summit in May 1998 (EU, 1998) is exogenous (similar to CP) in the sense that *bilateral* (not Euro) conversion rates are fixed in advance at the central parities of the ERM.

But it could also be considered endogenous (similar to CUR) in two respects (despite qualifications in each case). First, technically, for conversion rates *to the Euro* are to be set at market rates as of 31 December 1998. At the same time, central banks are, however, obliged to ensure that the envisaged (exogenously) fixed bilateral rates obtain on the last trading day before the start of the real world EMU. Second, economically, bilateral central parities (which are to be used as real world conversion rates) do actually reflect economic fundamentals and correspond to market rates. When there was a large deviation, central parities were (at least partially) adjusted. In the case of the Irish pound, a revaluation of 3 % was conducted shortly before the EU Summit (cf. McRae, 1998, in The Independent, and Oldag, 1998, in the Süddeutsche Zeitung, 17 March 1998). For smaller deviations from economic fundamentals, however, we can see that market rates, basically, stick to central parities. Indeed, Finland is an example for undervalued exchange rates – measured by real effective exchange rates

[22] EU (1992)-Treaty, article 109 l (4).

(OECD, 1998b) – where market rates stayed close to central parities, nonetheless. In these cases, markets appear to have deemed credible policy makers' commitment for preserving (exogenously set) central parities.

3.3 Money Demand

In MULTIMOD, real money demand is estimated jointly for all industrial countries in the model (only intercepts differ):

$$\ln \frac{M}{PA} = m_0 + m_1 * \ln A + m_2 * i + m_4 * \ln \left(\frac{M_{-1}}{PA_{-1}} \right) \quad (7)$$

The logarithmic real demand for money (PA is the absorption deflator) depends (log-)linearly on a constant, absorption A, the nominal interest rate i, and the previous period real money demand. Note that money refers to both supply, i.e. the stock of money, and demand, because the central bank is presumed to provide the demanded quantity of money at all times.[23]

There has been a vast literature on the (aggregation of) European money demand.[24] Here, the objective is to find a consistent aggregation procedure within the given underlying model. On the

[23] Furthermore, it may be considered a weakness of MULTIMOD (and other multi-country models) that money refers to high-powered money, not to M1 or alike money aggregates. However, Turnovsky (1995, p. 28) argues "that in fact little is lost by abstracting from the commercial banking system."

[24] Among many others cf. Hayo (1997) for narrow money and Wesche (1998) for a variety of monetary aggregates. Excellent surveys on methods and results are Cassard, Lane, and Masson (1994), Falk and Funke (1995), and Browne, Fagan and Henry (1997).

one hand, European money demand must be stable[25] as a prerequisite for the feasibility of a central bank strategy oriented towards monetary targeting (the assumption for the strategy of the European Central Bank maintained throughout this treatise). On the other hand, the magnitude of the European money demand as well as its stability properties depend on the conversion rates used in the procedure for aggregating national money demand functions.

For the hypothetical EMU scenarios defined in the previous subsection, national money demand functions are preserved, and – following Fagan and Henry (1997, appendix) – the European money demand is calculated as a sum of the estimated money demand in member countries k expressed in Euro (which equals DM due to normalization). Using the conversion rate obtaining under the hypothetical EMU scenario under consideration, the value for the European money demand is obtained by $M^U = \sum \frac{M^k}{e^{k,G}_{t \geq 1983}}$.

This definition has considerable conceptual advantages: first, no separate estimation (beyond the underlying model) is required for deriving an aggregated European money demand function; instead MULTIMOD provides the data for each national money demand used in the aggregation; and second, by virtue of being the sum of stable national money demand functions the European money demand is stable, too.[26]

---

[25] (Structural) stability of a money demand function is defined as invariability of estimated coefficients with respect to the time period (Fair, 1994, p. 75).

[26] This is true for MULTIMOD, because parameters (except for the constant) in log-linear national money demand functions are pooled estimates, i.e. identical across countries.

However, constructing European money demand from national functions has at least two theoretical drawbacks. The first one refers to central bank revenues which are modeled as seigniorage in MULTIMOD. Since money creation ($M - M_{-1}$) features in each government's budget constraint, we are assuming (unrealistically) that in the EMU each country's seigniorage still depends on the quantity of money attributable to that country, i.e. its change in fictitious "national" equilibrium money demand. Redistribution gains and losses as calculated in, for instance, Sinn and Feist (1998) are neglected. Wealth transfers of any kind are abstracted from (even though it would be technically possible to include them in the model).

The second weakness refers to the implicit assumption that the private agents' behavior concerning money demand does not change in hypothetical EMU scenarios (compared to the baseline) despite structural and policy changes in the hypothetical EMU, i.e. that the Lucas (1976) Critique on econometric policy evaluation were not relevant. However, in reality large effects are conceivable. (There is no conclusive evidence though – cf. question 2 in section 7.) On the one hand, further – potentially more rapid – financial innovations may raise the interest-sensitivity of money demand and/or reduce the need for holding money altogether (expressed in the constant term). On the other hand, a countervailing effect would be that agents in (previously) high inflation countries like Italy may desire to increase their demand for real balances (for given levels of interest rates and absorption) due to the presumably higher credibility of anti-inflationary policies in the EMU. Given that the objective of the treatise is to analyze transmission mechanisms caused by the EMU per se, the assumption of behavioral invariability seems the best feasible approach to the problem.

3.4 Monetary Policy

In the baseline model of MULTIMOD, the short term nominal interest rate i for each country is determined by its national central bank. There is no distinction between market rates and central bank rates. Short rate i is derived by the following central bank reaction function:

$$i^k = i^k_{-1} + \left[\left(r_2 * \ln \frac{e^{k,G}}{par^k}\right)^3\right] + \left[r_1 * \frac{\ln \frac{mt^k}{M^k}}{m_2}\right] \tag{8}$$

Central bank monetary operations of country k are either geared to the bilateral exchange rate vis-à-vis the DM (exchange rate targeting; response parameters are set to: $r_1 = 0$, $r_2 = 200$) or to the national money supply (monetary targeting; $r_1 = .333$, $r_2 = 0$). Exchange rate targeting is very severe due to the cubic formulation. A 1 % positive deviation of actual exchange rate $e^{k,G}$ (e.g. $[\frac{FF}{DM}]$) from its target value *par* (for instance, a depreciation of the FF) is resisted by an 8 % upward change in the interest rate, $i - i_{-1}$. Monetary targeting depends on $m_2 = -.005402$, the pooled estimate for the interest semi-elasticity of money demand in all industrial countries. A 1 % overshooting of M relative to its target mt causes a rise in the interest rate by 60 basis points.

In the baseline model, the behavior of the Bundesbank and the non-ERM central banks is described by monetary targeting. All other ERM member countries are assumed to commit to exchange rate targeting vis-à-vis the DM. MULTIMOD's strong interest rate response to exchange rate deviations from their targets guarantees that exchange rates stay near the prespecified target value *par*, thereby counterfeiting the ERM.[27] Empirically, the characterization of the ERM (in MULTIMOD) as an entirely "unidirectional" exchange rate union with Germany as the center (who dominates interest rates in member countries without being affected herself) is rejected for the period prior to the German unification. However, Gardner and Perraudin (1993), and Henry and Weidmann (1995) do find evidence for an "asymmetric" union (i.e. the influence on interest rates from Germany to other members is stronger than the other way round).

Leaving the ERM is interpreted as switching from exchange rate to monetary targeting. This is possible in MULTIMOD, because exogenous monetary targets are specified for each country. In fact, monetary target levels in period t correspond to actual baseline values for the money supply in period t.[28] The unrealistic implicit assumption is that central banks were 100 % successful in achieving their targets in the historical baseline period.[29] Given the baseline level of money M in equation 8, the interest rate is determined by the monetary target. An expansionary (contractionary) policy – implying lower (higher) interest rates – is modeled by increasing (lowering) the level of mt relative to the level of M.

---

[27] However, it should be noted that MULTIMOD baseline values for *par* are not ERM parity rates, but historical average annual exchange rates.

[28] Changes of baseline interest rates, $i - i_{-1}$, are explained by deliberate deviations of policy from monetary targeting (cf. question 3 in section 4 on the methodical issues). Equation 8 can only be fulfilled, because it actually contains a residual which is not shown in the economic specification presented on page 31.

[29] The model was changed to replace levels for the monetary target by growth rates, and to smooth monetary targets (cf. question 1 in section 4, and scenarios V.2 on page 213). This did not, however, affect simulation results substantially.

In the following, the expression monetary stability orientation (or monetary policy stance) will be used – loosely – to refer to the time path (or growth rates) of the exogenous monetary target sequence $(mt_t)_t$. By contrast, the term monetary development relates to the time path (or growth rates) of realized endogenous monetary variables (e.g. inflation or the actual supply of money $(M_t)_t$). A monetary development with low (high) growth rates over an extended period of time is sometimes described as high (low) stability record (or in a similar way). In the baseline, the monetary development for $(M_t)_t$ and the monetary stability orientation correspond to one another – by construction. Under hypothetical EMU scenarios, it will be shown that $(mt_t)_t$ and $(M_t)_t$ change and do no longer coincide because of the structural shock caused by the hypothetical EMU.

Once the hypothetical EMU starts, the nominal interest rate in member countries is no longer determined by a national interest rate reaction function, but by the interest rate reaction function of the hypothetical European Central Bank (ECB). The ECB commits to monetary targeting. There is no conceptual change like, for instance, a switch to inflation targeting. The common European interest rate, too, is modeled as the instrument, and the European money stock as the (intermediate) target for obtaining its price stability objective. As for previously national central banks, the hypothetical ECB exercises full control over short term interest rates:

$$i^U = i^U_{-1} + \left[r_1 * \frac{\ln \frac{mt^U}{M^U}}{m_2} \right] . \tag{9}$$

Under the assumption of unchanged coefficients r_1 and m_2 (from national equations; m_2 is negative), the change of the union-wide common interest rate $(i^U - i^U_{-1})$ depends on the aggregation of the quantity of European money M^U (cf. previous subsection), and on the construction of exogenous European monetary target mt^U (see below). In the first year of the EMU, equation 9 also hinges on assumptions for i^U_{-1}.[30] To avoid this problem while describing monetary policy in a situation of structural break, the interest rate reaction function would have to be (but is not) replaced altogether, e.g. by a Taylor Rule (first published in Taylor, 1993b) incorporating inflation and output gap instead of a monetary target. However, this would not be a convincing strategy, because even a Taylor Rule has been shown to be empirically relevant only, if the previous period interest rate is included (Clarida, Galí, and Gertler, 1997).

EMU means – by definition of a monetary union – a single monetary policy, but allows for various levels of union-wide monetary stability orientation. In the approach chosen, the 'intermediate' monetary policy stance of the hypothetical EMU is based on the average of historical national monetary stability orientations which correspond to the development of actual money supply in the historical baseline. The hypothetical European monetary target is constructed endogenously by aggregating national baseline targets (analogous to the aggregation of the European money stock in the last subsection): $mt^U = \sum \frac{mt^k}{e^{k,G}_{t \geq 1983}}$.

This approach may be criticized from two angles. First, simply adding up national target values given in the baseline of MULTIMOD is a crude way for describing the hypothetical ECB policy as an average of historical European monetary policies. Nonetheless, this procedure suffices to capture a crucial feature of any

---

[30] To determine i^U_{-1} as a GDP-weighted average of national interest rates, i.e. $i^U_{-1} = \sum \left(\frac{GDP^k}{GDP^U} * i^k \right)$, seems the most appropriate assumption for the 'intermediate' monetary policy stance described in the following paragraphs.

monetary union, the equalization of short term nominal interest rates. Second, the real world EMU is expected to conduct a more stability-oriented monetary policy. For instance, the growth rate of the average annual monetary target could have been reduced by x %.[31] Alternatively, the historical monetary stability stance of the Bundesbank could have been used. However, any specification of the European stability orientation is arbitrary as long as we cannot observe the actual monetary policy of the real world ECB. Moreover, (qualitative) findings of this study do not depend on a realistic modelization of the ECB behavior.

The common monetary policy in the hypothetical EMU – based on average monetary stability orientation – can be expected to produce average interest rates across the union from 1983 onwards. Relative to national baseline rates, interest rates fall in some countries and go up in others thereby affecting interest-sensitive national money demand (hence M^U) as well as the real side. Some countries are likely to experience contractionary, others expansionary effects. Hence mere averaging of the monetary stability orientation in Europe produces macroeconomic effects in each year – relative to the baseline.

However, from the perspective of a national country, the link between a change in monetary stability orientation relative to the baseline and a change in interest rates is not straightforward. It depends on the relative level of interest rates in member countries. Typically, a country with a historically low monetary stability record (like Italy) exhibits high nominal interest rates in the baseline. Hence, if nominal interest rates are averaged in the union, they decrease for that country, even though its monetary stability orientation rises relative to the baseline, i.e. the stability

[31] This was suggested by von Hagen during the Bonn Summer School 1997.

orientation of the ECB is higher (lower growth rates of mt) by comparison to the (formerly independent) national central bank. (In subsection 6.4 it is shown that real interest rates do not necessarily go down as well.) – The following observation is the only one (in this treatise) that is derived on purely theoretical grounds (the others are all based on simulation results). However, nominal interest rate results presented in section 5 do confirm this finding for all three hypothetical EMU scenarios analyzed in part II.

Observation 1 (Interest Rate Impulse)
A member country of the hypothetical EMU experiences short term interest rate impulses due to the common monetary policy in the union. – Impulses for countries with a low monetary stability record are likely to be expansionary, even though – from a national perspective – the monetary stability orientation rises.

4 Methodical Specifications and Limitations (6 Questions)

As is usual for simulation studies, numerous technical problems must be overcome, many methodical queries must be answered, and a heavy computational load must be managed. Technical and methodical details include:

- the computer source code of the original solution software SLIM (cf. Fisher, 1990; on the concept, cf. appendix A.2);
- technical adjustments for setting it up, for developing it further, and for presenting results;
- trial simulations for testing the baseline and for examining technical convergence criteria and the solution behavior (cf. also question 5 further down);
- specific changes to account for modifications of the solution algorithm (cf. also questions 4 and 6 further down);
- the original source code of MULTIMOD and adjustments to capture the reality as of the 1980s (on the economic aspect, cf. subsection 2.1 and appendix A.1);
- source code changes to account for the hypothetical EMU (cf. also questions 2 and 3 further down; on the economic aspects, cf. section 3);
- sensitivity analyses on the hypothetical EMU (cf. also questions 1 and 3 further down); and
- source code changes for modeling a fiscal retrenchment in Italy (on the economic aspects, cf. subsection 8.1).

Background information on methodical specifications and limitations presented here is organized and selected according to two principles. First, this section focuses on selected questions thereby reducing the discussion of technical/methodical aspects to those which are relevant for judging quality and reliability of simulation results presented in this treatise. Second, essential information for understanding the economic discussion in parts II and III has already been given in section 2 (on the simulation framework). This section provides an extension of purely methodical interest.

Questions will be asked on model properties and sensitivity analyses (question 1), on the aggregation of residuals in the hypothetical EMU (questions 2 and 3), on terminal conditions (question 4), on technical convergence criteria of the solution algorithm (question 5), and on changes to the solution procedure (question 6). Other technical details – without potential bearing on simulation results – are not discussed here.

Question 1: *How well have the underlying properties of the model and sensitivities of simulation results been studied?*

Fair (1984 and 1994) presents elaborate tests for single equations as well as for complete models. He applies them to his own model and compares the properties of his model to simpler models. The Research Department of the IMF claims that MULTIMOD was also tested extensively. Official documentation on the model version used here (Masson, Symansky, and Meredith, 1990, and IMF, 1991) are not completely satisfactory though when compared with the tests suggested by Fair. Nonetheless, plausible economic properties have been obtained in numerous papers based on simulation analyses using MULTIMOD.[32]

---

[32] Quite a few papers are listed in subsection 2.1. Furthermore, there are prima facie tests of the model. Baseline residuals are small (except for ex-

Moreover, the fact that MULTIMOD produces convincing results for diverse questions (irrespective of the solution algorithm) may also be seen as an indicator for genuine properties of equilibrium solutions.[33] Existence of solutions does not seem to be a problem, although convergence is not always achieved easily under any solution algorithm (Juillard and Laxton, 1996). Uniqueness is inferred because no jumps between equilibria are reported for alternative start values or for changes in the scenario assumptions.

As for stability (in a dynamic sense meaning convergence to the long run equilibrium), one must distinguish between local and global stability. This is so, because *unchanged* terminal steady state conditions which are consistent with the baseline are imposed on model solutions (cf. question 4). For moderate exogenous, behavioral, and policy shocks, the model readjusts to given terminal conditions, because values of expectational variables are determined by them – under rational expectations. Hence the long run equilibrium is locally stable. However, there is no global stability, because some larger shocks or structural breaks do not allow convergence to the given long run equilibrium. In these cases, the long run must be adjusted as discussed in questions 4 and 6. Nonetheless, for a hypothetical EMU without announce-

---

change and interest rate residuals; cf. questions 2 and 3) indicating (though not proving) a good fit of estimations. Standard simulations reported by Masson, Symansky, and Meredith, 1990, produce theoretically convincing results. For instance, a temporary fiscal expansion produces a transitory demand stimulus, but has lasting negative effects on the capital stock relative to the baseline. A monetary shock leads to overshooting of prices and exchange rates, but is neutral in the long run – relative to the baseline.

[33] This is documented in aforementioned papers by and confirmed in personal discussions with Steve Symansky and Paul Masson of the IMF, Ralph Bryant of the Brookings Institution, Ken Wallis of the ESRC Macromodelling Group (Warwick), and Andrew Hughes Hallett and Yue Ma of Strathclyde University (Glasgow), who have all worked extensively with MULTIMOD.

ment period or with the ERM in place in the year prior to the start of the monetary union (as discussed in subsection 3.1), an equilibrium solution can still not be obtained.

The behavior of a model can also be tested in a more general way by examining responses to disturbances of any kind (sensitivity analyses).[34] Large models generally exhibit less sensitivity than small theoretical models (Malinvaud, 1981). Nonetheless, economic and technical sensitivities were also tested for scenarios studied in this treatise. Six variations to hypothetical EMU scenarios are listed under point V of the overview of scenarios (on page 213):

1. eliminating the announcement period or introducing the EMS in the announcement period (cf. subsection 3.1);

2. specifying the monetary target in terms of growth rates (and smoothing out growth rates over time) instead of using target levels which correspond to historical money supply levels (cf. subsection 3.4; cf. also subsection 9.4, footnote 78);

3. postulating effects of European inflation rates on wage setting behavior (cf. question 2 in section 7; the effects of changes to the money demand are also discussed, but not modeled);

4. aggregating and varying exchange rate residuals (aggregation alternatives are discussed under question 2 further down; simulation results for variations of residuals are presented under question 3 further down);

[34] Stochastic simulations (comparing various models) were done, for instance, in Bryant, Mann, and Hooper (1993).

5. changing the aggregation procedure for residuals in the interest rate reaction function of the hypothetical ECB (cf. question 3 further down); and

6. on a very technical level: experimenting with alternative technical parameters (effects on the solution are reported in question 5 further down).

Sensitivities have also been studied for model comparisons (e.g. Mitchell, Sault, Smith and Wallis, 1995) and for *policy* variations (e.g. Hughes Hallett and Ma, 1994). In the latter denotation, major aspects of this treatise can also be considered sensitivity analyses. First, economic differences for alternative conversion procedures are examined in part II. Second, effects of tighter or laxer fiscal retrenchments are scrutinized in part III. In both case, it is shown that differences in the outcome can be explained, even in the only case with a larger deviation from the other results (cf. the discussion of the outcome under CP in part II).

Question 2: *What is the role of exchange rate residuals and how can they be aggregated for the hypothetical EMU?*

The complete specification of the baseline exchange rate specification differs from its economic representation in equation 2 on page 24 in two respects: first, the equation for country k includes a residual term u^k which is not changed for other scenarios (as long as national exchange rate equations are preserved); and second, exchange rates are noted inversely (as is standard practice in the US and at the IMF):

$$\frac{1}{e^k} = \frac{\left(1+\frac{i^k}{100}\right) * \frac{1}{Ee^k_{+1}}}{\left(1+\frac{i^{US}}{100}\right)} + u^k \qquad (10)$$

(where exchange rate e^k is still represented in standard European format). Under hypothetical EMU scenarios, national equations for member countries are replaced from 1983 onwards by

$$\frac{1}{e^U} = \frac{\left(1 + \frac{i^U}{100}\right) * \frac{1}{Ee^U_{+1}}}{\left(1 + \frac{i^{US}}{100}\right)} + u^U. \qquad (11)$$

For the residual u^U and its relationship to the u^k, a number of choices are possible. They have potentially drastic implications for simulation results (cf. also question 3).

It could be argued that u^U must be set to zero, because a non-zero residual in the Euro exchange rate equation 11 is not justified by historically determined error terms. However, results would no longer be comparable to the baseline. Unlike other residuals, exchange rate residuals (and interest rate residuals – discussed in the next question) are very large, and, therefore, impact on simulation results.[35] In particular, during the period of extreme (temporary) appreciations of the US-$ in the mid-1980s, a comparison would be impossible. The problem could be overcome by producing a model solution based on non-zero residuals of national exchange rate equations. Such a reference scenario could be used instead of the baseline for comparing it to hypothetical EMU scenarios. However, due to the size of exchange rate residuals, the reference scenario would be far off the baseline. The impact of counterfactual developments (hypothetical EMU) on the historical economic development could not be examined any longer.

---

[35] It is known that exchange rates cannot be captured adequately by economic theory. On average, the uncovered interest parity used here, for instance, cannot explain some 10 % of actual exchange rates during the 1980s.

To determine an appropriate choice for u^U, one must scrutinize the nature of national residuals first. $(-u^k)$ is a monotonous transformation of the interest rate premium[36] $irpr^k$ which is determined according to following log specification[37] (in US format) of the interest parity equation: $i^k = i^* + \ln \frac{1}{e^k} + \ln \frac{1}{Ee^k_{+1}} + irpr^k$ (*). Following Frankel (1989), $irpr^k$ can be decomposed:

$$irpr^k = cpr^k + rpr^k + ee^k \tag{12}$$

A country premium *cpr* signifies a country's "incomplete capital market integration", i.e. institutional restrictions. The exchange rate risk premium *rpr* reflects "imperfect substitutability between comparable assets in different currencies", i.e. country risk or elevated variance of return. Expectational errors *ee* refer to the deviation of agents' true expectations from their representation by model consistent expectations.

The impact of residuals on exchange rates varies considerably. In Italy, the residual amounts to -36 % of the total exchange rate in 1985 and -21 % in 1986, but +21 % in 1980; for Germany, it is -23 % in 1985 and -19 % in 1986, but +20 % in 1980. Large fluctuations and the change of sign indicate that, historically, expectational errors *ee* dominated interest rate premia. If we assume a zero mean for *ee* over time, the arithmetic average of national interest premia in each country reflects the sum of average risk premium *rpr* and country premium *cpr*. On average, the impact on exchange rates of these two components in the residual

---

[36] Equation 10, page 41, can be expressed by its logarithmic approximation, $i = ln\left(\frac{1}{e} - u\right) + i^* - \left(ln \frac{1}{Ee_{+1}}\right)$, whereas equation (*) can be written as $i = ln\left(\frac{1}{e}\right) + irpr + i^* - \left(ln \frac{1}{Ee_{+1}}\right)$. It follows that $-u = \frac{exp[irpr]-1}{e}$.

[37] The log specification is also used in part II, where, however, the logarithm of the exchange rate is simply denoted by e, instead of ln e.

amounts to -0.8 % of exchange rates in France and Germany, and -3.1 % for Italy. Using the aforementioned monotonous transformation, actual (positive) risk and country premia can be calculated (but depend on the exchange rate to the US-$ used for each country). They are highest for France, followed by Italy, then Germany. This reflects capital mobility restrictions (i.e. high country premia *cpr*) in France and Italy in the 1980s. The so-called country risk due to high levels of debt (i.e. the risk premium *rpr* in Frankel's terminology) does not seem to be much elevated in Italy compared to France.

How can these results be used for obtaining a residual for the hypothetical Euro exchange rate equation 11? On the one hand, dominating expectational errors are still relevant in the hypothetical EMU. Since they vary considerably between countries, some kind of averaging would be desirable. On the other hand, capital restrictions (country premia) are eliminated in the EMU and risk premia do probably also go down, maybe even to the German level. In fact, the German residuals could be used in the hypothetical Euro exchange rate equation. However, to account for both aspects, a weighted average of national exchange rate residuals (with smaller weights for French and Italian residuals) is preferred for the aggregation. Converted into $ per Euro (based on the going conversion rate in each case), French, Italian and German residuals receive the relative (admittedly somewhat arbitrary) weights 1:1:2, respectively.

Question 3: *How do simulation results respond to changes of residuals in the Euro exchange rate equation and in the ECB reaction function?*

The most elaborate and most explicit sensitivity analyses on hypothetical EMU scenarios were performed on residuals of the

Euro exchange rate equation and of the hypothetical ECB interest rate reaction function. Since national residuals are large in the baseline and the aggregation procedure always contains an element of arbitrariness, there is some uncertainty in the determination of exchange and interest rates – which are the focus of this treatise. Both monetary transmission variables, obviously, effect the overall outcome of simulation results. Studying the impact of residuals provides information on the quality and reliability of simulation results and findings presented in this treatise.

As for variations on exchange rate residuals, the aggregation procedure itself is preserved, but the magnitude of aggregated residuals is reduced by 10, 20 and 30 %. Considering the discussion on the nature of residuals under the previous question, these are large shocks. In particular, it was shown that components of the interest rate premium which are likely to be reduced in the hypothetical EMU are small compared to expectational errors which will not disappear (e.g. during the period of strong appreciations of the US-$ in the mid-1980s). Moreover, the reduction of country and risk premia was (at least partly) taken account of by giving French and Italian baseline residuals a smaller weight in the aggregation procedure.

Box 1 epicts sensitivities (under the CUR scenario) – to variations of aggregate exchange rate residuals – of GDP growth and inflation in the announcement period 1982, and in odd years in the hypothetical EMU (1983 – 1991) as well as prices and GDP *levels* after 10 years (1993). Results are threefold. First, the general pattern of GDP growth and inflation is not affected by changes in aggregate residuals. Moreover, there are no erratic changes under varying levels of residuals (results for 80 % and 90 % residuals are typically between those for 70 % and 100 %). Second, in each year, results for growth and inflation do not deviate by more than

Box 1: **Sensitivities of GDP and Prices (under CUR) to Varying Aggregate Exchange Rate Residuals**

	residual	growth rates [in percent]						levels
Germany:		1982	1983	1985	1987	1989	1991	1993
Real GDP	100%	1,4	1,8	0,3	1,1	4,0	3,4	1927,3
	90%	1,5	1,8	0,2	1,3	3,8	3,4	1930,6
	80%	1,7	1,9	-0,1	1,4	3,5	3,4	1933,5
	70%	1,9	1,9	-0,3	1,5	3,3	3,3	1936,6
Prices	100%	9,6	10,1	7,0	2,6	2,8	3,9	1,91
	90%	9,6	10,0	6,7	2,9	2,7	4,0	1,91
	80%	9,7	10,1	6,5	3,0	2,6	4,0	1,91
	70%	9,8	10,1	6,2	3,1	2,5	4,1	1,91
France:		1982	1983	1985	1987	1989	1991	1993
Real GDP	100%	0,7	-2,1	3,5	4,1	4,1	0,3	3720,1
	90%	0,8	-2,0	3,4	4,1	4,2	0,4	3720,2
	80%	1,0	-1,9	3,2	4,2	4,2	0,6	3726,1
	70%	1,1	-1,7	3,0	4,2	4,2	0,7	3730,7
Prices	100%	5,6	0,1	-2,6	0,3	5,2	5,7	1,44
	90%	5,7	0,3	-2,6	0,2	5,0	5,7	1,44
	80%	5,9	0,6	-2,6	0,0	4,7	5,7	1,44
	70%	6,1	0,8	-2,7	-0,3	4,2	5,6	1,42
Italy:		1982	1983	1985	1987	1989	1991	1993
Real GDP	100%	0,5	3,5	3,1	2,8	3,4	2,0	545,0
	90%	0,4	3,6	3,3	2,9	3,2	1,9	546,0
	80%	0,3	3,7	3,4	3,1	3,0	1,9	547,6
	70%	0,2	4,0	3,6	3,1	3,0	1,8	550,3
Prices	100%	17,2	14,9	10,5	5,8	4,9	6,6	3,19
	90%	16,6	14,1	10,2	6,3	5,2	6,8	3,18
	80%	15,9	13,4	9,9	6,7	5,6	6,9	3,17
	70%	15,2	12,6	9,7	7,3	5,9	7,0	3,17

Source: own calculations (levels: real GDP [in national absorption] or GNP deflator [1980=1.0])

1 % when comparing simulation results based on 70 % to those for 100 % residual levels. Italian inflation rates are an exception, because baseline inflation is so high that small changes in the exchange rate can cause overly strong reactions.

Third, the overall effect of changes of residuals can be measured by comparing GDP and price levels as of 1993, 10 years after the start of the hypothetical EMU. The change in GDP levels, for instance, amounts to less than 0.5 % for Germany, less than 0.7 % for France, and less than 1.0 % for Italy. Similar results were obtained under PPP and CP scenarios. Effects are limited, but not negligible. One should bear in mind though that a 30 % reduction in the level of the aggregate residual is implausibly high. Furthermore, it will be shown in subsection 5.3 that the aggregation procedure chosen produces exchange rates under hypothetical EMU scenarios which reproduce US appreciations in the mid-1980s.

As for aggregate interest rate residuals, consider the situation under the baseline first. Residuals of national interest rate reaction functions represent deliberate deviations of policy from its rule (monetary or exchange rate targeting), because interest rates are assumed to be set by the central banks (central bank rates equal market rates; cf. subsection 3.4). These discretionary modifications are expected (known by agents) in advance, because MULTIMOD is a perfect foresight model.

Analogously, the aggregate residual for the hypothetical ECB reaction function reflects the known discretionary component of monetary policy. At least four assumptions on the aggregation procedure are conceivable. First, zero residuals could be postulated. It is not convincing, however, that the ECB should stick exactly to its rule given that historical central banks did not.

Moreover, a comparison to the baseline would be impossible (just as in the case for exchange rate residuals discussed under the previous question). Second, German residuals could be used to account for – as is sometimes argued – Germany's dominating influence on European monetary policy. This view ignores that German residuals reflect a response to the economic situation in Germany, whereas residuals for the hypothetical ECB refer to the union-wide domain. Moreover, the hypothetical ECB was modeled to conduct some kind of 'intermediate' monetary policy (cf. subsection 3.4).

The third approach acknowledges that the domain of the hypothetical ECB is the economy in all member states. Hence all three historical residuals are considered with their relative importance by using a GDP-based weighted average. Under the fourth and last approach, historical residuals are seen as a reflection of the difference in the national policy stance. If the aggregation is to reflect political decisions – in a hypothetical tripartisan ECB council – on discretionary deviations from the policy rule postulated for the hypothetical ECB, the median of the three residuals should be taken as the union-wide interest rate residual.

Comparing the latter two approaches shows that simulation results (in each year) do not differ much, because resulting nominal interest rates differ by no more than .5 % in any year (except in 1985 when the difference is .7 %). Moreover, the overall outcome is almost identical, because positive and negative differences and their effects almost cancel out over time. This sensitivity analysis is based on the differences in the aggregation procedure, not on changes in the magnitude of a residual under a given procedure – as in the case of sensitivities studied for aggregate exchange rate residuals. Simulation results presented in part II and III are based on the weighted average approach (the third approach).

Question 4: *What is the role of terminal conditions and why do they have to be adjusted?*

The solution of forward-looking (rational expectations) models requires that so-called terminal conditions are satisfied. MULTIMOD is solved up to the year 2040, but expectational data for five additional future (annual) periods is needed, i.e. there are five lead periods. (On the solution algorithm cf. appendix A.2.) The data for the last five years of the data set (2041 to 2045) is called terminal conditions because it is never changed and every solution to the model must be consistent with it.

Moreover, this data is part of a steady state which starts in 1997. Any change in the structural setting, in policy, in behavior, or in exogenous variables will typically disturb the baseline steady state in the first years after 1997, but there is convergence to this steady state before the end of the model horizon in 2040. This means that any change, not just monetary policy changes, are neutral in the long run. The long run is a purely theoretical concept which is meaningless in an economic sense because it cannot change. Under these technical conditions, shock-induced *changes of the long run* itself can typically not be studied within the framework of a simulation analysis.

This characteristic of any standard forward-looking simulation model is not really disturbing for the analysis of effects of most structural, policy, behavioral, or exogenous changes – as long as the focus is on short and medium term adjustments (cf. von Hagen and Lutz, 1996, p. 302). Results are typically not reported for more than 10 years after the occurrence of the shock. To distinguish it from the long run, 10 years after the start of the EMU is referred to as the "longer term" in this treatise. During these first ten years, the impact of terminal conditions is practically negligible. In fact, their effect on early results is so small that it suffices for most purposes to solve the model under a reduced model horizon. Generally, some 20 years after the shock are used.

Some authors do, however, suggest to change terminal conditions even for the analysis of standard policy shocks. "In addition, the terminal conditions themselves are adjusted to be consistent with the long-run responses of the model to the shock in question. ..." according to Masson, Symansky, and Meredith (1990, p. 22). They do, however, not clarify how these "long run responses of the model" are to be determined. Are they inferred from simulation results without adjustments to terminal conditions; or from preconceived opinions on how things should be? It is unsatisfactory, that – in either case – more or less ad hoc changes to the long run are imposed on the model. The approach of Powell and Murphy (1997) seems more convincing. In their simulation model, changes of the long run caused by fiscal and monetary policy are derived analytically. However, their approach is very complex and specifically applied to their model.

Given the alternatives, changes to the long run would have been avoided if feasible. However, a solution procedure based on *unchanged* terminal conditions cannot be used for hypothetical EMU scenarios here because the structural change caused by the hypothetical EMU imposes an additional link between the short and the long run. Under any monetary union, more or less variable bilateral exchange rates in the baseline are replaced by irrevocably fixed conversion rates. Hence rates in the long run must correspond to those in the short run. In subsection 6.1, it is argued from an economic point of view that baseline exchange rates for the long run cannot be the conversion rates because they are inconsistent with the short run. Furthermore, bilateral long run exchange rates under the hypothetical EMU must be – from an economic point of view – different from baseline rates because exchange rates must correspond to equalized monetary policies due to nominal neutrality. Hence terminal conditions and the steady state must be allowed to change. The approach used in this treatise is discussed in question 6. Basically, an extended solution procedure is used to generate (not impose) new terminal conditions consistent with the shock in question.

Question 5: *What is the role of technical convergence criteria and how tight do they have to be?*

The solution procedure for solving dynamic non-linear rational expectations models (under the software package SLIM which is used in this treatise) comprises the repetitive use of two intertwined algorithms. An iterative Gauss-Seidl algorithm for solving the inner model (that is for given values of expectational variables) alternates with a Fair-Taylor component for dealing with the outer model, i.e. for resetting expectational values to actual values produced by the previous Gauss-Seidl solution of the inner model (cf. appendix A.2 and Fair and Taylor, 1983).

Each component requires a number of technical parameters which are controlled by the user. To obtain a solution for a particular scenario, one must experiment with various combinations of these technical parameters. Irrespective of how these parameters are set, a solution algorithm cannot produce complete convergence to the theoretical equilibrium of a large non-linear model. Most technical parameters only determine the iteration path leading to the (unique) solution.

This is, however, not true for the relative technical convergence criterion applied to the Gauss-Seidl as well as for the relative technical convergence criterion used for the Fair-Taylor component of the solution procedure. They determine the accepted percentage deviation in the value of an endogenous variable for two consecutive iterations.[38] If the convergence criteria are set too small (say 0.01 %), the model will never converge to such a degree. If too large convergence criteria (say 1 %) are permitted, the "solution" will probably not be close to the theoretical equilibrium. The dilemma is made worse by the fact that the tightest possible convergence criteria for obtaining a solution depend on the choice for the other technical parameters.

Two approaches for obtaining solutions close to the theoretical equilibrium are conceivable. First, a trial and error procedure can be used to find the tightest possible convergence under each scenario. Second (as done here), the interaction between the Gauss-Seidl convergence criterion, the Fair-Taylor convergence criterion, and the other technical parameters can be studied and used for deriving a procedure for obtaining solutions. This purely technical study of solution behavior comprised simulation runs for more than 100 combinations of convergence criteria and other technical parameters under various scenarios.

These (technical) simulations are not discussed in detail, but three results are reported. First, tighter convergence can be achieved more easily for certain combinations of the other technical parameters than for alternative sets of parameters. A combination of generally successful technical parameters is used in the procedure described under question 6. Second, it is easier to obtain tighter convergence for the Gauss-Seidl component than for the Fair-Taylor component. Realistically, one can get down

---

[38] There is no straightforward interpretation for relative convergence criteria. In particular, a convergence criterion for the Gauss-Seidl (Fair-Taylor) component of 1 % does not mean that actual (expectational) values are 1 % off the equilibrium (the actual equilibrium outcome).

to 0.1 % for Gauss-Seidl convergence, but only to 0.4 or 0.2 % for Fair-Taylor convergence. Third, occasionally, simulation results change considerably for different levels of convergence. As a consequence of the latter two results, the following conditions for an acceptable simulation run are postulated for this treatise (satisfied by all reported simulation results):

- Solution Tightness: Simulation results for the tightest possible convergence criteria are used as long as a certain minimum standard is achieved (0.1 % for Gauss-Seidl and 0.4 % for Fair-Taylor).
- Solution Sequence: There must not be a qualitative or large quantitative change to another simulation run under slightly laxer convergence criteria.

Question 6: *Which solution procedure is used to account for the structural shock, for sufficiently tight convergence criteria and for the necessary change of terminal conditions?*

The stepwise procedure employed for obtaining solutions (under all scenarios discussed in part II and part III) makes multiple use of the aforementioned Gauss-Seidl—Fair-Taylor solution algorithm. Box 2 shows that the algorithm (as described in appendix A.2) is repeated up to 8 times (first column), as long as solutions can be obtained for each repetition. Each time, the solution values of the previous repetition are used as start values for the new repetition of the algorithm. Technical parameter settings are either kept constant or changed as listed in the table.

Column two lists the end year of each intermediate solution. The time periods for repetitions 2 to 5 are reduced in steps of five

Box 2: **Technical Parameter Settings**

repetition	end year	EMU	FairCC	GaussCC
1	2039	25%	1.0	0.2
2	2034	50%	1.0	0.2
3	2029	75%	1.0	0.2
4	2019	100%	1.0	0.2
5	2009	100%	1.0	0.1
6	2009	100%	0.4	0.1
7	2009	100%	0.2	0.1
8	2009	100%	0.1	0.1

End year: last year of model horizon under the given repetition;
EMU: partial or full introduction of the hypothetical EMU scenario;
FairCC / GaussCC: percentage convergence criterion for Fair-Taylor/ Gauss-Seidl component of the algorithm.

or ten years to permit a change of terminal conditions. Previous terminal conditions are simply cut off and earlier data which has only partly adjusted to the previous terminal conditions (under lax technical convergence criteria – see below) is now used as terminal conditions for the next repetition. For repetitions 6 to 8, terminal conditions are kept so that values in previous periods can adjust (under tighter and tighter convergence criteria – see below) to a near steady state which is consistent with the new terminal conditions. The final end year 2009 is 26 years after the introduction of the hypothetical EMU, so that the time span suffices for the adjustment process.

Column three refers to a parameter that has not been discussed so far. The introduction of the hypothetical EMU produces a large structural shock which cannot be accommodated by the solution algorithm as is. Therefore, all hypothetical EMU scenarios are technically decomposed. They are formulated in a way that all EMU variables can be phased in partially. Under repetition 1, for instance, changes for the hypothetical EMU apply to 25 % only. Obviously, this is purely technical, without any meaning in economic terms. Together with slicing off chunks of five years in repetitions 1 to 3 (column 2), the purpose of this phasing-in is to avoid a failure of the solution algorithm.

Columns four and five depict the relative technical convergence criteria for the Fair-Taylor and the Gauss-Seidl component of the solution algorithm. They are only tightened systematically from repetition 5 onwards, once the hypothetical EMU has been phased in fully and the new terminal conditions are in place. Based on this procedure, acceptable solutions according to the conditions laid out in question 5 (solution tightness and solution sequence) can be obtained for all hypothetical EMU scenarios as well as for all scenarios studied in part III. All of these solutions were obtained after repetitions 6 or 7.

PART II

Results and Applications

5 Simulation Results

Based on the simulation framework, the methodical specifications, and the hypothetical EMU scenarios discussed in part I, simulation results for the hypothetical EMU are scrutinized in part II. A three-stage process is required to work out simultaneous effects and their relevance for today. This section (section 5) concentrates on merely *presenting* selected results. In section 6 the focus shifts to *discussing* impulses (shocks) caused by the hypothetical EMU, and to revealing causal connections between nominal and real variables. Finally, section 7 ponders on *applying* the findings to the real world EMU.

As is customary in comparative simulation analyses, results presented in the following figures capture deviations from, or ratios to, baseline data (henceforth referred to as 'relative to the baseline'). Picking the outcome under the market conversion procedure (henceforth "CUR") as point of departure, results for the other two procedures for fixing conversion rates at the start of the hypothetical EMU in 1983 are used by way of comparison: exogenously fixing at purchasing power parities (henceforth "PPP"), or at ERM central parities (henceforth "CP"), respectively. For baseline data, additional figures for CUR, and for CP and PPP diagrams consult the appendix.

The first two subsections of this section focus on the two key macrovariables output and inflation. In subsection 5.1, the development and cyclical pattern of short and medium term results are discussed with figures comprising the announcement period 1982, and the hypothetical EMU between 1983 and 1993. In subsection 5.2, the "longer term" is captured by comparing economic conditions at the end of the aforementioned period, i.e. ten years after the start of the hypothetical EMU.[39] Furthermore, a prima facie assessment of macroeconomic effects of the hypothetical EMU is offered.

In subsection 5.3, results for nominal interest and exchange rates are presented. Interest and exchange rate changes are interpreted later on (in section 6) as impulses caused by the hypothetical EMU and responsible for effects on the real economy. Before that step, subsection 5.4 offers a discussion of international competitiveness (in terms of real effective exchange rates) and implications for foreign indebtedness – based on inflation, output and exchange rate results presented in the first three subsections.

5.1 Output and Inflation Cycles

Figures (a) and (b) in box 3 present the CUR solution for GDP growth and for inflation in the hypothetical EMU scenario, expressed as deviations of simulated values from the baseline (i.e. as percentage point differences to baseline rates).[40] Magnitudes of EMU-induced changes are large for all three member countries Germany, France, and Italy (e.g. deviations of some ±2.5 % in growth in all countries). However, the impact for non-EMU members, here represented by the UK, is very small.

Consider figure (a) first. Starting in announcement year 1982, the introduction of the hypothetical EMU produces (real) cycles

[39] The expression "longer term" is used to distinguish results after a lengthy period of time (10 years) from those related to the theoretical concept of the long run (cf. question 4 in section 4).

[40] There are, obviously, no deviations from the baseline before 1982, the start of the simulation horizon. All curves originate in 0.0 (or 1.0 for figures based on ratios to the baseline).

Box 3: **GDP Growth and Inflation under the CUR Scenario**

(a)

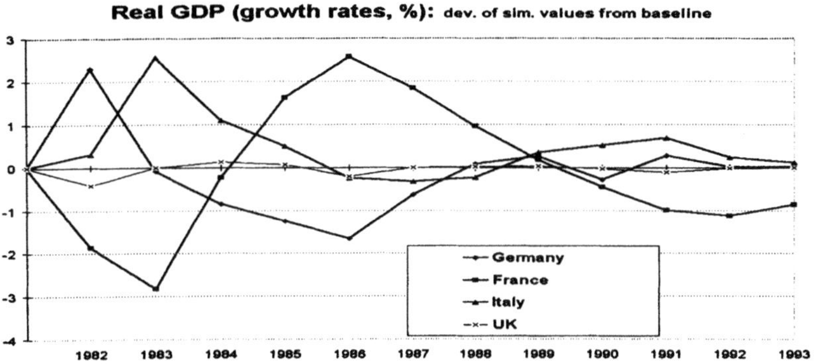

(b)

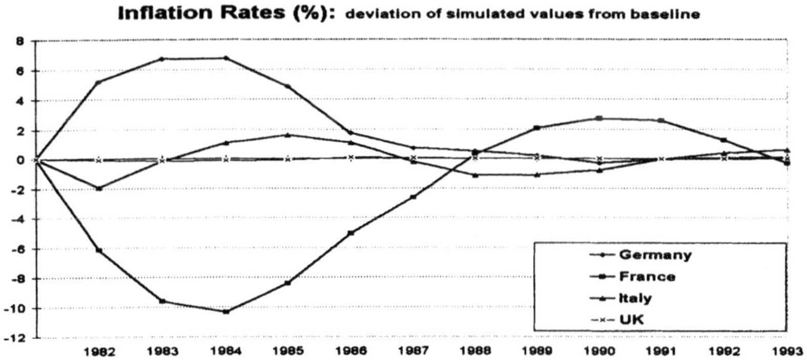

on top of already existing baseline cycles (henceforth called superimposed business cycles).[41] On the whole, the historical business cycle in France is reinforced, but it is partially offset in Italy and Germany. Over time the impact smoothes out, but fluctuations continue well beyond 1996, the year in which the steady state is reached for the baseline. The fact that results take well beyond the simulation horizon (1982 to 1993 in this treatise) to converge to steady state values is an indication that terminal conditions (cf. question 4 in section 4) are not a decisive factor for the simulated outcome presented here.

Member countries are affected by the EMU in different ways. The hypothetical EMU causes a sustained expansion in Italy – relative to the baseline – with a peak in 1985 and a mild trough in 1988 that still keeps GDP levels far above the baseline (though growth rates are, temporarily, below baseline rates). France experiences a sharp recession – relative to the baseline – reaching its bottom in 1984, then an expansion followed by another downturn beginning in 1990. In Germany, except for a strong expansion – relative to the baseline – in announcement year 1982, growth rates are below or close to baseline rates throughout. From 1985, there are net output losses (in levels) relative to the baseline.

As for figure (b), there are strong effects on inflation in the short run, which are more or less wearing off after 1986/1987 relative to the baseline. France experiences very strong disinflation up to 1988, but exceeds baseline inflation thereafter. Germany starts out with a considerable inflationary impact that is not counterbalanced by a cyclical swing in later years. Inflationary and disinflationary effects for Italy – relative to the baseline

[41] An explanation for cycles is offered at the end of subsection 6.4 (on the transmission of impulses).

– are confined to a ±2 % band, throughout, starting with disinflation in the announcement period and additional inflation from 1984 to 1986.

GDP growth and inflation results for PPP (cf. appendix B.4) are, qualitatively, identical to those for CUR. For France, deviations from the baseline are considerably smaller though. The picture changes for CP (cf. appendix B.3): results clearly differ from the outcome under CUR, but, depending on the country in question, to varying degrees. For instance, French inflation and GDP growth under CP are, qualitatively, identical to those for CUR (and largely correspond to results under PPP). In contrast, for Germany, CP results are completely inverted compared to the outcome under CUR.

A closer look at growth rates under CP reveals that the economic downturn (relative to the baseline) in Italy in the middle of the 1980s is much stronger than under CUR (annual negative growth relative to the baseline of about 1 % from 1985 to 1988). For Germany, the superimposed business cycle – relative to the baseline – is reversed. As a result, it is almost exactly countercyclical to the one for Italy and procyclical (with a lead of one or two periods) to the superimposed French business cycle.

As to prices under CP (in contrast to CUR), large inflation cycles relative to the baseline persist for about 10 years. Similar to the picture for GDP growth, French and German inflation rates are basically procyclical (with a lead of one to three periods though) and countercyclical to Italian rates. The Italian inflation cycle relative to the baseline is magnified and starts with additional inflation in 1982. In contrast, Germany does not experience large inflation rates at the beginning any more. Instead, she disinflates up to 1985 relative to the baseline, but experiences higher

Box 4: GDP Growth and Inflation after 10 Years

		baseline	changes to baseline:		
			CUR	PPP	CP
GDP growth:	Germany	2,37	-0,14	-0,19	-0,17
(in %)	France	2,39	-0,11	-0,13	-0,07
	Italy	2,35	0,48	0,44	0,33
	EMU	2,37	0,03	0,02	-0,03
inflation:	Germany	3,01	2,16	1,69	0,65
(in %)	France	5,00	-2,82	-1,72	-1,46
	Italy	8,78	-0,07	-0,12	0,02

Source: own calculations (average annual growth/inflation rates or changes thereof from 1981 to 1993 [percentage points])

inflation rates under CP (than under CUR) in the following years.

5.2 "Longer Term" and EMU Prospects

In this subsection, longer term results (i.e. – as mentioned before – 10 years after the start of the hypothetical EMU) are scrutinized for the three conversion procedures. The comparison is not used for ranking conversion procedures, but for pointing out similarities. In fact, CUR, CP, and PPP may have different effects in the short and medium run, but in the longer term they produce very similar results. The table in box 4 presents mean annual inflation and GDP growth rates for Germany, France and Italy from 1981 to 1993. Since the figures refer to averaged *yearly* changes relative to baseline rates, accumulated effects are considerable. By 1993, Germany has lost approximately 2 % of GDP relative to the baseline (CUR: -1.7; PPP: -2.1; CP: -2.0), and France at least 1 % (CUR: -1.2; PPP: -1.5; CP: -1.0). Italy is the clear winner with some 5 % additional growth after 10 years (CUR: +5.7; PPP: +5.3; CP: +4.0).

Given that GDP effects have opposite signs, we could ask for the net aggregated effect, i.e. can Italy compensate France and Germany? Under the three hypothetical EMU scenarios outlined in this treatise, the net effect for all three EMU countries together can be positive or negative depending on the procedure for fixing conversion rates. We conclude that, in principle, the compensation of losses in some countries by gains in others is possible. We should be careful with further interpretations though, because the net effect is rather small (by 1993, the aggregate effect under CUR and PPP amounts to less than ±0.5 percent of union-wide GDP levels).

The table also shows that, on average (between 1981 and 1993), Germany has experienced additional inflation (strong for CUR and PPP), hence an overall stagflation over the longer term – relative to the baseline. In contrast, Italy's price level is almost unchanged, and France has disinflated strongly relative to the baseline. There are obvious questions: first, why is the Italian response to output strong, but inflation stays put; second, why are output changes in Germany and France similar, but there are opposite signs for strong (dis-)inflation responses? To understand these results, the transmission of impulses caused by the hypothetical EMU must and will be discussed in section 6.

Inflation and GDP growth rates can also be scrutinized when they are not compared to the baseline. In a monetary union, by virtue of concurring monetary policy, we might falsely expect that inflation rates must be practically identical. However, in the real world, we do find (at times, very large) inflation differentials in monetary unions. For instance, consider different federal states in the USA (e.g. effects of the oil shocks on Texas and other states) or different Länder in Germany (e.g. comparing the East to the West after the unification). In theory, identical inflation rates can only prevail, if business cycles are harmonized and idiosyncratic (country-specific) shocks are absent.

The results in this treatise contradict the common view that business cycles will be harmonized soon after the start of the EMU (e.g. Welfens, 1998). In fact, it is shown that a somewhat synchronized business cycle (in the baseline) may be disrupted by the EMU itself. The forced equalization of nominal interest rates and the fixing of conversion rates amount to permanent idiosyncratic shocks for member countries – relative to the baseline. The effect on inflation rates is perpetuated because of asynchronous superimposed business cycles caused by the hypothetical EMU. Indeed, even after 10 years and more, simulated inflation rates (not relative to the baseline) for Italy, France, and Germany are still quite different from one another. By 1993, they vary by up to 5 %.

On the whole, simulation results for GDP and inflation suggest three potentially dangerous negative aspects of any EMU, be it hypothetical in 1983 or real in 1999. First, cyclical effects on the real economy could be induced. Large swings in output and unemployment would bear the risk of social instability. Second, the relative fall in output for individual countries (in this case, for France and Germany) might be limited in the longer term. Nonetheless, the clear prospect of losses on average (relative to a situation without EMU) – coupled with increased cyclical instability – might be politically unacceptable or even prompt social unrest. Third, a sustained rise in inflation may be hard to digest in any country, but particularly in Germany. This corresponds to fears in Germany that are being expressed more and more openly in the run-up to the start of the real world EMU.

5.3 Nominal Interest and Exchange Rates

This subsection presents simulation results for interest and exchange rates, but leaves the discussion of causes and effects of interest and exchange rate impulses to section 6. Under all conversion procedures, interest and exchange rate changes relative to the baseline are large for the (hypothetical) EMU member countries Germany, France, and Italy, but small for other countries. Therefore, the presentation and discussion of results focuses on countries participating in the hypothetical EMU. Box 5 depicts short and long term nominal interest rates (percentage point differences from baseline rates) and nominal exchange rates to the US-$ (as a ratio to baseline rates) under CUR, both after and immediately before the start of the hypothetical EMU in 1983.

Figure (a) shows that the common interest rate policy of the ECB (cf. subsection 3.4) translates – relative to the baseline – into rising interest rates in low-interest country Germany, but decreasing rates in Italy and France.[42] Towards the end of the reported period, changes relative to the baseline become less pronounced, because interest differentials in the baseline are considerably smaller towards the end of the 1980s and beyond. From 1991, French interest rates – relative to the baseline – turn positive, because that was the time, historically, when French rates approached low German rates. (Stability-oriented – Franc fort – policies started showing effects at the end of the 1980s.)

The development of union-wide nominal short term interest rates is similar under all conversion procedures, because interest

[42] Despite a large drop in nominal interest rates (not compared to the baseline), real rates turn negative only in a few case in 1983 and 1984 depending on the conversion procedure.

Box 5: **Nominal Interest and Exchange Rates under the CUR Scenario**

(a)

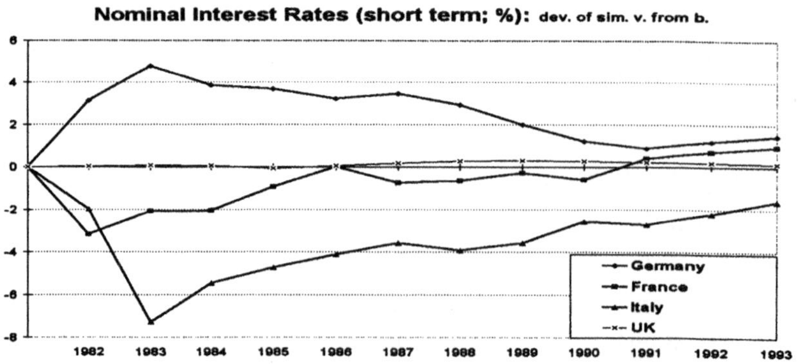

(b)

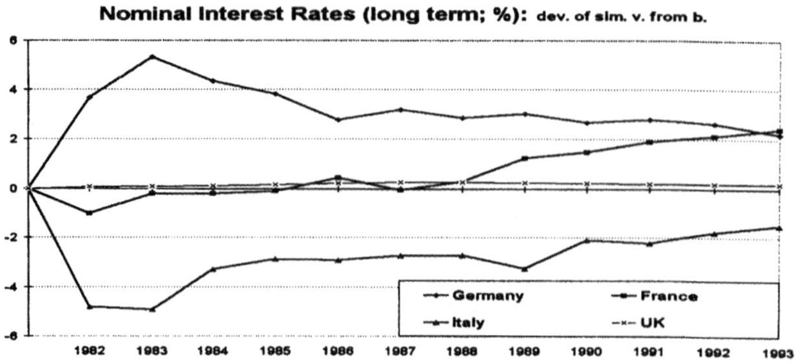

(c)

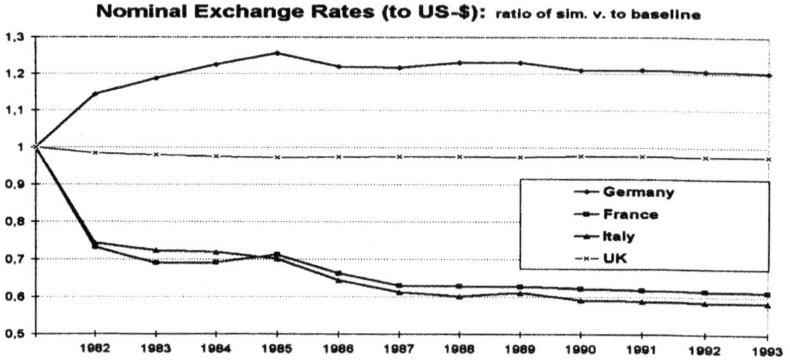

convergence does not depend on how bilateral exchange rates between EMU member countries are fixed. Once the hypothetical EMU has started, simulated interest rates as such (i.e. not compared to the baseline) do not differ among conversion procedures by more than one percent in any year. Under PPP, the common interest rate is almost identical to the one under CUR until 1988, but up to 1 % higher thereafter. Under CP, it is smaller in the first few years and – similarly to PPP – higher in the later period. Effects in the announcement period, too, are similar for CUR and PPP, but a perverse result obtains for CP. Italian interest rates increase somewhat, and German rates fall so that historical interest differentials are (slightly) enlarged in 1982.

Under all conversion procedures, nominal long term interest rates (relative to the baseline), basically, resemble short rates (except for the announcement period). For CUR, they are presented in figure (b) of box 5. Long rates in all EMU countries equalize around 13 % (CP: 12.5) in 1983, the first year of the hypothetical EMU. In the announcement year 1982, they are between 13 % (CP: 11.5) in Germany (up from 9 % in the baseline) and 15 % (CP: 12.5) in France and Italy (down from 16 and 20 % respectively). Even under CP, there is no widening of the long term interest rate gap between Germany and Italy as there was for short rates. The harmonization of long term interest rates is not surprising, because they are derived from short rates (by using the term structure argument that long rates correspond to an average of today's interest rate and future expected rates).

Figure (c) in box 5 presents Euro exchange rates vis-à-vis the US-$ in terms of DM, FF, and Lira – relative to the baseline – in the same way as for non-EMU currencies. Recall from subsection 3.2 that the new *European* currency Euro can be equally expressed in terms of Lira (= LiraConversionRate * Euro), FF (= FFConversionRate * Euro), or DM (= 1 * Euro – due to normalization). Hence, the performance of the Euro – under any hypothetical EMU scenario defined in this treatise – can be evaluated in comparison to each one of the original *national* currencies. (In fact, vis-à-vis the US-$, the Euro is stronger than the historical Lira or FF, but weaker than the one of the DM.)

In figure (c), changes in nominal exchange rates denote a depreciation relative to the baseline, if data points are above the 1.0 line. Positive slopes of a curve (above 1.0) stand for reinforced depreciations relative to the baseline. (Analogous interpretations apply for points below the 1.0 line and negative slopes above and below 1.0.) By scrutinizing results *relative* to the baseline, the temporary appreciation of the US-$ in the mid-1980s does not obscure the findings.[43]

Non-EMU currencies are hardly affected by the hypothetical EMU. In figure (c), they are represented by the Sterling–$ exchange rate. (It is not shown that there is a minor depreciation – relative to the baseline – of the non-European currencies US-$ and Japanese Yen vis-à-vis the European non-EMU currencies, that is the Sterling and the fictitious currency of the small industrialized country aggregate.) In contrast, simulated Euro–$ rates (DM–$, FF–$, Lira–$) change substantially relative to the respective national baseline.

Under CUR, there is a strong depreciation in Germany relative to DM–$ baseline exchange rates, whereas Italy and France

---

[43] This result does actually depend on the aggregation of exchange rate residuals in the hypothetical EMU (cf. question 2, section 4). The fact that simulated exchange rates – relative to the baseline – in periods with large exchange rate residuals in the baseline are in line with simulated exchange rates from other periods indicates that the chosen aggregation procedure was appropriate.

experience even stronger relative appreciations. For each country, exchange rate adjustments relative to the baseline already happen in announcement period 1982, because 1983 conversion rates are irrevocably fixed at 1982 bilateral exchange rates (i.e. bilateral rates do not change from 1982 onwards). Appreciations (depreciations) – relative to the baseline – are sustained throughout the entire time horizon considered despite a couple of minor countermovements. In the early years of the hypothetical EMU, deviations from the baseline become stronger, but from 1987 (1986 for Germany) they remain almost unchanged (historically, there were no realignments between 1987 and 1992).

The development of exchange rates vis-à-vis the US-$ — relative to the baseline – largely reflects changes in the baseline due to realignments within the framework of the EMS. From 1982, the distance between each pair of curves for Germany, France, and Italy in figure (c) is given *invariably* by the ratio of their bilateral conversion rate to the corresponding historical baseline exchange rate. The FF-DM and Lira-DM rates change by more than $\frac{1}{3}$ prior to the start of the hypothetical EMU. This is only possible, because flexible exchange rates are assumed for announcement period 1982 – as justified in subsection 3.1.

In a real world setting, narrow or even wide ERM bands[44] would not suffice to accommodate such exchange rate shocks. There would be a rationale for additional speculative pressure on ERM parities so that it seems unrealistic for central banks to be able to defend ERM parities in 1982. However, simulation results

[44] The narrow bands of the ERM (Exchange Rate Mechanism) of the EMS (European Monetary System) allow for a target zone of up to $\pm 2\frac{1}{4}$ % fluctuations of exchange rates around a central parity. Though officially extended to ± 15 % in August 1993 (wide bands), the exchange rate criterion of the Maastricht Treaty is sometimes still related to previously narrow ERM bands.

presented here tend to overstate the shock, because the anticipation period is limited to one year only, and because MULTIMOD presupposes full credibility of the EMU project (cf. subsection 3.1).

For procedures with exogenously fixed conversion rates (CP and PPP), exchange rate results (vis-à-vis the US-$) differ from those under CUR. For both procedures, bilateral exchange rates (between prospective EMU member countries) in announcement period 1982 do not have to correspond to conversion rates from 1983 onwards. Under PPP, results are, nonetheless, qualitatively identical to those under CUR. The appreciation of the Euro in terms of Lira is stronger than for the FF under PPP, but rates for the Lira are very similar under both conversion procedures. Under CP, there are two differences compared to CUR (cf. the discussion in subsection 6.3): (i) the Euro starts out with an appreciation relative to *all* underlying baseline currencies including the DM (i.e. the Euro is stronger – vis-à-vis the US-$ – compared to the historical DM until 1986); (ii) exchange rate adjustments under CP are not as large as for the other conversion procedures, because central parities of the EMS are close to actual baseline rates.

5.4 International Competitiveness

This subsection focuses on changes to international competitiveness (measured by real effective exchange rates) and their impact on the net foreign asset position (to capture the accumulated effect of the current account; cf. appendix A.1) in member countries of the hypothetical EMU. It is then shown that there are no longer losses for Germany, if real effects are measured in terms of GNP instead of GDP. Box 6 presents real effective exchange rates, net

Box 6: Real Exchange Rates, Net Foreign Assets, Real GNP under the CUR Scenario

(a)

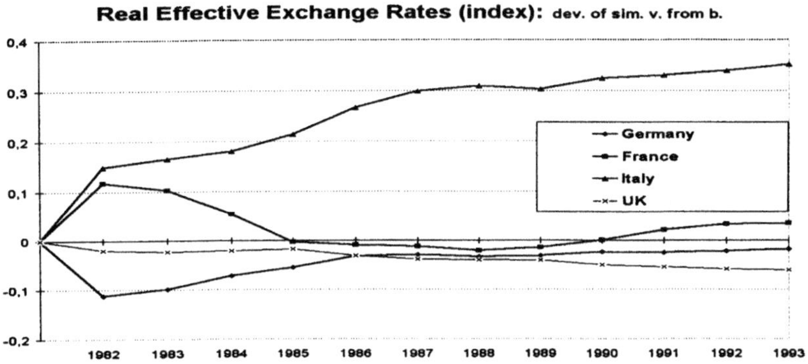

(b)

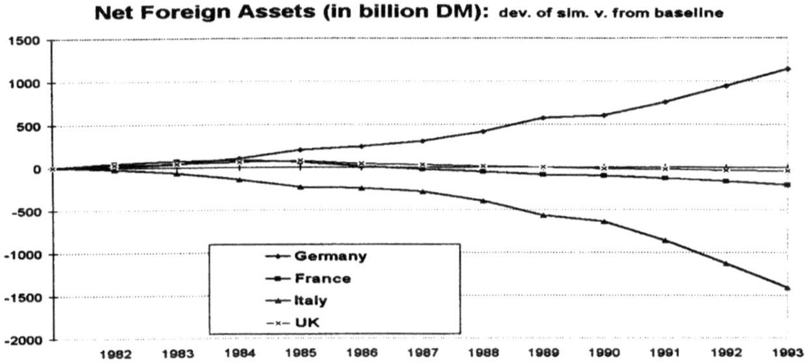

(c)

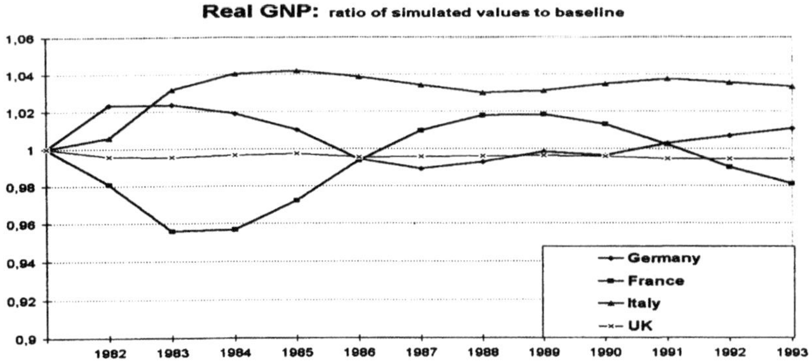

foreign assets, and real GNP under CUR relative to the baseline.

In subsection 5.1, it was discussed that there are inflation cycles relative to the baseline (as well as inflation differentials between the countries forming the hypothetical EMU). At the same time, we have just seen that nominal European exchange rates are strongly affected – relative to the baseline. This applies to exchange rates for the Euro-$ (represented, for instance, by the Lira-$ rate) as well as to bilateral rates (e.g. $\left[\frac{Lira}{FF}\right]$; conversion rates under the hypothetical EMU compared to baseline exchange rates). Hence, relative to the baseline there must be effects on bilateral real exchange rates, both between member countries of the hypothetical EMU and with reference to outside countries. The real exchange rate, $\lambda = \frac{e * P^*}{P}$, appreciates relative to the baseline ($\lambda \downarrow$), if there is a nominal appreciation compared to the baseline ($e \downarrow$), or if inflation at home increases by more than abroad, i.e. $P \uparrow > P^* \uparrow$ (given $P = P^*$ initially).

In a multi-country setting, overall international competitiveness is captured by real effective exchange rates. In MULTIMOD, they are index numbers fluctuating around 0.0. A positive deviation from the baseline represents a real appreciation. Figure (a) presents simulation results for real effective exchange rates under CUR – relative to the baseline. In France, there are countervailing effects of a strong disinflation relative to the baseline and a relative nominal appreciation that is caused by fixing exchange rates in 1983. As a consequence, there is only a limited effect on real effective exchange rates in the medium and longer term. The French net foreign asset position is somewhat worsened under CUR (-273 billions of DM) compared to the baseline (-65 billions of DM).[45]

---

[45] In MULTIMOD, negative national net foreign assets are not surprising,

In Italy, the relative nominal appreciation due to the hypothetical EMU directly translates into a sustained real appreciation relative to the baseline, since there is almost no inflationary impact in the longer term. Exports become relatively more expensive. In addition, the demand for imports increases due to the rise in GDP. As a consequence, Italy's trade balance and net foreign asset position (figure b) dramatically worsen over time relative to the baseline. By 1993, net claims on the Italian economy rise from 197 in the baseline to 1610 billions of DM under CUR.

The loss of assets in Italy is mirrored by a similarly large gain in Germany (baseline: 568 billions of DM; CUR: 1724). The nominal depreciation in Germany relative to the baseline is only partially offset by additional inflation, so that there is a small, but sustained real depreciation relative to the baseline leading to gains in competitiveness in each period. In addition, again mirroring Italy, the German demand for imports decreases due to the fall in GDP.

The outcome for real effective exchange rates is, qualitatively, similar for all conversion procedures. This is even true for CP, because differences in results for inflation and nominal exchange rates to those under CUR have opposite effects on real effective exchange rates. In particular, under CP (in contrast to CUR), Germany experiences a nominal appreciation (vis-à-vis the US-$ relative to the baseline) in the first years of the simulated period. But since there is also a stronger disinflation under CP than under CUR, the outcome of a small sustained real depreciation (relative to the baseline) prevails. As to Italy, the CUR result of continued real appreciations obtains for CP as well, because stronger infla-

---

since world-wide net foreign assets are defined such that they add up to approximately zero.

Box 7: **Net Foreign Assets after 10 Years**

		baseline	changes to baseline:		
			CUR	PPP	CP
NFA in 1993:	Germany	586	1725	1624	1253
(in bil. DM)	France	-65	-273	-43	-88
	Italy	-198	-1610	-1667	-889
	EMU	323	-158	-86	276

Source: own calculations (net foreign asset levels or changes thereof in 1993 [in billions of DM])

tion in the medium term (compared to CUR) is counterbalanced by a smaller nominal appreciation.

The longer term outcome for net foreign assets is presented in box 7. Again, results are very similar qualitatively. Under CUR, the losses for France are larger than under CP and PPP. Under CP, gains in Germany and losses in Italy are less important (compared to the other conversion procedures) and do not balance out. As a result, the change of aggregated net foreign assets for all hypothetical EMU countries is clearly positive under CP, but negative for the other two conversion procedures.

To evaluate the significance of the loss of assets for Italy, compare the 1993 stock of net foreign claims on Italy to the 1993 baseline value for Italy's GDP (2119 - also in billions of DM) and her capital stock (5093 billions of DM). Italy's high indebtedness to other countries, in particular to Germany, could also be expressed more provocatively: by 1993, a large part of Italy is owned by Germans. Since we are in a monetary union (with irrevocably fixed exchange rates), this is not a problem economically, but it may be politically unsustainable.

It should be conceded that this result hinges on the assumption of unchanged entrepreneurial behavior in Italy. Under sustained depreciations of the Lira (as captured in the baseline), incentives for restructuring and rationalization are weak. But locked conversion rates and non-depreciating Euro-$ exchange rates should be expected to induce behavioral changes (of firms and governments) in the upcoming real world EMU, thus reducing the loss of competitiveness in Italy. To some extent, the drive for mergers in industry and services in the real world in recent years may be attributed to the increased competitive pressure due to the expected formation of the real world EMU.

Due to these drastic effects on net foreign assets, the overall change in (real) GNP – relative to the baseline – is distinctly different from the one for GDP. Factor incomes accrued by nationals abroad are included in GNP, but not in GDP. MULTIMOD does not incorporate external labor income by nationals, but interest paid on capital invested in other countries is accounted for. Hence changes in net foreign assets affect GNP. Figure (c) (box 6, page 73) depicts real GNP levels under CUR as ratio to the baseline. The outcome for Italy is favorable throughout; for Germany, GNP is mostly above the baseline; but there are strong cycles around the baseline in France.

The figure cannot be compared directly to the graph on real GDP, because growth rates were used in box 3, page 61. Nonetheless, its purpose is to illustrate that the picture of gains and losses for member countries of the hypothetical EMU changes when we judge by real GNP instead of GDP. In 1993, real GNP in Germany is 1.1 % higher under CUR than in the baseline, whereas real GDP is 1.7 % below its baseline level (cf. subsection 5.2). The opposite applies to Italy: simulated real GNP under CUR is 3.3 % higher, but real GDP is 5.7 % higher. (For France, the difference is not so important.)

6 Interest and Exchange Rate Impulses

In the previous section, we saw that – relative to the baseline – the hypothetical EMU produces nominal shocks and affects real variables. In this section, it is shown that effects caused by the hypothetical EMU can be mostly understood by studying underlying causalities, even though the simulation analysis is based on a large system of simultaneous equations. Conceptually, (i) the causes for nominal interest and exchange rate impulses, and (ii) their transmission into the real economy can be distinguished. As for the interest rate impulse, the link between the common monetary policy and equalized short term interest rates (interest equalization effect) is straightforward and was already discussed in subsections 3.4 and 5.3.

As for the exchange rate impulse, causes are scrutinized in three steps. In subsection 6.1, changes of exchange rates caused by the market conversion procedure CUR are represented in a stylized graph and justified verbally. This effect (market conversion effect) is captured analytically in subsection 6.2. Subsection 6.3 contrasts CUR with exogenous conversion procedures PPP and CP. Based on differences in the underlying causality, the effect of exogenous conversion procedures (exogenous conversion effect) is compared to the market conversion effect, and actual simulation results are discussed. The remainder of this section is devoted to the transmission of impulses into real variables. In subsection 6.4, the relevant transmission effects are discussed for all three conversion procedures. In subsection 6.5, it is shown that there is typically a trade-off between interest and exchange rate impulses.

Box 8: **Exchange Rates under CUR (Stylized)**

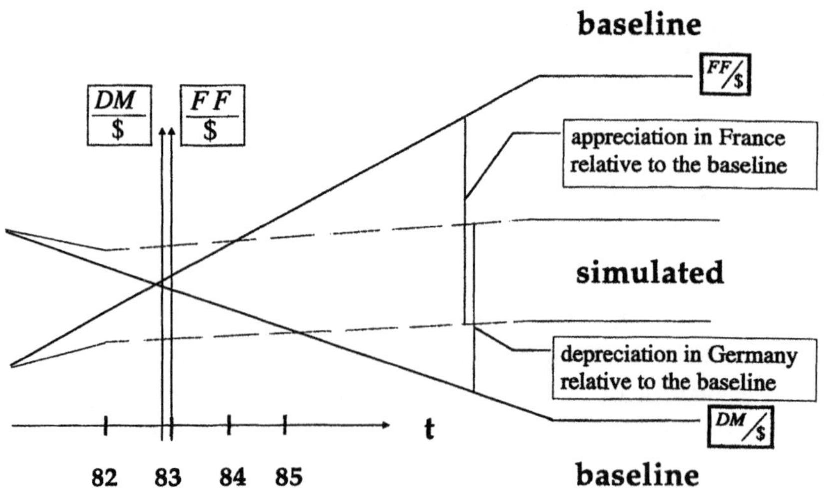

6.1 Exchange Rates under Market Conversion

Box 8 offers a stylized representation of exchange rate impulses caused by the hypothetical EMU (exchange rate impulses) under the market conversion procedure CUR (cf. simulated data in box 5, page 68). The figure captures the interdependence between exchange rates to the US-$ (henceforth outside rates) and bilateral exchange/conversion rates between hypothetical EMU member countries (henceforth both bilateral exchange rates under the baseline as well as simulated conversion rates will be referred to as inside rates). The downward and upward sloping straight lines depict baseline outside rates for a stronger currency (DM) and a weaker currency (FF or the Lira), respectively. The figure contains two diagrams: one for FF-$ rates, one for DM-$ rates. Ordinates are adjusted (scales differ) so that the two baseline curves intersect in 1983, the start year of the hypothetical EMU.

The two dashed lines represent outside rates for the simulated outcome (under CUR) from 1982 onwards; they are two representations of the Euro-$ exchange rate (according to subsections 5.3 and 3.2): DM-$ (= 1 * Euro-$ – due to normalization), FF-$ (= FFConversionRate * Euro-$). Since the conversion rate (from 1983) is fixed at simulated inside rates as of 1982, the distance (more precisely, the ratio) between the two curves capturing simulated outside rates must be constant from 1982 onwards. Under CUR, there is an appreciation relative to the baseline for the FF and a depreciation for the DM, throughout. This applies for the anticipation period, too. In 1983, simulated inside rates (conversion rates) differ from baseline inside rates (bilateral exchange rates), so that the curves for the simulated outside rates in box 8 do not intersect any more. These two curves (for simulated outside rates) lie between their two corresponding baseline curves when moving out to the right. Steady state outside rates are represented by the horizontal part of each curve (in this stylized presentation, there are unrealistic dips where the steady state begins). The figure shows that simulated steady state exchange rates are lower in France and higher for Germany compared to baseline rates.

It is intuitively appealing that the merger of stronger and weaker currencies – under intermediate monetary policy conditions (cf. subsection 3.4) – produces a common currency which is weaker than its strongest member (DM), and stronger than its weaker component currencies (Lira and FF as of the 1980s). This implies, for instance, that previous appreciation expectations in Germany are reduced or eliminated. As a result, Germany attracts less foreign capital, so that nominal short term market interest rates must go up – relative to the baseline. The opposite happens in countries with previous depreciation expectations. In the end, market rates should (almost) equalize in a monetary union with a common monetary policy.

It is not straightforward to capture these effects in a simulation model with rational expectations, because steady state conditions are typically fixed in advance or changes are imposed from the outside (cf. questions 4 and 6 in section 4). Exchange rate impulses and changes of the steady state under CUR are, therefore, justified in two steps. First, it is shown that long term (steady state) exchange rates under market conversion (CUR) must be allowed to change (unrestrained from imposed steady state conditions) – as shown in box 8. Second, the direction of changes – produced by the model – for short and long run outside rates relative to the baseline is discussed for each currency and summarized in observation 2.

As for the first issue, a (unrestrained) shift in steady state exchange rates is required to ensure the consistency of the dynamic system while coping with the structural break implied by the formation of the hypothetical EMU. This is so, because exchange rate expectations also change when the steady state shifts. To see why simulated steady state rates must differ from corresponding baseline rates, let us assume for a moment that the steady state did not change. In a monetary union, inside rates (conversion rates) must be consistent with members' outside rates at any time, i.e. also when the steady state is reached. If the steady state remained unchanged (or if changes were imposed), simulated outside rates in the beginning of the monetary union would have to be as far apart from one another as they are in the long run (as pictured in box 8). In other words, prespecified steady state conditions would determine conversion rates under CUR. Clearly, this would be unsatisfactory.[46]

Moreover, if the steady state remained unchanged, (at least one of the) simulated outside rates in 1982 would necessarily differ very much from their corresponding baseline rates in 1981 (prior to the announcement of the monetary union). The necessary appreciation for the DM (depreciation for the FF) in announcement period 1982 would produce an enormous shock the economy can typically not cope with. In fact, successful simulation runs for this treatise could only be produced once the simulation algorithm was modified so that changes to the steady state are determined by the model (cf. section 4, questions 4 and 6).

The second issue refers to the direction of change for short and long run outside rates under CUR relative to the baseline. Simulated steady state outside rates in Germany (France and Italy) depreciate (appreciate) relative to the baseline reflecting a change in the monetary development in hypothetical EMU member countries. In the historical baseline, Germany (France and Italy) exhibit low (high) money growth and inflation rates over an extended period of time (i.e. before the steady state is reached). In contrast, under CUR, the common monetary policy of the hypothetical EMU matters (cf. subsection 3.4). It is intermediate in the sense that the hypothetical ECB permits higher monetary growth than the Bundesbank (lower monetary growth than the Banque de France and the Banca d'Italia). Under nominal neutrality, DM (FF and Lira) long run outside rates must have

---

[46] Under exogenous conversion procedures (CP or PPP), the argument for changes in the steady state is more fundamental in nature, because unchanged steady state rates are always (generically) inconsistent with exogenous conversion rates. Furthermore, changes to simulated steady state rates must be larger under exogenous conversion procedures compared to CUR, if exogenous conversion rates are close to baseline rates at the beginning of the hypothetical EMU. This applies to results under the CP conversion procedure.

risen (fallen) in the same proportion as other monetary variables. Henceforth, this effect is called monetary equalization effect.

Under the uncovered interest parity condition ($e = i^* - i + Ee_{+1}$, where i is the interest rate, and e is the logarithm of the exchange rate)[47], short term exchange rates are affected by changes of the long run (i.e. the monetary equalization effect) through changes in expectations. This effect is well established in the theoretical rational expectations literature (for instance to capture announcement effects), but ignored in many applications. If long term exchange rates were assumed to remain unchanged, rising interest rates (caused by the common monetary policy) would imply appreciations. However, since the long run is allowed to change, a very different result obtains. Under CUR, the effect of interest rate changes relative to the baseline (interest equalization effect) is actually overcompensated by the countervailing effect of changes to exchange rate expectations (monetary equalization effect). Moreover, this applies in virtually every year and in each member country of the hypothetical EMU.

Simulated exchange rate data in box 5 (page 68) shows that exchange rate impulses become stronger from period to period in the early years of the hypothetical EMU. This basically reflects baseline changes capturing repeated realignments in the historical EMS until 1987. Mirroring a period of exchange rate stability in the ERM thereafter (no realignments between 1987 and 1992), exchange rate impulses persist on a more or less constant level from 1986/1987, i.e. outside rates relative to the baseline remain constant. Considering the magnitudes of appreciations in Italy and France relative to the baseline, and relative depreciations in

---

[47] In part II, the open interest parity is used in its logarithmic format, whereas in part I it is presented in terms of rates – as in the underlying model MULTIMOD (cf. page 24, equations 2 and 3).

Germany, this is a strong empirical result (based on an econometric model and the conditions of the 1980s). Even though it is intuitive for the CUR scenario, it is summarized in an observation, because it is needed for the discussion in the following subsections.

Observation 2 (Exchange Rate Impulse under Market Conversion)
In the hypothetical EMU with conversion rates determined by the market (CUR), a country with an originally weak (strong) national currency experiences appreciative (depreciative) exchange rate impulses – relative to a situation without monetary union – over an extended period of time. This is so because the interest equalization effect is dominated by the countervailing monetary equalization effect.

6.2 Market Conversion Effect

In this subsection, changes of outside rates of a stronger and a weaker member currency – caused by market conversion CUR – are linked by a formal condition. Thus exchange rate impulses in the hypothetical EMU under CUR – relative to the baseline – can be compared to exogenous conversion procedures (CP and PPP) in the next subsection. By subtracting simulated and baseline cross rate identities and using bilateral open interest parities (analogous to exchange rate equations in MULTIMOD)[48], changes of outside rates in two member countries, for instance Germany and France, can be linked for each year $t \geq 1982$ to yield:

$$e_t^F(s) - e_t^F(b) = \left(e_t^G(s) - e_t^G(b)\right)$$

$$+ \underbrace{\left(i_{82}^G(s) - i_{82}^F(s)\right) - \left(i_t^G(b) - i_t^F(b)\right) + \left(e_{t\geq 83}^{F,G}(s) - E_t e_{t+1}^{F,G}(b)\right)}_{\text{market conversion effect}}, \quad (13)$$

where 'b' represents the baseline (no monetary union) and 's' the simulated outcome (hypothetical EMU under CUR).

For any particular period, call the change in outside rates in France (left hand side) 'relatively appreciative' compared to Germany, if $\left(e_t^F(s) - e_t^F(b)\right) < \left(e_t^G(s) - e_t^G(b)\right)$. This definition includes the aforementioned case of an appreciation in France and a depreciation in Germany. (It does, however, also capture two other cases which are discussed below: an appreciation [depreciation] in France and a weaker appreciation [stronger depreciation] in Germany.) Whether the change in French outside rates is relatively appreciative or not depends on what is called market conversion effect (see further down). Applying the definition (for relative appreciativeness) to equation 13 yields that French outside rates are 'relatively appreciative', throughout, if and only if

[48] For the baseline 'b': $e_t^F(b) = e_t^G(b) + e_t^{F,G}(b)$ with $e_t^{F,G}(b) = i_t^G(b) - i_t^F(b) + E_t e_{t+1}^{F,G}(b)$;
for the simulated outcome 's': $e_t^F(s) = e_t^G(s) + e_t^{F,G}(s)$; by definition of CUR, the conversion rate equals the simulated exchange rate ($e_{t\geq 83}^{F,G}(s) = e_{82}^{F,G}(s)$), so that $e_t^{F,G}(s) = i_{82}^G(s) - i_{82}^F(s) + E_{82} e_{83}^{F,G}(s)$ for $t \geq 1982$; however, the expected inside rate in the monetary union corresponds to the endogenous, but constant conversion rate ($E_{82} e_{83}^{F,G}(s) = e_{t\geq 83}^{F,G}(s)$); cf. also Bohn (1998b).

– in each period – the market conversion effect in equation 13 is negative, i.e. if and only if

$$\underbrace{\left(i_t^F(b) - i_t^G(b)\right)}_{:=\Delta i_t(b)} - \underbrace{\left(i_{82}^F(s) - i_{82}^G(s)\right)}_{:=\Delta i_{82}(s)} < \underbrace{\left(E_t e_{t+1}^{F,G}(b) - e_{t\geq 83}^{F,G}(s)\right)}_{:=\Delta E e_{+1}(b-s)} . \quad (14)$$

The left hand side represents the aforementioned interest equalization effect, because it captures the impact of vanishing interest rate differentials in a monetary union. It consists of two components, the baseline interest differential in period t ($\Delta i_t(b)$) and the simulated interest differential in announcement period 1982 ($\Delta i_{82}(s)$).[49] For France and Germany (or Italy and Germany), each component is positive in the 1980s, i.e. countervailing because of the minus sign (cf. box 5, page 68, together with appendix B.1). The net effect of interest equalization is also (mostly) positive, because $\Delta i_{82}(s)$ is comparatively small.

The right hand side captures the aforementioned monetary equalization effect, because the difference of baseline expected inside rates and conversion rate (also) reflects changes in the simulated monetary development in France and Germany relative to the baseline. Given that inflation rates increase in Germany and decrease in France over an extended period of time (before the steady state is reached), there must be an appreciation of the FF vis-à-vis the DM so that $\Delta E e_{+1}(b-s)$ must be positive in each year.

---

[49] According to the (theoretical) open interest parity between France and Germany, $\Delta i_{82}(s)$ should be zero under CUR. However, in the model, the uncovered interest parity only applies with qualifications (cf. section 4, question 2). Interest rates of member countries of the hypothetical EMU are still different in the announcement period, because residuals differ before the start of the monetary union. In the real world, too, short term nominal interest rates have not completely converged (especially when the average is taken) in 1998, the year prior to the start of the EMU.

All in all, condition 14 (page 87) is satisfied, throughout, under CUR. In each year, the FF and the Lira are 'relatively appreciative' vis-à-vis the DM. In years with a positive interest equalization effect, there is a trade-off between the two equalization phenomena, but the monetary equalization effect dominates. The virtue of condition 14 is that it captures the determinants of exchange rate changes under CUR analytically (and can be compared to PPP and CP). Nonetheless, the result was clear in advance from the discussion of changes of outside rates (issue 2), because a depreciation of the DM and an appreciation of the FF (Lira), obviously, imply that condition 14 is fulfilled.

Theoretically, outside rates in France (and Italy) could be 'relatively appreciative' under CUR (condition 14 satisfied), but there could still be a (weak) appreciation in Germany relative to the baseline. In box 8, page 80, the curve representing simulated DM outside rates would pass below the baseline intersection point in 1983, but would not cut the simulated FF curve (which would be below the simulated DM curve). A similar outcome obtains under CP – as discussed in the next subsection. (Conversely, the FF and the Lira could depreciate vis-à-vis the US-$, but by less than the DM – relative to the baseline.)

Such an appreciation for all currencies – relative to the baseline – is possible, if the common monetary policy produces a monetary development close to the historical outcome for Germany. Then, the long run outside rate of the DM would not change much; instead steady state adjustments would have to be born by outside rates of the FF and the Lira. In the short and medium term, an appreciation for all currencies would even be possible for a slight depreciation of the German outside steady state rate, as long as the rise in interest rates in Germany (relative to the baseline) dominated the depreciative change in expected DM outside rates.

6.3 Causality and Exogenous Conversion Effect

To compare exchange rate results for the three conversion procedures, it is useful to distinguish three time periods: (i) anticipation period 1982; (ii) start period 1983, in which inside rates are irrevocably fixed; and (iii) the time from 1984 characterized by constant inside rates, but floating outside rates. The underlying causality explaining simulation results differs for endogenous (CUR) and exogenous (PPP and CP) conversion procedures.

The figure in box 9 illustrates one possibility to conceptualize causality links for exchange rates – under hypothetical EMU scenarios – over the three time periods considered.[50] Inside and outside rates are specified for France and Germany as examples. Horizontal arrows pointing to the left indicate the effect of expected outside rates on previous period outside rates in each period. Due to the structural break in 1983, the inside rate in 1982 is only affected indirectly by future inside rates. Instead, it can be understood to be determined by outside rates which depend, individually, on the open interest parity. For 1983 and for each year from 1984, however, the degrees of freedom for French and German outside rates together are reduced by one, because conversion rates are fixed.

Under CUR, conversion rates (inside rates) are fixed at bilateral 1982 exchange rates (inside rates). Thereby, inside and outside rates in 1982 and 1983 form a subsystem of simultaneous equations as indicated by the two intertwined loops of arrows

[50] From the point of view of systems dynamics, alternative system (impact) diagrams are possible (cf. Becker, 1995).

Box 9: **Causality in Exchange Rates**

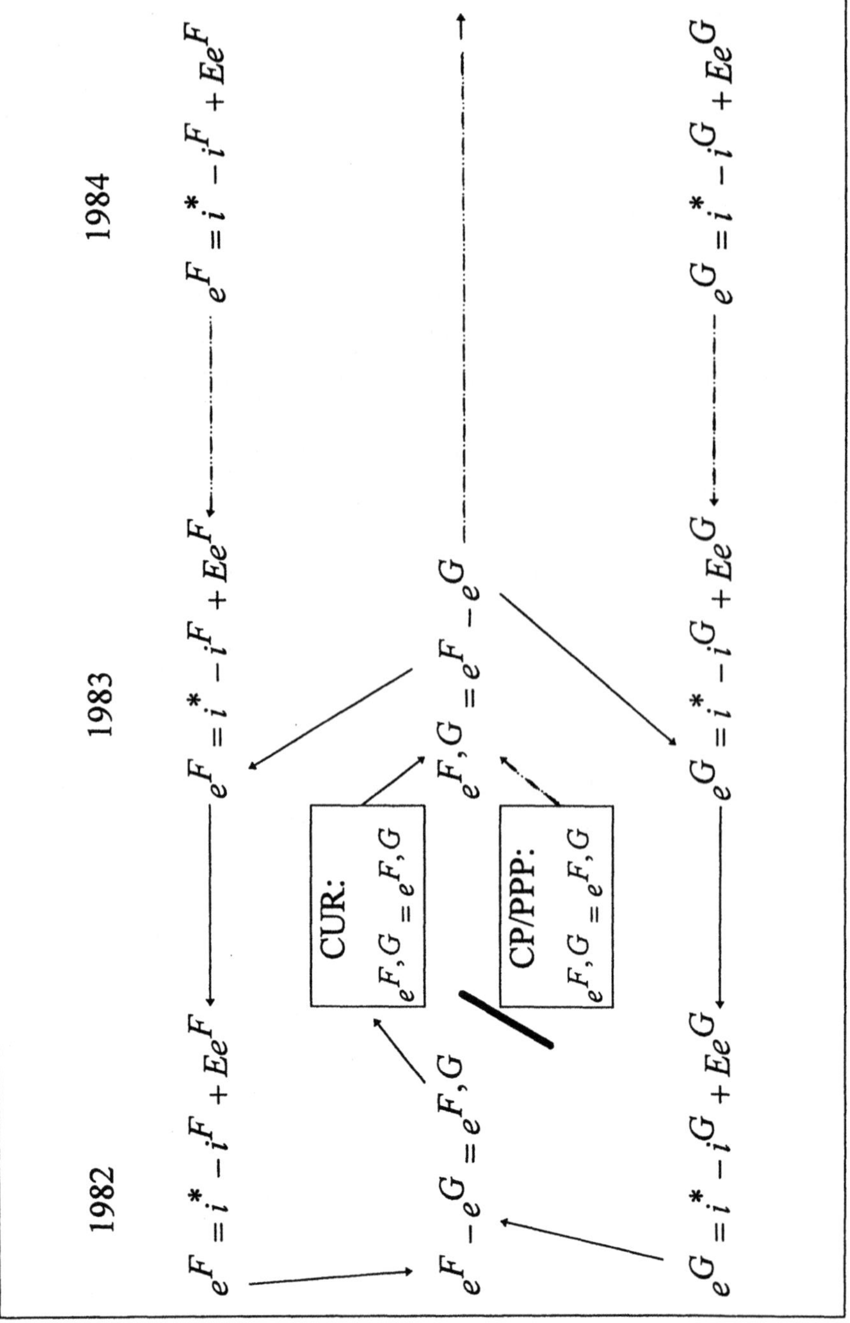

(with unbroken lines). Interest differentials in each period (interest equalization effect) and – long run – outside rate expectations (monetary equalization effect) are the 'external' impelling forces determining results as already shown in the previous subsection. Outside rates in the period from 1984 are determined on the basis of the relevant 'external' forces *and* under the restriction of given inside rates (conversion rates that were obtained in the 1982/1983 subsystem).

Under PPP and CP, there is no link between inside rates in 1982 and 1983, i.e. between 1982 bilateral exchange rates and 1983 conversion rates. Instead, conversion rates are exogenous. Hence, what applied for the period from 1984 under CUR is now relevant for 1983 as well as for 1984 and thereafter: outside rates are determined on the basis of the relevant 'external' forces *and* under the restriction of (now exogenously) given inside rates. 1982 outside rates emerge as a consequence of 1982 interest differentials and realized outside rates in 1983 (rationally expected in 1982).

All in all, the driving factors differ for endogenous and exogenous conversion procedures. Under CUR, the 'external' forces (in particular, the dominating monetary equalization effect captured by long run outside rates) determine the results for EMU outside rates. In contrast, under exogenous conversion procedures CP and PPP, the outcome is strongly affected by the exogenous inside rate (conversion rate).

The fundamental difference between exogenous conversion procedures (PPP and CP) and market conversion CUR can be illustrated by reviewing equation 13, page 86 (on the link between changes of outside rates in one member country and those in another). Formally, the trade-off between interest equalization and expected inside rates still applies for the announcement year.

However, in 1982, the simulated expected inside rate is no longer determined by the monetary development, but by the exogenous inside rate for those two countries as of 1983 (i.e. their conversion rate).

For the period from 1983 onwards, equation 13 must be replaced by the simple difference between baseline and simulated cross rate identities (since the simulated conversion rate $\overline{e^{F,G}_{t\geq 83}(s)}$ is exogenously set, the simulated bilateral open interest parity (for 1982) cannot be substituted in any longer):

$$\begin{aligned} e^F_t(s) - e^F_t(b) &= \left(e^G_t(s) - e^G_t(b)\right) \\ &+ \underbrace{\left(\overline{e^{F,G}_{t\geq 83}(s)} - e^{F,G}_t(b)\right)}_{\text{exogenous conversion effect}} \quad , \quad t \geq 83. \quad (15) \end{aligned}$$

Under PPP or CP, the French Franc (vis-à-vis the US-$) is 'relatively appreciative' compared to the DM, if and only if the simulated inside rate (conversion rate) is revalued relative to the corresponding baseline inside rate. This is a mere tautology. However, it pinpoints the difference between market conversion rates (CUR) and rates determined by PPP or CP. Here, the exogenous conversion effect (underbraced) replaces the trade-off under CUR between interest equalization and monetary equalization (market conversion effect; underbraced terms in equation 13). The next observation is straightforward, but again it is needed for the discussion in the following subsections.

Observation 3 (Exchange Rate Impulse under Exogenous Conversion)
In a monetary union with exogenously fixed conversion rates (CP or PPP), 'relatively appreciative' exchange rate impulses (applying over an extended period of time) can be produced by the (political) choice of the conversion rate.

Despite this difference in the underlying causality between CUR and exogenous conversion procedures PPP and CP, the outcome for the FF and the Lira is also 'relatively appreciative' compared to the DM – relative to the baseline. In fact, CUR results are very similar to those under PPP (cf. appendix B.4). Given that the FF and Lira are undervalued (and the DM overvalued) in the historical baseline (in terms of purchasing power parity; cf. Hill, 1986, and footnote 21), both conversion procedures account for corrections. Under PPP, purchasing power parity exchange rates are directly imposed. Under CUR, near purchasing power parity rates are produced, because markets are freed from depreciation (appreciation) expectations, i.e. from steady state conditions which strongly affected exchange rates in the historical baseline.

Under CP (cf. appendix B.3), there is a qualitative difference. The DM appreciates vis-à-vis the US-$ (not as much as the FF or Lira though) in the first years of the hypothetical EMU relative to the baseline. However, after 1985 the DM depreciates and in 1987 the unity line is crossed (i.e. there is no change relative to the baseline). Also note that Lira and FF outside rates remain almost constant between 1985 and 1987 relative to the baseline, although there was a somewhat reinforced appreciation under CUR.

These features result from the fact that exogenous CP conversion rates do not have a sound economic justification. There is a conflict between the steady state properties in the long run (as produced by the model) and imposed CP conversion rates from 1983 which are taken from outside the model. A split outcome obtains to reconcile the restriction in the short run and the long run requirement. In the long run, the DM (slightly) depreciates, and the FF and Lira appreciate relative to the baseline (similar to CUR and PPP). In the short run, they cannot diverge as much as required and possible under market conditions (CUR). All currencies appreciate. The medium term (most visibly, the years 1986 and 1987) is a period of adjustment. German exchange rates – relative to the baseline – appreciate by somewhat more, Italian and French ones by somewhat less than under CUR.

These considerations do not explain comprehensively, why, at last, the DM appreciates vis-à-vis the US-$ in the first years under CP. And there is probably no completely satisfactory answer. In particular, it cannot be explained by a dominant interest equalization effect (which would be the reason for a similar outcome under CUR – as described in the last paragraph of subsection 6.2). In fact, in the first few years, European interest rate levels under CP (not compared to the baseline) are lower than under CUR or PPP, which would rather point to a more depreciative outcome in the short run.[51]

However, it can be remarked that, under CP, curves of outside rates (including the steady state) are forced closer together than for CUR, because CP conversion rates are relatively near to corresponding baseline inside rates. Given that, under CUR, the Lira and the FF appreciate vis-à-vis the US-$ by more than

---

[51] Moreover, the strength of the Euro in the short run relative to the baseline DM cannot be explained by the appreciation of the US-$ in the mid-1980s (due to foreign exchange transactions out of the DM in the baseline), because no such effect appears under PPP or CUR.

the DM appreciates, it is not implausible that a narrowing of the distance between curves of simulated outside rates (in box 8, page 80) under CP produces an appreciation for *all* exchange rates in the early years of the hypothetical EMU. Economically, appreciative exchange rate impulses for all member countries suggest that overall monetary growth rates for the whole of the hypothetical EMU may have decreased under CP relative to the overall development under the baseline. This is corroborated by the fact that average inflation rates under CP are considerably smaller in Germany, but only slightly larger in France and Italy than under PPP or CUR (cf. box 4, page 64).

6.4 Transmission of Impulses

Causes for interest and exchange rate impulses produced by any monetary union have been summarized in observations 1, 2, and 3. The next two observations refer to their transmission in the real economy.

Observation 4 (Transmission Mechanisms)
Interest and exchange rate impulses produce real effects, which can largely be explained by three transmission mechanisms: a competition effect, a terms of trade effect on disposable income and wealth, and a real interest rate effect.

As an example for observation 4, effects of nominal interest and exchange rate impulses on the real economy are presented for Germany – under CUR – in box 10. The representation of simulation findings is simplified by focusing on the three already

Box 10: **Transmission of Impulses in Germany under CUR**

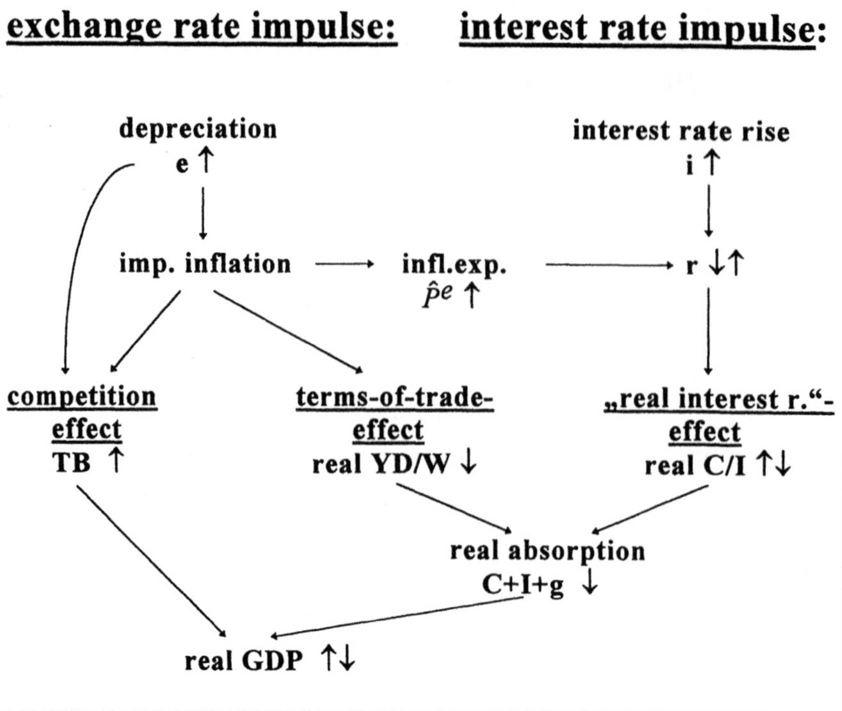

mentioned transmission mechanisms: a positive (i.e. expansionary) competition effect, a negative (i.e. contractionary) terms of trade effect on disposable income and wealth, and a real interest rate effect that is positive in the short run, but negative in the medium and longer term. The overall impact on GDP is positive at first, but turns negative after 1985 – as already seen in subsection 5.1.

Relative to the baseline, the depreciation raises prices for imports, thereby causing imported inflation. Since prices are sticky, future inflation goes up as well, so do inflation expectations ($\widehat{P^e} \uparrow$) due to rational expectations. Hence, by definition, real interest rates r are lowered. However, at rising nominal interest rates, the net effect on real rates is ambiguous a priori. In the short run, strong interest rate equalization effects are overcompensated due to even stronger effects on expected inflation. In the medium term, however, elevated nominal interest rates relative to the baseline dominate the behavior of real rates.

Even though real interest rates decrease in the announcement period and in the first years of the hypothetical EMU, private investment I and consumption C (government consumption g is exogenous) stay below baseline levels throughout. This is due to a negative terms of trade effect lowering real wealth W and real disposable income YD.[52] National purchasing power is reduced. Nonetheless, GDP increases up to 1985 because of a boost to trade caused by the depreciation (despite the increase in inflation). Notwithstanding the lasting nature of the positive trade effect (trade balance $TB \uparrow$), the contractionary impact of rising nominal *and* real interest rates determines the overall outcome in the medium and longer term.

---

[52] Wealth and income effects are discussed in more detail in subsection 8.2.

Supply side aspects (which are not captured in box 10) reinforce the inflationary impact of depreciations. Since the capital stock is systematically run down (relative to the baseline), and output increases in the announcement period and the beginning of the hypothetical EMU, capacity utilization rises until 1985 – relative to the baseline. Inflation caused by capacity utilization effects (according to the Phillips curve relationship) augments imported inflation. As a result, real interest rates decrease in the first years – as seen above – despite higher nominal interest rates. After 1985, capacity utilization returns to baseline levels, thus eliminating additional inflation effects.

The transmission of impulses in France is basically a mirror image of those in Germany except that the trade balance is positive in the first few years. Nonetheless, contractionary effects in the short run are stronger than corresponding expansionary ones in Germany. This is possible because of the rather moderate relative decrease of nominal interest rates reflecting the intermediate position of French interest rates in the historical baseline.

In Italy, results are much more clear-cut than in France and Germany. Throughout there is a negative competition effect, a positive terms of trade effect, and a very strong positive real interest rate effect. As a result, GDP is permanently above baseline levels. Despite a build-up of capital, capacity utilization increases. The ensuing inflationary impact (due to the Phillips curve relationship) is strong enough to cancel out imported disinflation effects. At inflation near baseline rates and sharply decreasing nominal interest rates, clearly, the real interest rate effect on output must be positive and very strong.

Most impulses, effects, and results (as discussed for CUR) prevail, qualitatively, under exogenous conversion procedures (PPP and CP). The interest rate impulse remains almost unchanged, because interest equalization invariably applies to all conversion procedures. In contrast to CUR, the PPP or CP exchange rate impulse is affected by exogenously fixed conversion rates. In particular, depreciation impulses are considerably smaller for France under PPP, and for France and Italy under CP. As a result, effects are dampened, but not drastically changed.

The situation is different for Germany under CP. There is a nominal appreciation until 1986 – in contrast to the permanent depreciation under CUR. The appreciation causes a switching of signs for most variables in the short to medium term in box 10. In the announcement period and the first few years of the hypothetical EMU, disinflation is imported and reinforced by capacity utilization below baseline levels. As a result, the real interest rate effect on absorption is negative in this period, not positive as under CUR. Despite a positive terms of trade effect in these first years (due to imported inflation), absorption falls throughout relative to the baseline. Overall economic activity measured by GDP permanently stays below baseline levels, although the trade balance is more positive during the entire period. (In the years with appreciations relative to the baseline, the competition effect remains positive because appreciations are overcompensated by the ensuing disinflation.)

Under all scenarios and for all countries, inflation plays a central role – as illustrated in box 10. Prices and inflation also account for most of the dynamics. Whereas the interest and exchange rate impulses hardly change over time, prices and inflation are above and below their baseline values in different years. This is so because prices do not fully adjust in the short run. Instead, prices are both sticky and forward-looking (cf. appendix A.1). Owing to the three aforementioned transmission effects, prices and inflation changes impact on real variables, on total aggregate demand as well as on investment which determines the change in (future) capacity output. Thus capacity utilization is affected and feeds back into price changes (according to the Phillips curve relationship).

6.5 Real Effects

Nominal impulses in terms of interest and exchange rates are the determinants of real effects caused by the hypothetical EMU – relative to the baseline. In the case of an appreciation combined with a rise in interest rates, as for Germany under CP, the effect was unambiguously negative (except for the smaller terms of trade effect). In all other cases, there was a potential trade-off, either between depreciations and interest rate rises relative to the baseline, or between appreciations and a drop in interest rates.

In a trade-off situation, real interest rates seem to be decisive, empirically, in the hypothetical EMU as of the 1980s. If one of the nominal impulses determines the effect on the real interest rate r *and* produces a large change in r relative to the baseline, then the overall outcome is governed by the real interest effect. As an example, take the nominal interest rate impulse in Italy. Under all conversion procedures, it is so powerful, that real interest rates clearly decrease in most periods (in some periods under CP and PPP, they are close to the baseline). As a result, Italy gains under all conversion procedures. These empirical findings are generalized in

Observation 5 (Real Effects)
Real macroeconomic effects for individual countries forming or joining a monetary union depend on a potential trade-off between interest and exchange rate impulses. Under the hypothetical EMU, a decisive change in real interest rates typically determines the overall outcome.

The trade-off – with respect to effects on the real economy – between interest and exchange rates is conventional wisdom. (It is also clear that it depends on the openness of a national economy.) However, there seems to be almost no empirical or model-theoretical literature. In particular, no attempt has been made, to my knowledge, to apply a formal trade-off argument to the real world EMU. McRae (1998) mentions – with wrong numbers though – a so-called "four-to-one rule of thumb that is sometimes applied to the UK (four percentage points on the [real] effective exchange rate are equivalent to one point on [real] interest rates)".

McRae presumably refers to an IMF (1997) illustration of the combined effect of *real* short term interest rates and *real* effective exchange rates. Describing the "easing of monetary conditions" in each country, their so-called Monetary Conditions Index "is defined as the percentage point change in the real short term interest rates and the percentage point change in the real effective exchange rates ... . Relative weights of 3 to 1 are used for Canada, France, Italy and the United Kingdom, 4 to 1 for Germany, and 10 to 1 for Japan and the United States ... to represent the relative impacts of interest rates and exchange rates on aggregate demand". The IMF is careful to stress the qualitative nature of the index when interpreted, and that the numbers used are not precise estimates.

Box 11: **Nominal Impulses and Real Effects (Stylized)**

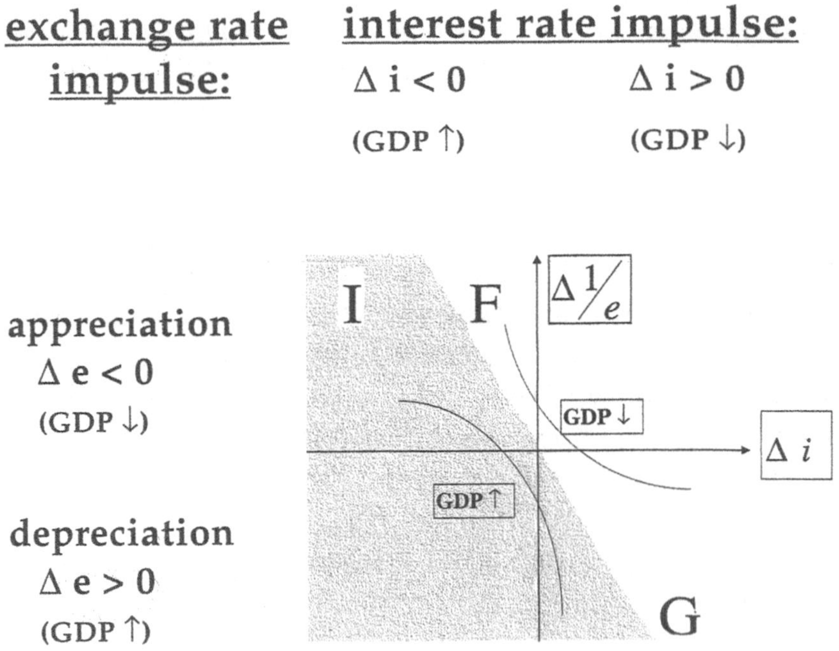

The trade-off discussed in this treatise is like a Monetary Conditions Index in nominal terms. Here, it is a qualitative description of simulation results. The diagram in box 11 presents the impact of nominal interest and exchange rate impulses on GDP – relative to the baseline – in a stylized way. It shows that effects are unambiguous in the first and third quadrant, but countervailing in the others. No quantitative results are presented, because it is not claimed that a regular relationship or even a law was discovered. In fact, the trade-off is likely to depend on economic conditions, the time period, and the temporal link (e.g. lags) to the original impulse. The dividing line between positive and negative GDP effects may be jagged (instead of straight).

Under CUR and within the framework of box 11, Italy (I) is positioned in the fourth quadrant and moves up right over time, but stays well within the area of positive GDP effects. France (F), in the same quadrant, starts out in the area of negative GDP effects, but ends up in the shaded area, although her position moves up right as well. (The overall GDP effect for France after 10 years remains negative though.) The German position (G) in the second quadrant changes from the shaded area to the area associated with negative GDP effects – despite the fact that the interest rate decreases relative to the baseline (leftward movement) and the depreciation slightly increases over time (downward movement).

Box 11 could also be interpreted in terms of the aggregated long term effect relative to the baseline. Notwithstanding theoretical objections concerning the aggregation over time of individual impulses in each period, we could determine positions for members of the hypothetical EMU under scenarios simulated in this treatise based on the long term results presented in subsection 5.2. Under all conversion procedures, France would have to be placed in the fourth quadrant, non-shaded area; Italy in the fourth, shaded area; and Germany in the second, non-shaded area. Under CP, Germany would move up towards or even beyond the abscissa (depending on the aggregation procedure).

By expanding the model and the analysis, it could be attempted to get a *quantitatively* better understanding of the actual trade-off between interest and exchange rate impulses in a monetary union relative to a situation without monetary union. For instance, simulations could be devised to calculate the exact trade-off for variations of underlying conditions (e.g. changes of the monetary policy stance of the ECB) which were shown to determine interest and exchange rate impulses. For the sake of analysis, interest and exchange rate impulses could also be controlled exogenously. However, this task must be left for future research. The scope of this treatise is deliberately limited to *qualitative* findings.

7 Assumptions and the Real World EMU (6 Questions)

So far, simulation scenarios were devised and their outcomes analyzed. It was intended to capture fundamental impulses and their transmission effects and trade-offs, not to provide a *quantitatively* correct description of the EMU as of 1999. Nonetheless, it is the logically last step that assumptions and findings are reviewed and compared to the real world. In this section, the relevance of *qualitative* simulation findings for the real world EMU is discussed by asking six questions. They relate to underlying implicit and explicit assumptions (question 1); the impact of policy and behavioral changes on simulation results (question 2); the existence of interest and exchange rate impulses in the real world EMU (question 3); anticipation effects in the run-up to the real world EMU (question 4); macroeconomic effects after its start in 1999 (question 5); and decisions associated with the EU Summit in Brussels on 2 May 1998 (question 6).

Question 1: *Which underlying implicit and explicit model assumptions do simulation results depend on?*

Implications of technical and methodical specifications and limitations have already been discussed in section 4. In addition, simulation results depend (i) on the historical baseline, (ii) on assumptions of the underlying model MULTIMOD, and (iii) on how the EMU is taken account of in this treatise. These assumptions will be screened in the following.

As for (i), specific baseline assumptions have rather small effects according to Fair (1994, p. 273). Simulations are constructed in such a way that historical shocks affect the baseline as well as alternative scenarios. By analyzing counterfactual outcomes relative to the baseline, effects of historical shocks, basically, cancel out in the difference. In principle, this is also true for historical economic policies which are embodied in the baseline. Examples are the French expansionary policies in the beginning of the 1980s (before the start of the hypothetical EMU), and the US-$ appreciation in the mid-1980s (which hardly seems to affect exchange rates – relative to the baseline – as presented in box 5, page 68; cf. also the discussion on exchange rate residuals in section 4, question 2).

In this treatise, historical policy assumptions (are not, but) could only be problematic, if they had a direct impact on changes brought about by the hypothetical EMU. For instance, a *temporary* strong monetary expansion in one of the hypothetical EMU countries (in the baseline) might have caused additional distortionary effects in the simulated outcome. This is so, because national expansionary policies in MULTIMOD can be put down to a higher growth rate for the exogenous national monetary target. Since the common monetary policy in the hypothetical EMU depends on an aggregate nominal monetary target which incorporates national target values, (baseline) expansionary effects in one country are passed on – by construction – to the entire hypothetical EMU. Relative to the baseline, there would have been contractionary effects in the country in question and expansionary effects in the other hypothetical EMU countries on top of effects which are typically caused by the hypothetical EMU (as shown in this treatise). If the effect for the union as a whole had been expansionary or contractionary is unclear.

As for (ii), results are affected by a large number of assumptions contained in the underlying model, in particular: by fundamental economic assumptions in MULTIMOD (e.g. price stickiness; Keynesian short term effects, but long term nominal neutrality); by the extend to which economic markets are captured (e.g. no financial markets, no labor markets, no direct investment); by the model specifications for institutional conditions (central bank and government reaction functions); and by the rational expectations and perfect foresight hypotheses (requiring perfect credibility for policy acts). Any of these assumptions could be altered to study their impact under baseline and/or under hypothetical EMU conditions.

The same applies to (iii), i.e. to changes of the underlying model which were conducted to account for the hypothetical EMU (cf. section 3). There are inexhaustible possibilities for alternative specifications of the hypothetical EMU, thus leaving scope for alterations and extensions of the simulation exercise. In this treatise, explicit and implicit assumptions cover inter alia: first, the structural break with the start of the EMU (structure of the ECB reaction function, conversion rate procedures); second, the choices of policy makers in the EMU (e.g. unchanged fiscal policy, intermediate monetary policy); third, the invariance of private agents' behavior (e.g. unchanged national money demand, unchanged wage setting behavior); and fourth, the lack of credibility problems with regard to policy decisions (in particular, that the hypothetical EMU happens with certainty). The second and third aspect are discussed under the following question.

Question 2: *What would be the impact on simulation results, if government policies and private agents' behavior in the hypothetical EMU changed?*

It is argued in the literature (e.g. European Commission, 1990) that the introduction of the EMU causes policy and behavioral changes. However, there is no compelling way to model these changes within the framework of a comparative simulation analysis. First of all, most of these changes are highly debatable. Secondly, it may be argued that changes would have partly happened, even if the real world EMU had not been envisaged to start on 1 January 1999. Thirdly, changes are likely not to apply in all countries to the same degree because, for instance, financial markets work differently in different countries or fiscal consolidations are not required. For example, the main future candidate for the real world EMU, Britain, does not have an excessive debt or a deficit beyond the limits set in the Maastricht Treaty.

There are controversial views on the direction of monetary and fiscal policies in the real world EMU. Fiscal policies may be contractionary to conform with obligations of the Maastricht Treaty, but there are also fears that the real world EMU could "undermine budget discipline of member governments" (Siebke, 1993, p. 154; cf. also, for instance, Kenen, 1995, p. 96). As a case study for Italy, fiscal consolidation policies as required by the Maastricht Treaty are simulated in part III.

Monetary policies in the real world EMU are generally expected to be more stability-oriented than assumed in this treatise (in terms of growth rates of the monetary target). At the same time, nominal short term interest rates might equalize at the low level observed in so-called core countries – Germany, France, Benelux, or Austria. (In the run-up to the real world EMU, an indication for such a development was the sharp reduction of central bank interest rates in countries with higher interest rates – Italy and Ireland – by 1 % in October 1998.) As an option for further research, these changes could be incorporated in an alternative hypothetical EMU scenario. In this treatise, a prima facie assessment is offered, instead, under question 5, page 115, where predictions for the real world EMU are discussed.

Changes of private agents' behavior could be incorporated in the analysis to account for the Lucas Critique. However, it is not straightforward to evaluate their outcome without modeling and simulating them explicitly, because effects are mostly countervailing. In the following, potential changes to wage setting and private money holdings caused by the EMU are discussed, and prima facie assessments are made where possible.

First, there may be changes to the wage setting behavior in a common market with a common currency: (i), wages and hence prices may become more flexible; and (ii), wage settlements may be affected by the European inflation rate instead of the national one.[53] The former aspect is likely to reduce the dynamic impact of the hypothetical EMU and lead to faster adjustments. In the short run, this could, however, produce even larger swings in output and unemployment and more social instability – as discussed in subsection 5.2.

The latter aspect was examined in a simulation series (under the PPP conversion procedure) with various degrees of influence of European inflation rates on national wage settlements (cf. question 1 in section 4, and scenarios V.3 on page 213). The idea was that the strong inflationary (disinflationary) impact in Germany (France) relative to the baseline (cf. subsection 5.1) might be smoothed out, if wage settlements were based on European instead of national inflation rates. This would be an indication that interest and exchange rate impulses are less powerful than claimed in this treatise, if only behavioral adjustments were incorporated in the analysis. However, the outcome is ambiguous.

---

[53] Yet another view is taken by Burda, Schmidt, and Galler (1997) who study the wage convergence between two regions of a monetary union in the context of the German unification.

On the one hand, the disinflation in France caused by the hypothetical EMU – relative to the baseline – is reduced; on the other hand, the inflationary impact in Germany is magnified. This is actually not surprising, because inflation rates in the baseline are so far apart that simulated German inflation rates are still – despite of rising by up to 7 % relative to the baseline – below the simulated European average.

Second, we could account for possible changes to the European money demand. In subsection 3.3, it was claimed that the higher degree of monetary stability which might be experienced in some countries (e.g. in Italy) due to the formation of the real world EMU is likely to raise private money holdings altogether (the constant term should be higher), and that additional financial opportunities (e.g. caused by more rapid financial innovations) could raise the interest sensitivity and/or decrease the constant term of money demand in individual member countries.

In a portfolio model capturing the impact of the EMU on European money demand both analytically and in a calibrated numerical analysis, Rother (1997) confirms that effects are largely ambiguous and countervailing. Based on specifications of agents' behavior, he derives a money demand equation which depends on the transactions benefit of money, returns and risks of securities, and wealth. His overall results for switching from the ERM to the EMU hinge on specific constellations of parameters and, in particular, on the level of wealth.

Findings for the absolute level of money demand are less ambiguous than those for interest and wealth elasticities. If one assumes a high level of wealth (by standards of Rother's model), the elimination of exchange rate risks (variance) and the equalization of interest rates produce an increase in the absolute level of money demand. Furthermore, the inflation risk (variance) may go up or down leading to an decrease or increase in money demand, respectively. Rother does not consider changes in the economic environment caused by the EMU, e.g. potentially more rapid financial innovations.

In the following, prima facie assessments for the impact (on the hypothetical EMU) of changes to the constant term or the interest sensitivity are offered. An increase in the constant term would cause a systematic monetary tightening in the hypothetical EMU, because the exogenous monetary target does not change. The overall outcome for the hypothetical EMU is likely to be more contractionary. Effects of the opposite situation, a systematic monetary loosening, are discussed in detail in the context of fiscal policies in part III (cf. page 153). – An increase in the interest elasticity of money demand would typically reduce fluctuations in the interest rate, because smaller changes of central bank rates are needed to achieve a desired change in money demand.

However, since changes to the European money demand or to the wage setting in the EMU are not conclusive, the assumption of behavioral invariability may be the best feasible strategy in this treatise. As extensions to the analysis, individual behavioral changes could be (but are not) examined as case studies. For a number of different specifications of the hypothetical EMU, their impact on interest and exchange rate impulses and real effects could then be compared.

Question 3: *Underlying economic (policy) conditions were shown to produce interest and exchange rate impulses in the hypothetical EMU. Do similar conditions also exist in the real world EMU?*

Before answering this and the following questions, note that simulation results and findings of the analysis are based on relating *hypothetical EMU scenarios* to a reference scenario, the *historical baseline*. However, for the observable *real world "scenario"* leading to the actual EMU in 1999, there is no readily available reference scenario. Instead, based on conjectures, a *conceptual scenario* with no plans for a monetary union must be constructed (in our heads).

In the simulations on the hypothetical EMU, economic and economic policy conditions cause nominal interest and nominal exchange rate impulses (relative to the baseline) which, in turn, trigger effects on the real economy. The economic (policy) conditions in the real world are likely to differ from those in the conceptual scenario. To assess their role in the actual EMU as of 1999 the question can be split into two parts: (i) would there have been noteworthy short term interest differentials, if the real world EMU had not been announced and set up in 1999 (i.e. in the conceptual scenario); (ii) are there reasons that justify deviations of conversion rates in the real world EMU from bilateral exchange rates in the conceptual scenario without monetary union? Questions (i) and (ii) are answered with a clear yes, even though the answers are based on conjectures for the conceptual scenario.

Consider nominal short term interest differentials first. Interest rates observed in the years prior to the start of the actual EMU in 1999 already incorporate policy changes in prospective member countries of the real world EMU. Box 12 shows that the interest differential for Germany and Spain, for instance, has shrunk to 1.13 % by January 1998. If interest rates for a situation without the EMU are to be conjectured, one must look at rates prior to the announcement of the real world EMU. In 1992, the year of the Maastricht Treaty, interest rate differentials

Box 12: Nominal Short Term Interest Rates

Three months interbank rates or yields on 3-months Treasury bills

	Germany	France	Italy	Spain	USA
Jan. 1982	10,46	15,07	20,96	n.a.	13,38
Jan. 1992	9,53	9,98	12,36	12,88	4,47
Jan. 1998	3,57	3,62	6,09	4,70	5,54

Source: OECD, Main Economic Indicators, July 1983, July 1993, and April 1998a (nominal short term interest rates [in percent])

were large between the Southern countries (e.g. Spain and Italy) and the more stability-oriented core countries, for instance Germany, but also France (since the 'Franc fort' policies eventually lead to small interest rates in the early 1990s). The data may be seen as evidence for considerable differentials (between European countries) that would probably have prevailed (maybe to a lesser degree) in a conceptual scenario without the EMU.[54] Hence the real world EMU is likely to cause interest rate impulses relative to the conceptual scenario – qualitatively identical to those found in the simulations.

As to exchange rates, consider changes in the monetary development (cf. subsection 6.1). Since 1992, a formidable effort towards harmonization of monetary policies – at a high level of stability – can be observed. In fact, central parities of the ERM which will be used as conversion rates in the real world EMU did

[54] It must be admitted that the data in box 12 could be interpreted differently. If we include earlier periods (e.g. 1982), we could argue that there is a trend towards smaller interest rates and smaller differentials, that would have prevailed with or without the EMU. However, this view ignores an additional impetus originating from obligations for the creation of independent central banks and from each country's desire to fulfill the (nominal) Maastricht Criteria.

not have to be changed for most countries during this period.[55] By contrast, in the conceptual scenario without monetary union, it is not likely that the monetary development would have harmonized to such a degree in so many European countries. Instead, considerable inflation differentials would have put pressure on exchange rates of the countries in question. Thus, bilateral exchange rates in a hypothetical situation without the prospect of the EMU (conceptual scenario) would probably have differed (at least in some countries) from actual conversion rates used for the real world EMU.

Question 4: *Do anticipation effects observed in the run-up to the real world EMU correspond to anticipation effects produced by the simulations?*

It has already been mentioned that the model does not exactly capture the real world situation. In reality, the period between announcement and actual start of the EMU is longer. Also, there is uncertainty about the prospect of the EMU project altogether. Hence, anticipated adjustments are likely to be more clear-cut in simulations, with stronger level effects, but less volatility (in an annual model) than in the run-up to the real world EMU.

However, qualitatively, there is strong real world evidence to confirm anticipation effects found in the simulations. Depending on political events and on market expectations on the prospects of the (real world) EMU as well as on participating countries, long run nominal interest rate differentials between potential real world EMU countries changed drastically (cf. IMF, 1998). For instance, the long rate differential for Germany and Italy came

---

[55] Ireland joined, Italy rejoined the ERM in 1996; the central parity of the Irish punt was *revalued* by 3 % in March 1998 (shortly before the EU Summit in May).

down to 3.2 % in 1994, widened again to 5.0 % in 1995 (when Italy's participation in the real world EMU seemed less likely) and was down at 0.3 % in February 1998 (when markets were convinced that Italy would be a member).

The effect of narrowing long run interest differentials is captured in the simulations. Under all conversion procedures, long rates in all hypothetical EMU countries equalize around 13 % (CP: 12.5) in 1983, the first year of the hypothetical EMU. In the announcement year 1982, they are between 13 % (CP: 11.5) in Germany (up from 9 % in the baseline) and 15 % (CP: 12.5) in France and Italy (down from 16 and 20 % respectively).

The validity of anticipation effects for both interest and exchange rates was shown most clearly, when there were rumors that Britain would join the real world EMU as of 1999. Within a few hours, the British-German (long) interest differential shrank by 22 basis points to only 96. At the same time, the Sterling depreciated by 4 Pfennige to an exchange rate of 2.83 DM, because an even lower conversion rate is said to have been expected.[56]

Question 5: *Can we make predictions for the macroeconomic effects of the real world EMU?*

Question 5 is based on a *comparison of* hypothetical EMU scenarios defined in this treatise relative to the historical baseline *with* (conjectures for) the real world situation after the start of the EMU in 1999 relative to (conjectures for) the conceptual scenario without monetary union from 1999. Hence, any prediction for macroeconomic effects in the real world EMU depends on conjectures as well as on assumptions used in the simulation analysis.

---

[56] Davies and Luce (1997) in the Financial Times; and Schulz (1997) in the Frankfurter Allgemeine Zeitung; both 29 September 1997).

Under these circumstances, such a prediction – as presented in the following – may be called, less pretentiously, a speculative answer (or "educated guess") for the real world EMU as of 1999.

In the answer to question 3, page 111, it was argued that nominal interest and exchange rate impulses observed in simulations conducted in this treatise do actually exist in reality, at least qualitatively. However, it was also suggested under question 2, page 107, that interest rates in the real world EMU might be lower, and that the monetary policy of the real world ECB is likely to be more stability-oriented than under hypothetical EMU scenarios described here.

As a result, Germany may experience greatly reduced or even eliminated depreciative exchange rate impulses in the real world (relative to the conceptual scenario) compared to CUR (relative to the baseline). Furthermore, assuming that union-wide nominal short term interest rates in the real world EMU correspond to – presumably low – German levels under the conceptual scenario (without the EMU) implies that interest rate impulses would also be slashed for Germany compared to CUR. Conversely, interest and exchange rate impulses would still be large in some other EMU member countries (who can be characterized by higher monetary growth and higher inflation as well as higher interest rates in the conceptual scenario).

On balance, Germany would no longer suffer from the formation of a monetary union as suggested by the analysis thus far. If there is, however, a (minor) depreciative exchange rate impulse, she might even gain from a (small) competition effect and also (due to imported inflation) from somewhat reduced real interest rates. Similar results will obtain for the other core countries as well. Countries (like Italy, Portugal, Spain) with a less unambiguous monetary stability record would appreciate relative to the conceptual scenario without monetary union, but enjoy reduced nominal and real interest rates. Italy with an excessively high nominal interest rate in the conceptual scenario (leveraging on her huge fiscal deficit) is likely to gain most by the introduction of the real world EMU – just as presented for the hypothetical EMU.

Prima facie, it seems likely that a Pareto-superior outcome (in terms of aggregate output over the longer term) obtains in the real world EMU compared to simulation results. This is caused by the larger expansionary interest rate impulse for Italy and the elimination of the contractionary interest rate impulse in Germany. As an extension to the analysis, it has already been mentioned that the aforementioned scenario could also be modeled for the hypothetical EMU. Alternatively, it could be asked (normatively) if the hypothetical EMU can be constructed so that the participation is advantageous for all member countries – possibly by allowing for side payments from gaining to loosing members. (Making more accurate predictions for the real world EMU may also require to include possible country-specific and/or union-wide shocks in the analysis.)

Question 6: *Was the interest-exchange trade-off (illustrated in this treatise) relevant for decisions associated with the EU Summit in Brussels on 2 May 1998?*

Question 6 calls for a normative application of simulation findings to real world politics. It examines if the knowledge of a potential trade-off between interest and exchange rate impulses was or could have been used for decisions on two levels: (i) by national governments of the UK, Denmark, and Sweden[57] not to participate in the EMU; and (ii) by the European Council on 2 May 1998 concerning membership and conversion rates of those countries willing to take part in the EMU.

The *actual choice* of conversion rates and the composition of member countries were political decisions from the beginning. After all, each country who wanted to participate (except for Greece) was admitted and unchanged central parities of the ERM[58] were used as conversion rates. Months before the Summit, this outcome was already generally expected and largely anticipated by markets. However, long term interest spreads had not fully converged yet, and market rates for the Irish punt were almost 6 % below central parities.

From a normative perspective, it would, however, have been desirable to evaluate costs and benefits of *possible policy choices* in advance. Two standards for assessing alternative options are conceivable. According to the first standard, the potential trade-off between interest and exchange rate impulses can be examined relative to the conceptual scenario, i.e. a situation without plans for a monetary union (as in question 5). Along these lines, participation in the real world EMU should be advantageous for most countries because interest rates in the union equalize at a lower level. Simulation results for Italy in the hypothetical EMU showed that the ensuing expansion (relative to the baseline) does not necessarily produce additional inflation – as long as there are

[57] Formally, only the UK and Denmark reserved the right to "opt out" of the EMU (ÖNB, 1995, pp. 114-121 – protocol 11 and 12). However, Sweden could also push through her desire to stay out of the EMU by not participating in the ERM of the EMS, one of the preconditions for membership.

[58] The central parity of the Irish punt was, however, revalued by 3 % in March 1998 (shortly before the EU Summit in May).

countervailing (appreciative) exchange rate impulses.

Awareness of these arguments would have made it harder for national policy makers (and their peoples) to claim potential advantages produced by the EMU (in particular, reduced interest rates) while refusing at the same time to do what is sometimes seen as a sacrifice, namely to revalue undervalued exchange rates (central parities). Instead, the discussion on the "right" conversion rates was nipped in the bud because policy makers wanted to avoid opening a Pandora's box.

As for the second standard, policy choices can be analyzed and compared to one another with respect to intertemporal consequences in the final transitional phase to the EMU (say, in 1998). In fact, it is argued that the interest-exchange trade-off could have also been used as a tool for cushioning short term adjustments. Scrutinizing decisions on membership and conversion rates leads to two (debatable) contentions. First, the political inflexibility of the real world conversion procedure hampered policy makers' willingness and ability to make economically justified adjustments to conversion rates for countries actually participating in the real world EMU – in the following discussed for Ireland and Finland. Second, the interest-exchange trade-off could have also been used to ease economic problems associated with the hypothetical participation of Britain in the EMU.

As for the first contention, it is often claimed that central parities are appropriate conversion rates because they proved to correspond to market rates. However, it could also be argued that the expectation of announcing central parities as conversion rates in the EMU helped to prevent deviations from central parities as long as depreciative or appreciative pressures stayed within a certain threshold. In any case, market rates for the Irish punt were far off central parities in early 1998. The realignment in March 1998 only narrowed the gap between market rates and central parities. Moreover, policy makers at the Brussels Summit in May 1998 did not dare to adjust conversion rates for the Irish punt fully to rates deemed right by the markets. They wanted to avoid politically motivated haggling over conversion rates.

Fixing at central parities of the EMS has, subsequently, produced an ongoing depreciation of market rates of the Irish punt since March 1998 until full correspondence with central parities was reached by 1 January 1999. As a result, Ireland is enjoying a competitive advantage in the EMU, but at the cost of parallel interest and exchange rate impulses which are fueling an already hot economy. Therefore, the competitive edge may not last long. Asset price inflation and imported inflation effects will lead to an appreciation of real exchange rates. Moreover, an economic downturn becomes even more likely. The effect of reduced interest rates (which is much stronger than the one caused by depreciating exchange rates) is corroborated in The Economist (1998b) as of 14 November 1998. These adverse effects could have been somewhat reduced, if the conversion rate had been adjusted at the start of the EMU.

One could have also argued for realignments of other currencies' central parities, but the argumentation is not compelling. For instance, Finland enjoyed a drastic improvement of her competitive position since 1990[59] which would have justified a revaluation of her central parities. However, since nominal short term interest rates were already as low as in the core countries in 1998, there would not have been a countervailing interest rate impulse.

---

[59] Measured by real effective exchange rates, cf. OECD, 1998b. This is also true, for instance, for the subperiod from 1995 to 1998.

As for the second contention, the interest-exchange trade-off could have also been exploited in Britain (along the same lines as for Ireland). The decision to stay out of the real world EMU was politically motivated. Nonetheless, the participation in the EMU would have produced economic problems, because business cycles in Britain (as in Ireland) and on the Continent were asynchronous in 1998. Lower (equalized) interest rates caused by the real world EMU would have lead to an overheating of the economy (as it did in Ireland). In principle (see qualifications in the next paragraph), it would have been possible though, on an *aggregate level*, to use an appreciative exchange rate impulse for curbing the ensuing overexpansion – just as in Ireland.

In reality, this was unrealistic for two reasons. First, there would have been considerable allocative and distributive effects, but this is also true for Ireland. Second, Britain was not likely to overcome its political rejection of joining at a high Sterling conversion rate, say at 2.9 or 3 $\frac{DM}{£}$. This view has some economic justification, because presently high exchange rates (of 2.7 to 3.0 $\frac{DM}{£}$ during 1998) are overvalued (in contrast to the situation in Ireland). For instance, purchasing power exchange rates are estimated at 2.4 or 2.5 $\frac{DM}{£}$ and real effective exchange rates have drastically risen since 1995 (OECD, 1998b), i.e. there has already been a considerable loss in competitiveness. All in all, the case for Britain to join the EMU at high rates was not as strong as it was to revalue the Irish punt in order to somewhat alleviate expansionary effects caused by the interest rate impulse.

PART III

Fiscal Policy in Italy – An Extension

8 Fiscal Consolidation Without EMU

As discussed in the last section, the relevance of interest and exchange rate impulses can be studied under various alternative scenarios. One of the possible extensions of the analysis is the introduction of fiscal consolidation (or retrenchment) policies as prescribed by the Maastricht Treaty, i.e. fiscal policies aiming at the reductions of "excessive" budget deficits and government debt.[60] The analysis is designed as a case study for a country such as Italy as of the 1980s. On the one hand, Italy exhibits undervalued exchange rates – relative to purchasing power parity (Hill, 1986) – and high interest rates (as seen in sections 5 and 6). On the other hand, Italy – already in the 1980s – suffers from a debt-to-GDP ratio of almost 100 %

Within the framework of part III of this treatise, this section (section 8) develops a fiscal consolidation strategy for Italy and applies it to the original baseline scenario. (The next section examines interdependencies between the fiscal consolidation program in Italy on the one hand, and interest and exchange rate impulses as well as effects caused by the hypothetical EMU on the other hand.) Subsection 8.1 proposes a fiscal consolidation strategy which can be applied equally to various previously specified scenarios. Lax, moderate, and tight fiscal retrenchments are defined. In subsection 8.2, the impact of a moderate fiscal retrenchment under baseline conditions is analyzed with reference to the original baseline. In subsection 8.3, observable effects are compared to those under tighter and laxer fiscal consolidation pro-

[60] The term fiscal policy will generally be used with this meaning, throughout part III. In the context of the EMU, the opposite definition, i.e. expansionary fiscal policies, in particular debt financed government expenditure increases, is also commonly used (e.g. Siebke, 1993).

grams as well as to effects under the original hypothetical EMU scenarios (without fiscal consolidations).

8.1 Fiscal Strategies

The fiscal convergence criteria of the Maastricht Treaty are specified in Protocol 5 (cf. ÖNB, 1995, pp. 107-108). They comprise a debt-to-GDP ratio of not more than 60 % and a ratio of the government budget deficit to GDP of not more than 3 % in each member country. There are numerous studies on the implications of the fiscal requirements (cf. the review article by Wyplosz, 1997). Previous simulation studies on fiscal consolidations in the EMU (Hughes Hallett and McAdam (1998a/b) based on MULTIMOD; and von Hagen and Lutz (1996) based on the Taylor (1993a) model) were mentioned in the introduction. They examine alternative policy strategies for achieving the fiscal Maastricht criteria. They do not, however, model the EMU itself, nor do they incorporate interest and exchange rate impulses caused by any monetary union.

Inter alia these authors demonstrate that fiscal consolidations are mixed blessings, since a fiscal retrenchment also reduces the denominator in the debt-to-GDP and deficit-to-GDP ratios.[61] Hence, they suggest (discretionary) "monetary loosening" to raise GDP along with the fiscal contraction to achieve a sustained reduction of debt and deficit ratios. Furthermore, Hughes Hallett and McAdam (1998a/b) find that tax increases are more effective than expenditure cuts. In contrast, von Hagen and Lutz (1996)

---

[61] In subsection 9.2, it will be shown that the role of GDP as the denominator can be favorable, because the hypothetical EMU produces overall expansionary effects in Italy.

argue (but do not model) along the lines of Alesina and Perotti (1995a and b) that tax rises should cause disincentive effects[62] (which are, however, not captured in the Taylor model – nor in MULTIMOD).

In this treatise, neither discretionary monetary relaxation nor alternative fiscal (consolidation) strategies are modeled. Only one fiscal consolidation strategy is chosen. It is implemented under baseline and hypothetical EMU scenarios so that the effect on the interest-exchange trade-off can be compared and evaluated qualitatively. The selected strategy should produce debt and deficit reductions à la Maastricht (and stay at these debt and deficit ratios) irrespective of the scenario it is applied to. As a precondition, it must be robust (and flexible) enough to produce equilibrium solutions under various scenarios.

MULTIMOD offers three alternative approaches for specifying fiscal strategies. First, *exogenous government sector variables* can be changed. This amounts to an (elementary) exogenous shock analysis. For instance, it can be applied to exogenous (real) government expenditures.[63] However, a trial and error procedure would have to be used to achieve (and stay at) specific debt or deficit ratios under various scenarios. For different paths of government expenditure cuts, a comparison of various scenarios

---

[62] "[T]ax increases (particularly labor and social security taxes) lead to a fall in competitiveness, as wage demands increase to compensate for an increased fiscal pressure..." (Alesina and Perotti, 1995a, p. 235). Cf. also the discussion by Tanzi and Zee (1997) on the "excess burden of taxing" referring to changes of "private economic agents' allocative decisions" caused by tax increases.

[63] Similarly, the exogenous debt target in equation 16 (see below) could be changed. However, since the baseline tax rate reaction function does not account for GDP ratios, modifying the tax equation may be more promising – as suggested by the third approach.

would not be straightforward.

Second, *endogenous government sector variables* can be exogenized. One option is to increase the tax rate exogenously (instead of using endogenous tax rate responses as modeled for the baseline) in order to raise additional revenues. But again the link to the actual debt or deficit ratios is precarious. Another option is to exogenize and directly control the level of public debt (or of government deficit). This is also difficult, because debt (or deficit) must still be consistent with its own dynamics and its constituent components: current government consumption (and investment), tax revenues, central bank profits (or seigniorage), and interest payments. Feedback rules would have to be modeled. But again, it is difficult to achieve (and stay at) the required debt (or deficit) ratio under various scenarios, but for comparable strategies (that is for similar paths of debt or deficit levels, respectively).

Nonetheless, this option was pursued by prospective real world EMU member countries in 1997, the year that mattered for applying the Maastricht Criteria and selecting members. They aimed at a specific deficit *level* which they considered to be consistent with the 3 % deficit-to-GDP *ratio* criterion. However, under changing levels of economic activity and revised estimates for government revenues, current government consumption (as well as the targeted deficit level itself) had to be adjusted several times. Up to the last minute, it was not clear, if the required deficit ratio could actually be achieved.

The third (and chosen) approach also works through tax revenues, but it is based on a *modified tax rate reaction function* (of the underlying model). In MULTIMOD, the *average* tax rate t governs tax revenues thereby affecting government debt and deficit. The original (baseline) tax rate equation is a feedback rule based on an exogenous target variable for endogenous debt and deficit levels. A fiscal consolidation can be conducted by exogenously changing the target variable bt in equation 16. However, this amounts to the first approach (relating to exogenous government sector variables) which has already been rejected.

The baseline tax rate reaction function is given by:

$$t = t_{-1} + \tau_1 * \frac{B - bt}{gnp * p} + \tau_2 * \frac{(B - B_{-1}) - (bt - bt_{-1})}{gnp * p}. \quad (16)$$

Each year, t changes in response to deviations of nominal debt (B) and deficit ($B - B_{-1}$) from corresponding exogenous target values (bt and $bt - bt_{-1}$) depending on response parameters τ_1 ($= 0.04$) and τ_2 ($= 0.3$) as well as the value of nominal GNP (gnp is real GNP, and p is the GNP deflator).[64] In proportion to nominal GNP, the tax rate response to deviations from the targets is identical in each country. Equation 16 only allows to target debt and deficit *levels* – relative to GNP. Again, it would be difficult to achieve (and stay at) specific debt (or deficit) *ratios* – relative to GDP – under various scenarios, but for comparable strategies (that is for similar sets of paths for debt *and* deficit targets bt and $bt - bt_{-1}$).

In the modified tax rate reaction function used in this treatise, fixed *ratios* of debt-to-GDP and deficit-to-GDP (capturing the Maastricht requirements) are targeted explicitly:[65]

---

[64] In the baseline, bt corresponds to the actual historical debt level. Only changes to the baseline cause a response to the tax rate reaction function. – Parameters τ_1 and τ_2 are justified by a stability analysis based on these values (Masson, Symansky, Meredith, 1990, p. 12).

[65] Incidentally, a similar (not identical) rule was independently developed by Hughes Hallett and McAdam (1998a/b). They apply it to all prospective EMU member countries as of the 1990s, whereas here it is only used for Italy.

$$t = t_{-1} + \tau_1 * \left(\frac{B}{gdp * p} - 0.6 \right) + \tau_2 * \left(\frac{(B - B_{-1})}{gdp * p} - 0.03 \right) \quad (17)$$

A fiscal consolidation strategy described by equation 17 only makes sense for countries with 'excessive' debts or deficits – as described by the Maastricht Treaty. Given the 1980s as simulation period in this study, it can only be applied to Italy. (For Germany and France, equation 16 is not changed.)

This fiscal consolidation rule allows for flexible policy responses; there are no prespecified debt or deficit levels (or ratios) that must be achieved at a particular point in time during the adjustment process. Even though the same rule is applied to the baseline and hypothetical EMU scenarios, it is robust enough to produce solutions under various (though not all) alternative conditions.

The fiscal consolidation path prescribed by equation 17 depends on the relative as well as on the absolute weight of the response parameters. Baseline weights of $\tau_2 = 0.3$ for the deficit and $\tau_1 = 0.04$ for the debt component imply that a 1 % deviation from the targeted deficit ratio (of 0.03) causes the same tax rate response as a 7.5 % deviation from the debt target ratio (of 0.6). A fiscal consolidation plan based on these weights is henceforth called "moderate". For Italy with almost 40 % above the debt target and more than 6 % above the deficit target in the 1980s, both (debt and deficit) terms in the tax rate reaction function carry a similar weight. Hence limited changes of *relative* weights (in opposite directions) do hardly affect the simulation outcome.[66]

To obtain results for tighter and laxer tax rate reactions, it suffices to change response parameters proportionately. The ac-

---

[66] A "mixed" strategy referred to in section 9 is defined by a tight deficit response [$\tau_2 = 0.5$], but a lax debt response [$\tau_1 = 0.0133$]. Compare to "lax" and "strict" strategies defined further down in the next paragraph.

tual response of tax rates to a tighter or a laxer rule depends on the overall economic constellation, because growth affects the denominator of debt and deficit ratios (cf. observation 7, p. 156). Henceforth, "tight" refers to $\tau_2 = 0.5$ and $\tau_1 = 0.0666$ (baseline values multiplied by $\frac{5}{3}$), "lax" to $\tau_2 = 0.1$ and $\tau_1 = 0.0133$ (multiplied by $\frac{1}{3}$). Fiscal consolidation strategies for Italy under baseline conditions are called lax, moderate or tight fiscal-baselines. Analogously, lax, moderate or tight fiscal-CP (or fiscal-CUR) scenarios are defined.[67] Any fiscal consolidation program for Italy under hypothetical EMU conditions is called fiscal-EMU.

The basic dynamics of the adjustment path hinges on the fact, that the debt and deficit components may have opposite signs (the same applies to the baseline tax rule, equation 16). Given that the Italian debt ratio exceeds its targeted value of 0.6 %, the tax rate goes up at the outset. Raising government revenues typically pushes the deficit ratio below its target, eventually. Nonetheless, the tax rate continues to go up as long as the tax rate increasing effect of the debt component (above its target ratio) outweighs the tax rate decreasing effect of the deficit component (below its target ratio). When the debt ratio approaches its target value (but is still above), the deficit ratio (still below target) dominates, thus causing the tax rate to go down again. A relatively smooth landing is achieved. However, the tax rate might still not respond fast enough to avoid some undershooting of the debt ratio. A debt ratio below target pushes the tax rate further down, thus lowering tax revenues and raising the deficit ratio again. Once the initial adjustment has been completed, the development of debt and deficit is cyclical, but stays near target ratios – by construction

---

[67] No simulation experiments were carried out for fiscal-PPP scenarios. Furthermore, under the CUR scenario, only the lax fiscal strategy produced a satisfactory solution. Cf. questions 4, 5, and 6 in section 4 on the methodical and technical limitations for obtaining solutions.

of the tax rate reaction function.

8.2 Moderate Fiscal Retrenchment

The effects of a fiscal consolidation program can be investigated from the perspective of Ricardian equivalence (formally put by Barro, 1974, and Buchanan, 1976): does tax financed expenditure produce the same effects as higher government expenditure funded by increased government debt (vis-à-vis the public)? Bernheim (1987) reconsidered Ricardian equivalence by asking if there are macroeconomic effects of deficit financed tax cuts. In this subsection, the question is inverted: are there macroeconomic effects of tax financed debt reductions? The answer will be used in the next section as the basis for examining effects of a fiscal consolidation on the potential interest-exchange trade-off in monetary unions established in part II.

Box 13 depicts simulation results under the moderate "fiscal-baseline" scenario. It means that Italy (not France and Germany) carries out a moderate fiscal consolidation program under baseline conditions otherwise. The tax rate reaction is characterized by values for the response parameters τ_1 and τ_2 which are kept at their baseline levels (0.04 and 0.3, respectively). Figures (a), (b) and (c) present debt-to-GDP and deficit-to-GDP ratios as well as average tax rates as deviations of simulated values from the baseline (i.e. as percentage point differences).

Figures (a) and (b) show that Italy obtains a gradual decline in debt and deficit ratios relative to the (original) baseline. Other countries do not commit to debt reduction policies; their curves coincide with the abscissa, which means that baseline values are

Box 13: **Debt, Deficit and Tax Rates under the Moderate Fiscal-Baseline**

(a)

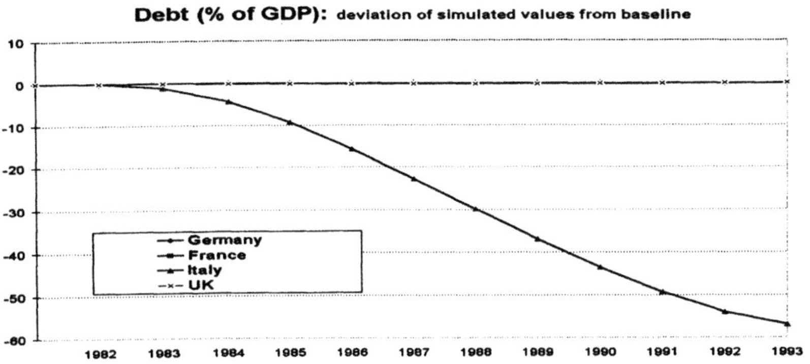

(b)

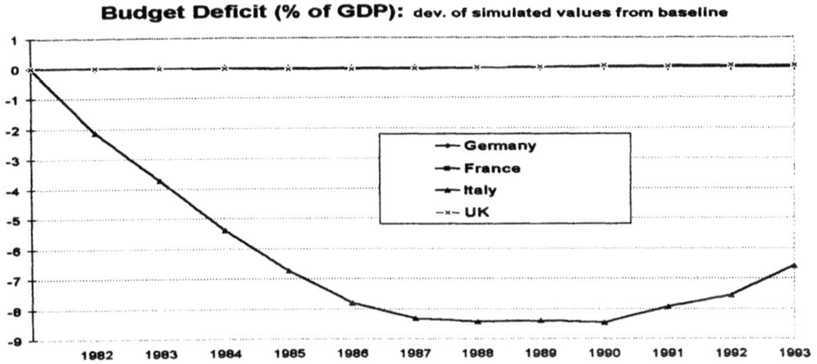

(c)

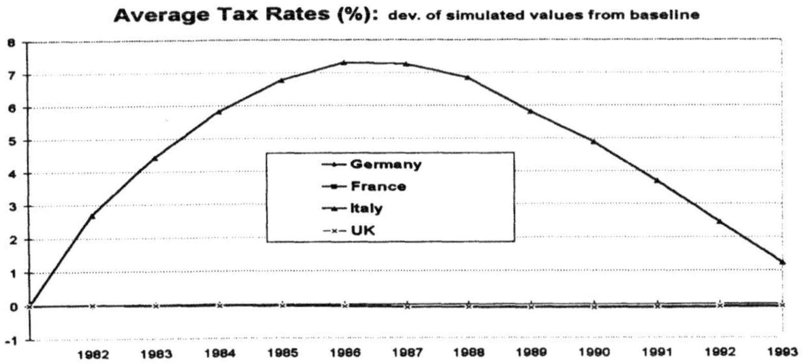

not changed. The Italian fiscal consolidation plan is successful in the sense that target ratios are achieved in 1986 for deficit and in 1989 for debt (not shown). The tax rate – relative to the baseline – goes up, temporarily, by more than 7 %.[68] The peak of tax rate changes (+7.3 %) is in 1986, the first year of a deficit-to-GDP ratio below target.

Even though the deficit ratio decreases by more than 2 % in 1982, the debt ratio is practically not affected. This is so for two reasons. First, the tax rate can only rise gradually – as shown in figure (c). Second, given unchanged ratios of tax revenue to GDP (tax), and of government expenditure to GDP (e), we know from Domar's (1944) seminal article on "The Burden of Debt" that the change in the debt ratio b ($= \frac{B}{gdp*p}$; cf. equation 17, page 130) depends on nominal interest rate i and nominal GDP growth rate g ($= \widehat{gdp * p}$). The government balance sheet identity can be rewritten as follows (cf. also Lech, 1993): $b - b_{-1} = def - (g * b_{-1})$, where government budget deficit $def = e - tax + i * b_{-1}$ (primary deficit $e - tax$ plus interest payments on debt $i * b_{-1}$). For any g, only one deficit ratio def is consistent with a constant debt ratio b. Since the debt ratio does not change under a fiscal-baseline scenario relative to the baseline in 1982 despite a decline in the deficit ratio, g must decrease in the moderate fiscal-baseline compared to the original baseline (as confirmed in the next paragraph).

Box 14 depicts simulation results for real GDP growth, inflation and capacity utilization (as percentage point differences to

---

[68] Tax rates – relative to the baseline – are reported, throughout, in terms of percentage point changes $t(s) - t(b)$, i.e. as the difference of the simulated average tax rate $t(s)$ and the baseline average tax rate $t(b)$, *not* as percentage changes ($\frac{t(s)}{t(b)} - 1$).

Box 14: GDP Growth, Inflation, and Capacity Utilization under the Moderate Fiscal-Baseline

(a)

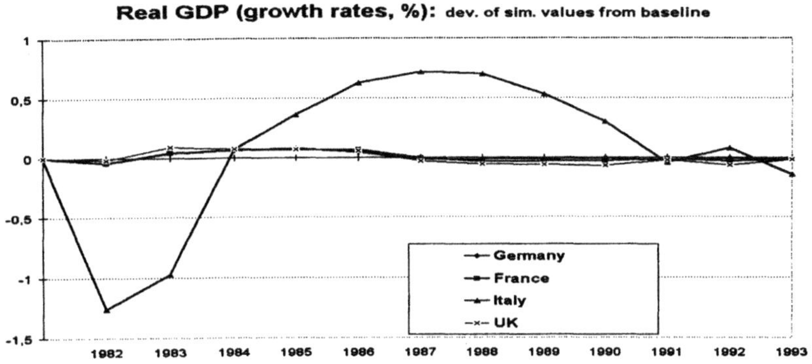

(b)

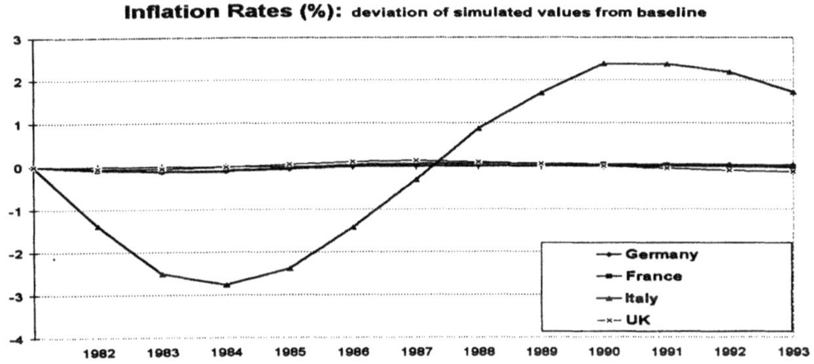

(c)

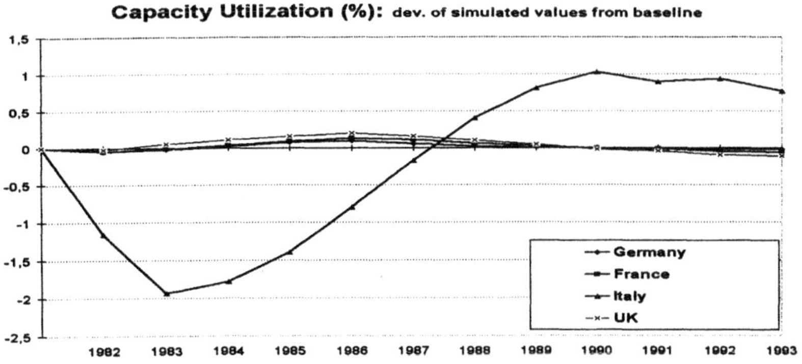

the baseline). Countries without fiscal consolidations are practically not affected. For Italy, figure (a) shows the first wave of a cyclical adjustment path for changes of GDP growth relative to the baseline. Thereafter, superimposed business cycles continue, but die out eventually. Relative to the baseline, there is a contractionary effect in the short run, but an expansionary one in the medium term. However, GDP levels stay below baseline levels until 1987 (not shown).

Capacity utilization (figure c) is also reduced (until 1987), because the loss in actual output (GDP) exceeds the reduction in capacity output caused by a shrinking stock of capital. At lower levels of capacity utilization, inflation rates (figure b), too, remain under their corresponding baseline values during these first years of the fiscal consolidation phase. Despite rising inflation rates, thereafter, the price level is still below its baseline value by 1992.

How can the changes in economic activity relative to the (original) baseline be explained? The fiscal consolidation program produces primary effects through real disposable income and real wealth (cf. box 15). Figure (a) on real disposable income is almost a mirror image of the tax rate curve (figure (c) in box 13). Relative to the baseline, (real) net-of-tax labor and capital income is diminished in years with elevated tax burdens due to the fiscal consolidation program.

Figure (b) of box 15 shows that total (real) private sector wealth is reduced permanently relative to the baseline. Wealth is affected by countervailing effects, which are not quantified in the following discussion. On the one hand, the present value of the stream of current and future after-tax capital and labor income may be higher than under original baseline conditions (despite lower capital and labor income in early periods) because lower tax rates are required in future periods once the debt burden has been successfully reduced. Also, (real) net foreign assets are build up compared to baseline levels (see discussion below). On the other hand, there is – relative to the baseline – a reduction in the real stock of money (see discussion below) and, particularly, in public holdings of real government debt. In MULTIMOD, government bonds are modeled as net wealth, reflecting the majority view of economists on the question, in contrast to Barro's (1974) "basic conclusion ... that there is no persuasive case for treating government debt ... as net component of perceived household wealth".

Reduced levels (relative to the baseline) of private sector wealth and income cause a decrease in investment and consumption, at least in the first years of the fiscal consolidation plan. Since aggregate demand decreases faster than capacity output, there is a strong disinflation – as already discussed. Changes in price levels and inflation rates produce secondary effects relative to the baseline: competition effects (real effective exchange rates are presented in box 15, figure c) and real interest rate effects (cf. box 16, figure b). The competition effect is countervailing to the income and wealth effects. It is expansionary for the entire period until 1993. It originates in reduced price levels (nominal exchange rates do not change; cf. box 16, figure a) and leads to a real depreciation (box 15, figure c) relative to the baseline, an improvement of the trade balance, and a lasting build up of net foreign assets (not shown).

Figure (b) in box 16 illustrates that percentage point differences in real interest rates relative to the baseline exhibit contractionary effects until 1985, but expansionary ones from 1986 onwards. Real interest rates are basically driven by (rationally expected) next period inflation rates, because nominal interest

Box 15: Disposable Income, Wealth, and Real Exchange Rates under the Moderate Fiscal-Baseline

(a)

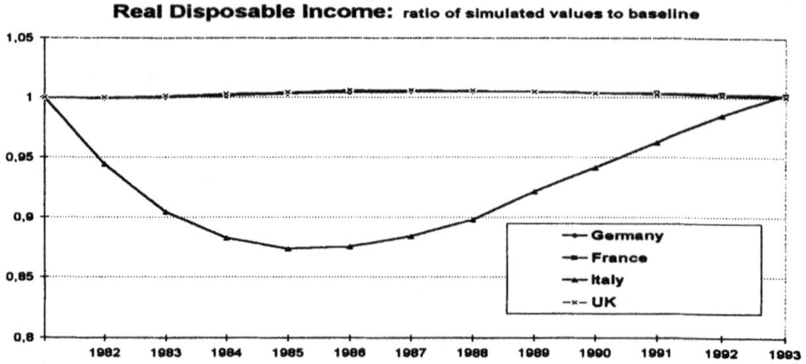

(b)

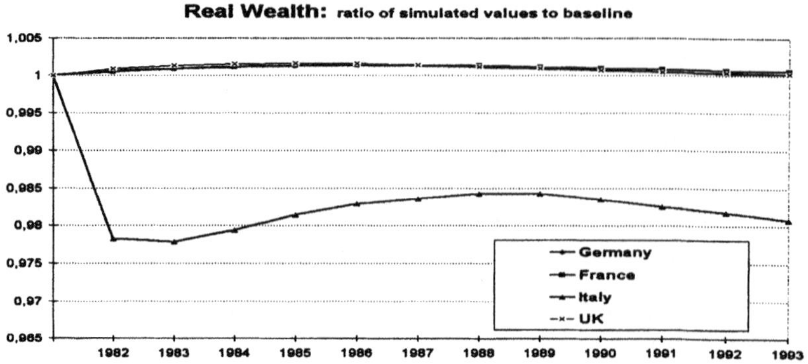

(c)

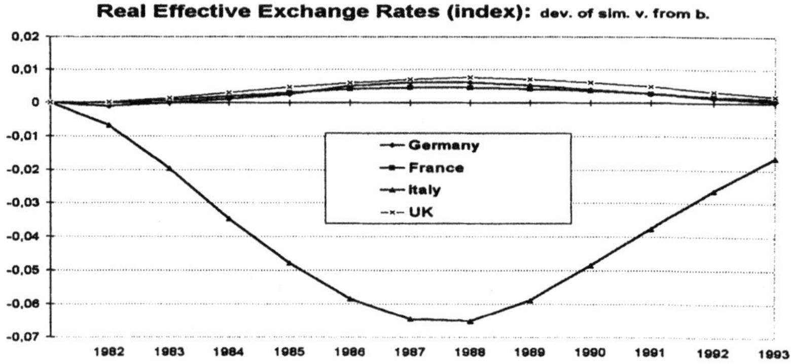

Box 16: Interest Rates and Nominal Exchange Rates under the Moderate Fiscal-Baseline

(a)

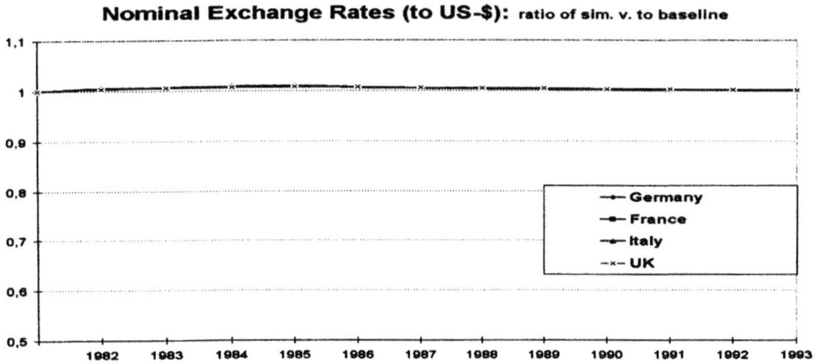

(b)

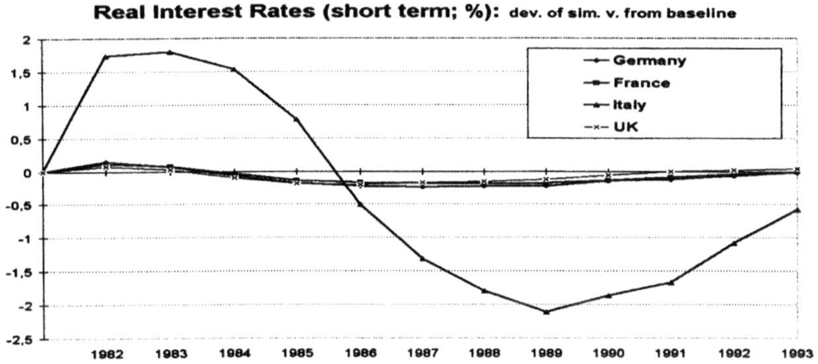

(c)

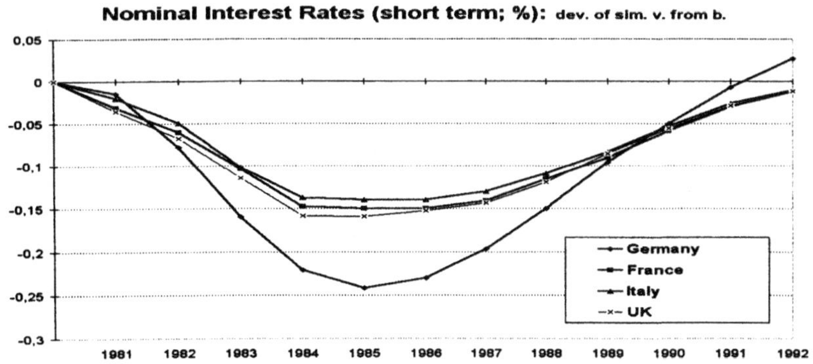

rates hardly change (cf. box 16, figure c). This is so because, under (baseline and) fiscal-baseline conditions, Italy is a member of the ERM adhering to exchange rate targeting vis-à-vis the DM. Interest rates are only reduced, because there are (relatively small) contractionary spill-overs into Germany. Lower economic activity in Germany (Italy, and other countries) – relative to the baseline – causes reductions of private sector real money holdings. Given that monetary targets of the Bundesbank are not changed from (exogenous) baseline target values for the nominal money stock, there is an automatic monetary loosening. In fact, German nominal interest rates are reduced during the entire period under scrutiny (cf. box 16, figure c). To stay close to the central parities of the ERM, the Italian central bank must also reduce interest rates. However, in Italy, the largest deviation to the baseline is only -0.15 % which occurs between 1985 and 1987 (for Germany, it is almost -0.25 %).

The combined impact of all effects on aggregate demand – relative to the baseline – is not expansionary before 1986, the first year in which real interest rates fall below baseline rates. (Whereas investment rises above baseline levels in 1987, it takes consumption until 1992.) As in the discussion on the transmission of impulses caused by hypothetical EMU scenarios (cf. subsection 6.4), the real interest effect dominates the other effects. The overall outcome for Italy is favorable in the sense that, by 1993, real GDP is up 0.8 % from its original baseline level (at almost zero percent additional inflation). There are short term losses, but aggregate demand rises above the baseline in the medium run, while prices stay below baseline levels until 1993 – as shown in box 14. In sharp contrast, the impact on the other countries is very small.

To counterbalance the economic slump in the early years of the fiscal consolidation plan, a (discretionary) monetary loosening as suggested by Hughes Hallett and McAdam (1998a and b) would certainly have a stimulating effect on aggregate demand. Along these lines, it would be recommendable, from a national perspective, to leave the ERM so that expansionary monetary policies could be pursued. However, monetary tightening seems advisable in the later years to preserve disinflation gains which were accrued in earlier years.

8.3 Fiscal Policy Effects Compared

Consider the effect of tightening or loosening the fiscal consolidation program for Italy (response parameters are increased or decreased, respectively). Simulation results are similar, but some differences are caused by the fact that occurrence, strength, and cycles of wealth and income, competition, and real interest rate effects depend on the phasing-in of fiscal consolidation measures. The total outcome as of 1993, the last year presented in the figures, is reported, but should not be used for ranking lax, moderate, and strict fiscal strategies. An evaluation at a specific point in time, say 1993, does depend on phase differences in adjustment cycles. A previously less favorable strategy may appear to be the better strategy if evaluated a few years later or earlier.

A laxer plan (cf. appendix B.5) implies that debt and deficit ratios are reached three years later. The debt-to-GDP ratio actually rises until 1985 (for reasons discussed in the previous subsection). The peak in tax rates, too, occurs three years later – at a reduced rate compared to the moderate fiscal retrenchment plan. As a result of these policy measures, the contractionary income effect is weaker at first compared to the moderate plan, but lasts longer (due to the delayed effect of tax rises). The negative wealth effect is slightly stronger throughout though. The positive competition effect is stronger and lasts longer (because prices are lower and nominal exchange rates are hardly affected). Real interest rates are higher throughout compared to the moderate plan (because of reduced expected inflation rates and almost unchanged nominal interest rates).

The overall effect on GDP is that adjustments are smoother, but growth rates turn clearly negative in 1991. In 1982 and 1983, GDP growth rates are above those of the moderate plan, because disposable income is not so badly affected by tax increases. After that, the more unfavorable real interest rate effect (compared to the moderate plan) dominates so that, by 1993, GDP is actually more than 1 % lower than under moderate fiscal policies. Inflation exceeds baseline rates one year later (in 1988) compared to the moderate plan and rates are lower so that, by 1993, prices are still more than 5 % below those of the moderate fiscal consolidation plan.

A stricter fiscal consolidation plan (cf. appendix B.6) produces, by and large, the opposite picture: the targeted debt ratio is reached in 1988, one year earlier; the deficit ratio is almost at its target by 1983, the start of the hypothetical EMU. To achieve this, taxes reach their peak as early as 1985 with 7.8 % above the baseline (+7.3 % in 1986 under the moderate plan). As a result, the contractionary income effect – relative to the baseline – is stronger at first, but turns positive in 1991. Compared to the moderate consolidation plan, the contractionary real wealth effect is weaker at first, but deteriorates thereafter (due to a steeper rise in inflation rates). The positive competition effect is stronger at first because of powerful disinflation effects, but weakens when inflation grows faster than under the moderate fiscal-baseline. For the same reason, real interest rates rise by more until 1986 and drop more sharply thereafter.

Compared to moderate fiscal policies in Italy, there is more volatility in growth rates, inflation, and real interest rates – relative to the original baseline. Overall, there are stagflationary effects compared to the moderate fiscal-baseline. By 1993, GDP is reduced by more than 1 % relative to the baseline, but prices are some 6 % higher. The contractionary effect is larger in the early years due to stronger contractionary income and real interest rate effects. In the medium term, a strong expansionary real interest rate effect (relative to the baseline) dominates and makes up for the higher GDP losses in the earlier years. At lower levels of capacity output, the strong expansion leads to higher inflation rates though (according to the Phillips curve relationship). Towards the end of the reported period, the real interest rate actually turns positive again (to start another cycle) and the wealth position worsens, but additional inflation (on top of baseline inflation) is reduced only gradually. As a result, output is lower and prices higher (after 10 years) than under the moderate fiscal consolidation plan.

Though not the primary objective of this study on interest and exchange rate impulses in monetary unions, some policy recommendations for fiscal consolidation programs can be derived. They are not based on the fact that short term results are, obviously, more advantages under the lax fiscal strategy; nor do they rest on the favorable performance of the moderate strategy after 10 years (slightly more expansionary than the baseline at an almost unchanged price level). Instead, they focus on the role of supply side effects under laxer and tighter fiscal-baseline scenarios. Tighter fiscal consolidations cause a more severe depletion of capital and a stronger reduction of capacity output in the short run. When GDP grows again in the medium term, capacity utilization is much higher under a tighter fiscal strategy. Hence price levels (and largely inflation rates, too) are more unfavorable over an extended period of time. In 1993 (only as an example), the price level difference between the lax and the strict strategy amounts to 10 %, even though GDP levels are similar. From the perspective of this study, lax or moderate fiscal contractions are recommendable due to smaller supply side effects.[69]

Despite these differences, the comparison of laxer and tighter consolidation programs for Italy in a historical simulation period (until 1993) reveals a clear pattern of effects and aggregate outcomes for all fiscal strategies. Relative to the baseline, there is an expansionary competition effect, a contractionary wealth and income effect, and a change of sign for the real interest effect around 1986/87 from contractionary to expansionary. Irrespective of the actual fiscal consolidation program, the real interest rate effect largely dominates the outcome, even though income and wealth effects ignite the adjustment process. Under all strategies, there are short term losses, but aggregate demand rises above the baseline in the medium run. If the consolidation program is stricter, cyclical swings are larger and the first peak occurs sooner. The following observation summarizes these empirical results:

---

[69] From the perspective of political economy, there are arguments, however, which favor a rather energetic consolidation with tighter contractions because of beneficial expectation effects: economic agents perceive government policies as more credible and respond more optimistically to the expected success in the consolidation effort.

Observation 6 (Fiscal Consolidations)
Irrespective of the tightness of tax rate responses to achieve targeted debt and deficit ratios, macroeconomic effects of fiscal consolidations conducted by Italy show the same pattern. They cause primary income and wealth effects (contractionary) which, in turn, produce competition effects (expansionary) and – largely dominating – real interest rate effects (contractionary first, then expansionary). The outcome is contractionary in the short run, but expansionary in the medium run.

Comparing transmission impacts described here (obtaining under a fiscal-baseline) to those resulting from hypothetical EMU scenarios (cf. subsection 6.4 and box 10) reveals some fundamental differences. Fiscal consolidations trigger changes in income and wealth (one of the three aforementioned transmission effects), which immediately spread to the other transmission effects. In contrast, under hypothetical EMU scenarios, the three transmission effects are induced by (additional) impulses in terms of changes in nominal interest and exchange rates.

The role of nominal variables (prices, exchange and interest rates) can be scrutinized in more detail. First, under both sets of scenarios, prices and inflation rates play a central role in the dynamics of the economies. However, under hypothetical EMU scenarios, changes in inflation are strongly affected by imported inflation (cf. subsection 6.4), whereas here, they are almost exclusively determined by capacity utilization effects (according to the Phillips curve relationship). Second, under hypothetical EMU scenarios, the competition effect hinges on changes in nominal exchange rates; here, price changes are the main cause. Finally, under hypothetical EMU scenarios, real interest rates result from a trade-off between changes in nominal interest rates and expected inflation. In contrast, nominal interest rates are practically not affected by fiscal consolidation policies (under baseline conditions otherwise), so that expected inflation governs real interest rates.

9 Fiscal Retrenchment and Hypothetical EMU

This section links a fiscal retrenchment in Italy (examined in the previous section) and hypothetical EMU scenarios (studied in part II). A heuristic approach is chosen: subsection 9.1 discusses generally expected results for fiscal-EMU scenarios, presents specific results for the lax fiscal-CP scenario[70], and pinpoints discrepancies between actual and expected results. In subsection 9.2, these discrepancies are reassessed and interpreted as interdependencies between the fiscal consolidation program in Italy on the one hand, and interest and exchange rate impulses as well as effects caused by the hypothetical EMU on the other hand. It is shown that there is a general pattern applicable to all fiscal-EMU scenarios. Subsection 9.3 pursues the implications of these interdependencies for the interest-exchange trade-off illustrated in section 6. Possible policy recommendations are derived. Subsection 9.4 discusses scope and limitations of the analysis in part III.

9.1 Expected Results and the Lax Fiscal-CP Scenario

Any specific fiscal-EMU scenario consists of two scenario components: first, the hypothetical EMU scenario under a particular conversion rate procedure (here, CP or CUR); and second, a fiscal strategy (be it lax, moderate, strict, or mixed) to fulfill the fiscal Maastricht Criteria. When examining these components as

---

[70] This is a lax fiscal consolidation program for Italy under hypothetical EMU conditions – as defined in subsection 8.1.

separate scenarios it is possible to extract characterizing effects – as done for the hypothetical EMU in section 6 and for the fiscal-baseline in section 8.

For instance, results for Italy under any EMU scenario (without fiscal consolidation policies) are characterized in each period by a (dominating) expansionary real interest rate effect, a weaker positive income and wealth (terms of trade) effect, and a countervailing (contractionary) competition effect. Any fiscal retrenchment strategy largely exhibits opposite effects in each year: an expansionary competition effect, a contractionary wealth and income effect, and a contractionary real interest rate effect until 1986/87; thereafter, the real interest effect turns expansionary and parallels the real interest effect under the hypothetical EMU.

It is clear that results of any specific fiscal-EMU scenario must be affected by effects of both scenario components. The simplest intuition is to expect that they correspond to an addition of quantitative effects of the two respective scenario components (henceforth called additive overlay). Although there is a considerable number of non-linearities in the underlying model MULTIMOD (cf. appendix A.1, and Masson, Symansky, and Meredith, 1990), this expectation is largely confirmed by simulation results. Discrepancies between actual results and the additive overlay of corresponding scenario components can be accounted for by interdependencies between the fiscal component and the hypothetical EMU components (not by non-linearities of the model).

The analysis of results for fiscal-EMU scenarios starts out with the *lax* fiscal strategy (unlike section 8) under a *CP* scenario (unlike section 5) because the lax fiscal-CP scenario is very close to the additive overlay and effects can be explained more easily than for a fiscal-CUR scenario. In the following boxes, simulation results under the lax fiscal-CP scenario relative to the baseline are compared to the (additive) overlay of its two scenario components, i.e. to a straight sum of the outcome under CP (relative to the baseline) and the outcome under the lax fiscal-baseline (relative to the baseline). There is no theoretical justification for adding up both results; it is purely indicative. The analysis of results concentrates on Italy, but spill-overs on other countries caused by the fiscal consolidation plan in Italy will be mentioned.

Box 17 depicts GDP growth rates, inflation, and capacity utilization for Italy under the lax fiscal-CP scenario. Growth rates (figure a) exceed those of the overlay in the first two years, but are smaller in the medium term. It seems that the divergence of inflation (figure b) between the lax fiscal-CP and its additive overlay can be explained in most cases, qualitatively, by the divergence in GDP growth.[71] In years with higher (lower) growth rates under the lax fiscal-CP, capacity utilization (figure c) for the lax fiscal-CP goes up (down) by more – larger slope – than for the additive overlay. A steeper rise (fall) in capacity utilization causes a stronger change in inflation rates in the same direction (according to the Phillips curve relationship).

It remains to be explained though, why GDP growth rates under the lax fiscal-CP differ from the additive overlay. Part of GDP differences can be put down to the fact that real interest rate, competition and income and wealth effects are affected when inflation rates under the lax fiscal-CP deviate from the additive overlay. In particular, higher expected inflation at the outset causes lower real interest rates (cf. box 18, figure a), thus a more expansionary effect compared to the additive overlay. At

---

[71] However, in the next subsection, it will be argued that there is an additional effect caused by imported inflation

Box 17: GDP Growth, Inflation, Capacity Utilization in Italy under the Lax Fiscal-CP Scenario

(a)

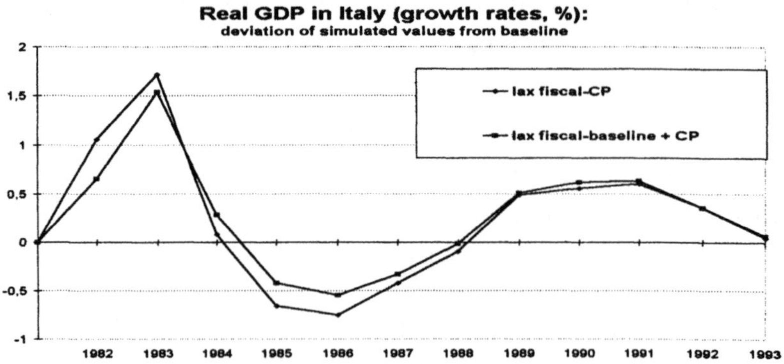

(b)

(c)

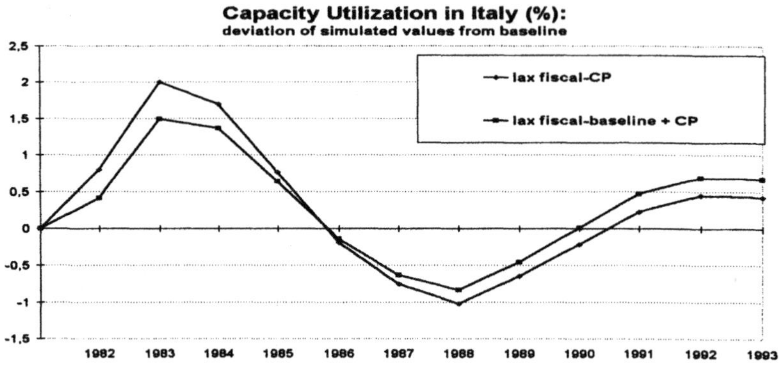

the downturn of the inflation cycle, lower expected inflation rates have the opposite effects: they produce higher real interest rates which can partly be held responsible for the more contractionary effect on GDP growth rates produced by the lax fiscal-CP scenario compared to the additive overlay. This part of the story relates to the consistency requirement of any equilibrium solution.

However, there are two further discrepancies (between the lax fiscal-CP and the corresponding additive overlay) which account for the shift from one equilibrium to the other: first, nominal exchange rates vis-à-vis the US-$ (of all hypothetical EMU currencies) under the lax fiscal-CP do not appreciate as much as the additive overlay may suggest (for Italy, cf. figure b in box 18); second, tax rates in Italy cannot be explained by adding up the values for each scenario component (figure c).

As for the first discrepancy, figure (b) shows that the initial appreciation of the Lira vis-à-vis the US-$ is significantly weaker than suggested by the additive overlay. As a result of the less dramatic appreciation, the negative competition effect under the lax fiscal-CP is weaker than for the additive overlay (which consists of the expansionary effect under the lax fiscal-baseline and the contractionary effect under the original CP). Nonetheless, real effective exchange rates (cf. appendix B.7) still appreciate (though less) relative to the original baseline, and the loss of net foreign assets amounts to almost 450 billions of DM by 1993 relative to the original baseline. Under the original CP scenario, the loss is twice as large (889 billions of DM).

Since conversion rates are fixed at central parities, the weaker nominal appreciation of the Lira vis-à-vis the US-$ also implies higher DM and FF exchange rates to the US-$ under the lax fiscal-CP compared to the additive overlay. Remember that even

Box 18: Real Interest, Nom. Exchange, and Tax Rates in Italy under the Lax Fiscal-CP Scenario

(a)

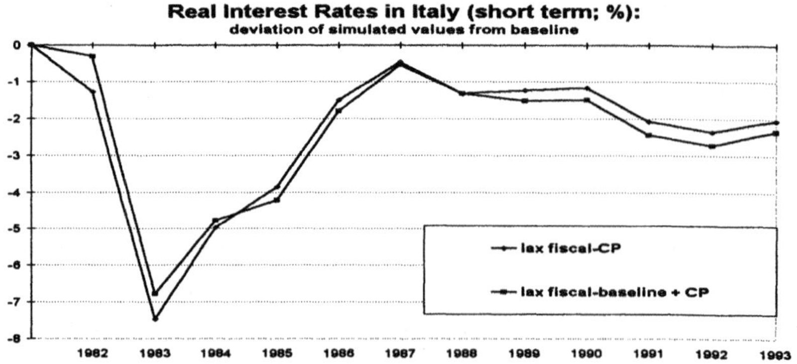

(b)

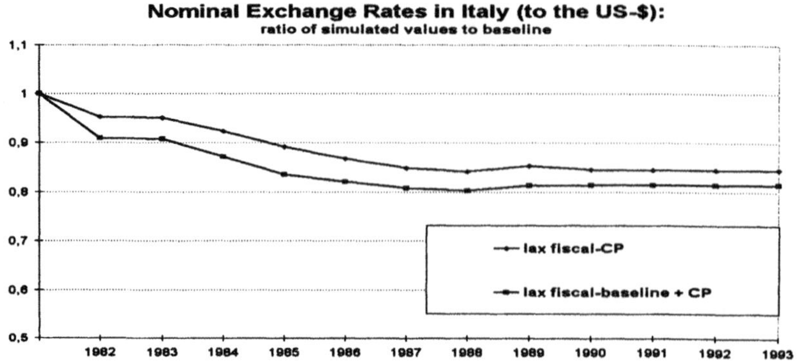

(c)

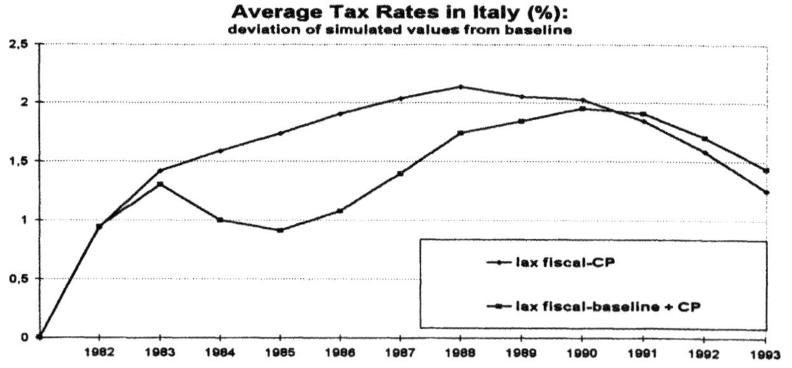

the DM appreciates under the original CP relative to the baseline (in contrast to CUR and PPP) during the first years of the EMU. The appreciation for the DM almost disappears under the lax fiscal-CP. According to subsection 6.1, higher exchange rates to the US-$ reflect higher levels of monetary variables in the long run – compared to the additive overlay.

The basic mechanism to account for higher monetary growth or inflation over a longer period of time (compared to the additive overlay) rests on changes to money demand and different responses of central banks under different scenarios. A (lax) *fiscal-baseline* (which is one component of the additive overlay) incorporates exchange rate targeting within the ERM. Under such conditions, fiscal consolidations in Italy produce lasting reductions in the nominal money demand, which do not trigger *direct* interest rate responses by the Italian central bank to restore the initial volume of nominal money in the economy (as argued in subsection 8.2).

By contrast, under a (lax) *fiscal-CP scenario*, there is monetary targeting conducted by the ECB (based on an exogenous aggregate nominal money supply target). Reductions in the union-wide nominal money demand (merely caused by the fiscal contraction in Italy) induce automatic monetary loosening (reduced interest rates) in all hypothetical EMU countries such that the effect on the nominal money demand is limited. Hence the level of nominal money is likely to be higher in the longer term under a (lax) fiscal-CP scenario – compared to results suggested by the additive overlay.

The second discrepancy between the lax fiscal-CP and the corresponding additive overlay refers to tax rates in Italy. Figure (c) in box 18 illustrates that fiscal consolidations are tighter in the period from 1984 to 1989. This is so (cf. also next subsection), because the modified tax rule is applied to the combined scenario under the lax fiscal-CP, whereas it only applies to the lax fiscal-baseline component of the additive overlay. As a result, real disposable income and real wealth (cf. appendix B.7) are lower under the lax fiscal-CP, throughout, thus producing a less expansionary effect compared to the additive overlay.

Effects of discrepancies in nominal exchange, average tax, and real interest rates can be put together to explain the deviations of GDP growth rates in Italy under the lax fiscal-CP (relative to the baseline) compared to the additive overlay (relative to the baseline) – as presented in box 17, figure (a). Basically, lower real interest rates and less contractionary competition effects (due to higher exchange rates) produce higher GDP growth rates in the first couple of years. In the period from 1984 to 1989, higher real interest rates and less expansionary income and wealth effects (caused by higher tax rates) determine that growth rates are below those suggested by the additive overlay.

Higher nominal and real exchange rates under the lax fiscal-CP (compared to the additive overlay) produce different impacts for Italy and for the other hypothetical EMU countries France and Germany. Whereas higher exchange rates magnify – in Italy – initial expansionary effects and subsequent cyclical swings (compared to the additive overlay), they reduce initial contractionary effects and dampen ensuing cyclical swings in Germany and France. (For a comparison to the original CP scenario, cf. box 22, page 165. For lax fiscal-CP data as such, cf. appendix B.7).

9.2 Impact of Fiscal Strategies on EMU Scenarios

So far, the lax fiscal-CP scenario and its results have been dissected into components, their effects, and deviations from expected results. On this basis, interdependencies between fiscal consolidations in Italy and effects caused by hypothetical EMU scenarios are scrutinized in this subsection. However, fiscal-EMU scenarios are now compared to corresponding original EMU scenarios, no longer to additive overlays.

The analysis covers two issues. First, it is shown that different fiscal strategies for Italy produce results for tax rates, and for debt and deficit ratios which are much more similar to one another under fiscal-CP scenario conditions than under fiscal-baseline conditions. The comparison of various fiscal-CUR scenarios is not possible, because only a lax fiscal-CUR scenario is available, but the same line of reasoning can be applied in principle. Second and most importantly, the impact of fiscal consolidations on nominal interest and exchange rate impulses will be discussed for the lax fiscal-CP and then compared to the other fiscal-EMU scenarios.

As for the first issue, consider implications for tax rates, and debt and deficit ratios caused by the application of fiscal strategies to the hypothetical EMU instead of the baseline. These changes only affect Italy. On the one hand, tax rates of a fiscal-CP scenario are higher than those obtaining under the corresponding original CP scenario. This is so because the *modified* tax rate reaction function is applied to fiscal scenarios. Since lower debt and deficit ratios are targeted, tax rates must be higher under the fiscal-CP scenario.

On the other hand, tax rates of any fiscal-CP scenario are lower than those under the corresponding fiscal-baseline. Peak rates occur two to three years earlier, and they are more than 3.5 percentage points lower. The reason is that the EMU produces an expansionary effect on aggregate output in Italy (cf. subsection 5.1), which contributes to the reduction of debt-to-GDP and deficit-to-GDP ratios. Since deviations from debt and deficit ratio targets produce stronger tax rate responses for stricter fiscal rules, tax rates are reduced by more under a stricter fiscal-CP compared to its corresponding fiscal-baseline, even though the expansionary effect caused by the hypothetical EMU is the same under all fiscal strategies.[72] As a result, the difference in peak rates for lax, moderate, strict, and mixed fiscal strategies is .5 percentage points smaller under the fiscal-CP compared to the fiscal-baseline (cf. appendices B.7-B.9).

Deficit and debt ratios in Italy under lax, moderate, strict, and mixed plans become even more alike than tax rates. Each figure in box 19, considers debt ratios under a particular fiscal strategy (lax, moderate, or strict) and compares results for its fiscal-baseline and the corresponding fiscal-CP scenario. Comparing the three figures illustrates that laxity or tightness of the *fiscal-baseline* do have a significant effect on the debt ratio, whereas these differences are almost leveled out under *fiscal-CP scenarios*. (Given the reasoning of the last paragraph, the same should hold for fiscal-CUR scenarios as well.) This finding illustrates the role of the denominator in debt and deficit ratios:

[72] Compared to the corresponding additive overlay, tax rates are higher under the lax fiscal-CP (cf. last subsection), but lower under the moderate and strict fiscal-CP, because the tax rate reducing effect produced by the overall expansion in the hypothetical EMU is stronger for stricter fiscal plans.

Box 19: **Debt in Italy under Lax, Moderate, Strict Fiscal-CP Scenarios**

(a)

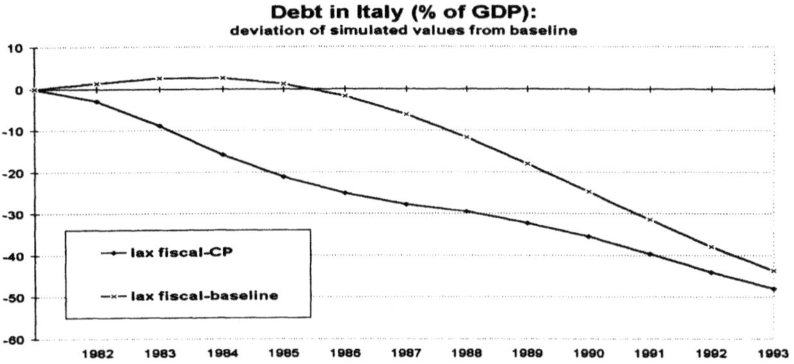

(b)

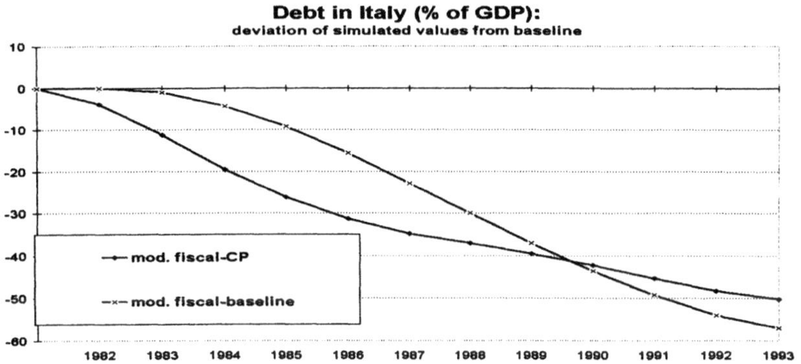

(c)

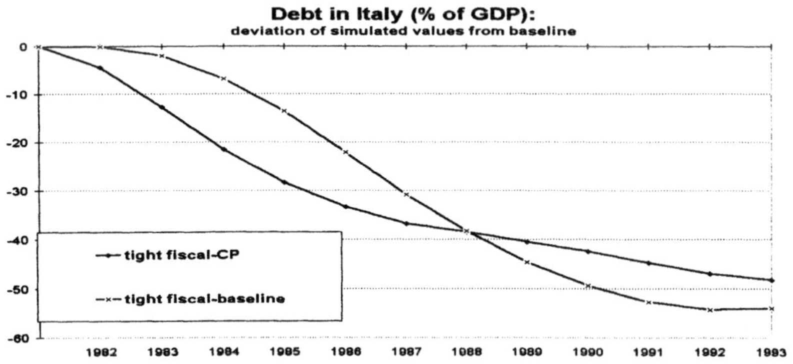

Observation 7 (Denominator Effect under Fiscal-CP Scenarios)
Despite differences in tightness, alternative tax rate responses in Italy (to achieve targeted debt and deficit ratios) produce similar effects on debt and deficit ratios under a given fiscal-CP scenario. This is due to the denominator effect, i.e. the reduction of debt and deficit ratios merely caused by output expansions induced by the hypothetical EMU.

In the hypothetical EMU, the expansionary impact on aggregate output is so strong in Italy that much smaller tax rises are required to bring debt and deficit ratios down. Furthermore, the increased similarity in tax rates and debt and deficit ratios under alternative fiscal strategies implies that effects of fiscal consolidations will also be similar. In fact, it is shown in the next subsection that the impact of fiscal policies on the hypothetical EMU does practically not depend on the strictness of the underlying tax rule.

As to the second issue of this subsection, consider the impact of fiscal consolidations on nominal interest and exchange rate impulses, first for the lax fiscal-CP scenario, then for other scenarios. The analysis of the lax fiscal-CP in the previous subsection has shown that *exchange rate impulses* observed for the original CP scenario[73] are affected by the introduction of fiscal consolidations. Exchange rates vis-à-vis the US-$ under the lax fiscal-CP are higher in Italy, but also in the other hypothetical EMU member countries – compared to the original CP scenario. It was argued that this is due to higher monetary growth and inflation

---

[73] Nominal exchange rate results for the original CP scenario correspond to those of the additive overlay, because the fiscal- baseline (component) does practically not affect exchange rates.

over a longer period of time caused by fiscal contractions in Italy which prompt monetary loosening.

A more expansionary monetary policy by the hypothetical ECB should be reflected by larger *interest rate impulses* in Italy, i.e. union-wide nominal interest rates should be lower under the lax fiscal-CP compared to the original CP. This is true for most years, but not for the first years of the hypothetical EMU. From 1983 to 1986, a paradoxical result obtains: monetary policy is tighter (interest rates are higher) than under the original CP. This is so despite the contractionary impact of higher taxes which should cause automatic monetary loosening (given that there is an exogenous nominal monetary target for the hypothetical ECB). However, since exchange rates are higher compared to the original CP, prices and inflation are higher, too (due to imported inflation effects on the one hand, and a more positive competition effect leading to higher GDP, higher capacity utilization and an additional inflation effect based on the Phillips curve relationship on the other hand). When GDP and prices go up, the public desires to increase its nominal money holdings. The central bank, however, tries to bring them down again (to the level of the exogenous nominal monetary target) by raising nominal interest rates.

As for the other fiscal-EMU scenarios (moderate fiscal-CP, strict fiscal-CP, mixed fiscal-CP, and lax fiscal-CUR), the impact of fiscal consolidations on nominal interest and exchange rates is very similar. Nominal exchange rates for three of these scenarios are depicted in box 20. In each case (even for the lax fiscal-CUR), the change in exchange rates relative to the baseline is about 5 percentage points smaller than under the corresponding original EMU scenario.

Box 20: Nominal Exchange Rates in Italy under Lax, Strict Fiscal-CP, and Lax Fiscal-CUR

(a)

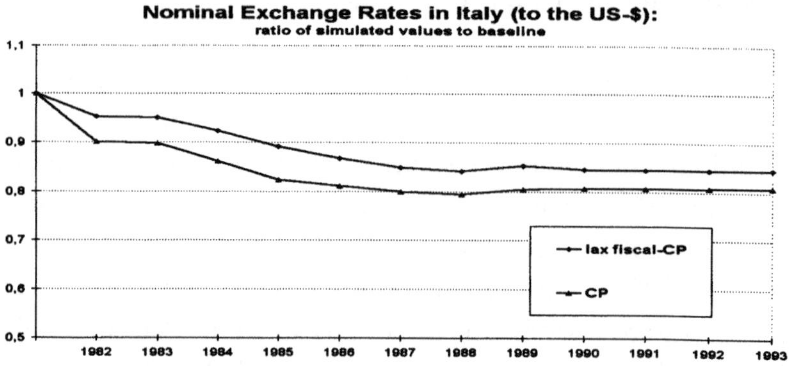

(b)

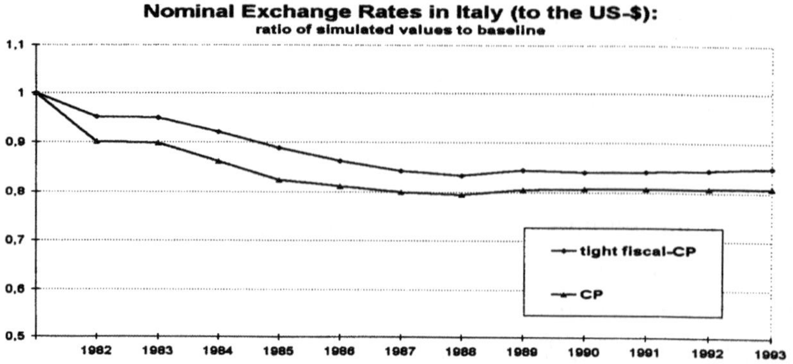

(c)

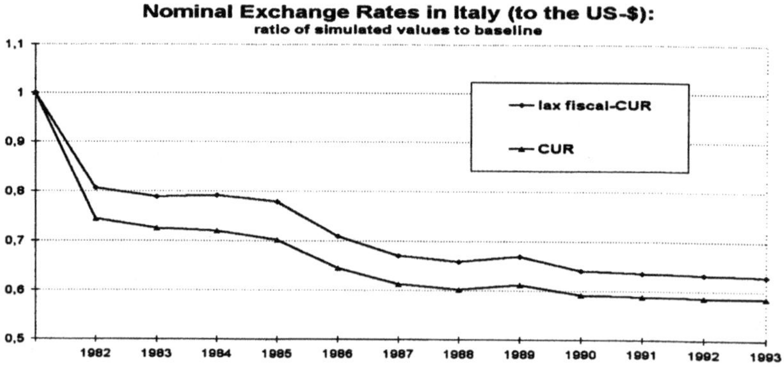

Since exogenously fixed central parities are used as conversion rates under fiscal-CP scenarios, bilateral *conversion rates* cannot be affected by a more expansionary monetary development – compared to the original CP scenario. Under the lax fiscal-CUR, however, there is an additional weakening of the Lira (by 3 percentage points compared to the original CUR) in terms of a reduced appreciation vis-à-vis the DM. This is possible, because – under CUR – bilateral conversion rates are based on freely floating 1982 market exchange rates. As a result, the (positive) impact on the competition effect (measured by real effective exchange rates; cf. appendices B.7-B.9) is very similar in all EMU countries under fiscal-CP scenarios, whereas it is more expansionary for Italy under fiscal-CUR scenarios.

We know from part II that member countries experience nominal exchange rate impulses caused by the formation of the hypothetical EMU (without fiscal consolidations). The following observation recapitulates the finding that fiscal consolidations in Italy alter nominal exchange rate impulses:

Observation 8 (Exchange Rate Impulse under Fiscal-EMU Scenarios)
Irrespective of the tightness of tax rate responses in Italy and of the hypothetical EMU scenario (fiscal-CP or fiscal-CUR), fiscal consolidations produce an additional depreciative impact on nominal exchange rate impulses. Over an extended period of time, exchange rates are higher in all member countries because of a more expansionary monetary development union-wide. As a result, there is an additional expansionary competition effect over and above effects caused by the fiscal strategy and by the hypothetical EMU on their own.

Since changes of the exchange rate impulse are almost identical under various scenarios, the impact on interest rates is very similar, too – as illustrated in box 21. For all fiscal-EMU scenarios, interest rates are (approximately 0.5 %) higher than those of the corresponding original EMU scenario in the first three to four years of the hypothetical EMU, but below thereafter. It should be remarked though that – under all fiscal-EMU scenarios – the impact of changes in nominal interest rates on real rates is practically eliminated by the aforementioned higher rate of (expected) inflation. These findings are simplified in the following observation:

Observation 9 (Interest Rate Impulse under Fiscal-EMU Scenarios)
Irrespective of the tightness of tax rate responses in Italy and of the hypothetical EMU scenario, there is only a weak impact of fiscal consolidations on nominal interest rate impulses in all EMU countries. Its bearing on aggregate demand is small.

9.3 Fiscal Policy Implications for Monetary Unions

In this subsection, findings of the two previous subsections are condensed and real effects of fiscal-EMU scenarios are summarized in observation 10. On this basis, the impact of fiscal consolidations on hypothetical EMU scenarios is compared to the impact of a fiscal retrenchment on the baseline. Finally, some policy recommendations for fiscal consolidations in monetary unions are extracted (based on results from sections 8 and 9).

Box 21: **Nominal Interest Rates in Italy under Lax, Strict Fiscal-CP, and Lax Fiscal-CUR**

(a)

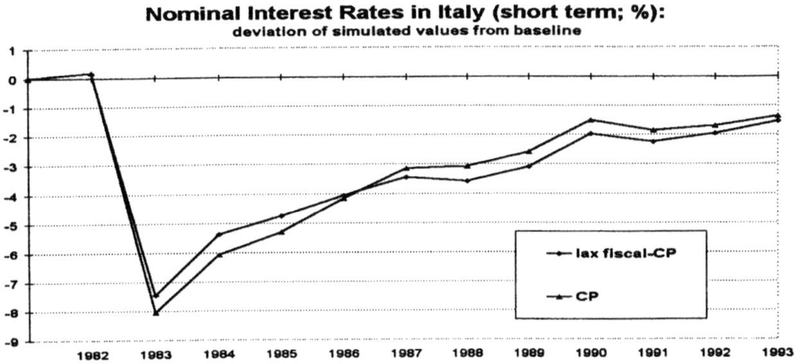

(b)

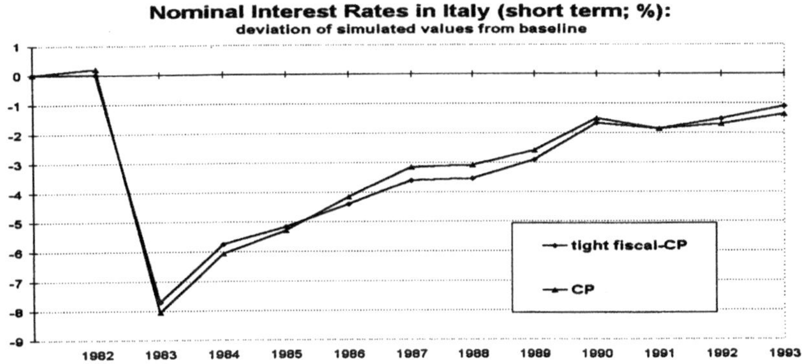

(c)

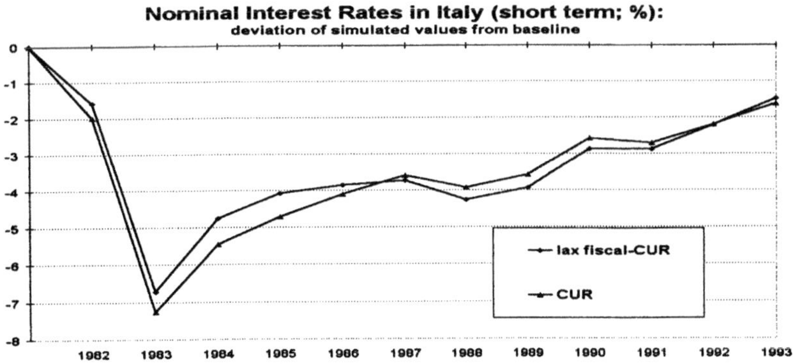

Findings of the previous two subsection are twofold. On the one hand, fiscal-EMU scenarios produce results that can be largely explained by adding up results for fiscal strategies per se (fiscal-baseline) and those for hypothetical EMU scenarios per se. On the other hand, interdependencies between fiscal consolidations in Italy and the hypothetical EMU do affect the overall outcome of fiscal-EMU scenarios in three respects: first, lax, moderate, tight, and mixed fiscal strategies amount to similar debt and deficit reductions (in terms of ratios to GDP) under any fiscal-EMU scenario (fiscal-CP or fiscal-CUR); second, all fiscal strategies produce a similar impact on interest and exchange rate impulses; third, changes to exchange rate impulses entail an additional expansionary effect over and above effects caused by the fiscal retrenchment on its own on the one hand, and by the hypothetical EMU on its own on the other hand.

Box 22 depicts the overall impact on real GDP of various fiscal consolidation strategies under CP conditions. In separate figures for Italy, France, and Germany, GDP levels – under various scenarios – are presented as ratios to baseline values. The figures confirm that – for each country – the simulated outcome for all fiscal strategies is very similar. Upcoming comparisons of fiscal-CP scenarios to the original CP scenario talk about more expansionary/contractionary effects or gains/losses. These findings do not contradict results discussed in subsection 9.1, because there a lax fiscal-CP scenario was compared to the additive overlay, not to the original CP.

For Italy, fiscal contractions lead to short term losses in aggregate output (of up to 1.5 % in 1984) – compared to the original CP. These losses would be even larger without the additional expanionary effect stemming from the more depreciative exchange rate impulses under fiscal-CP conditions compared to the original

Box 22: Real GDP in Italy, France, and Germany under CP and Fiscal-CP Scenarios

(a)

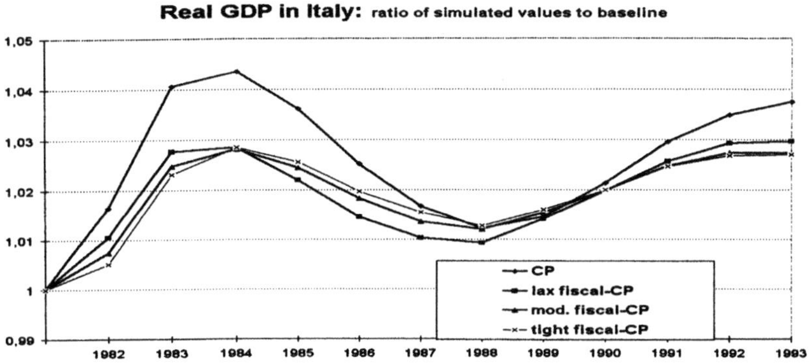

(b)

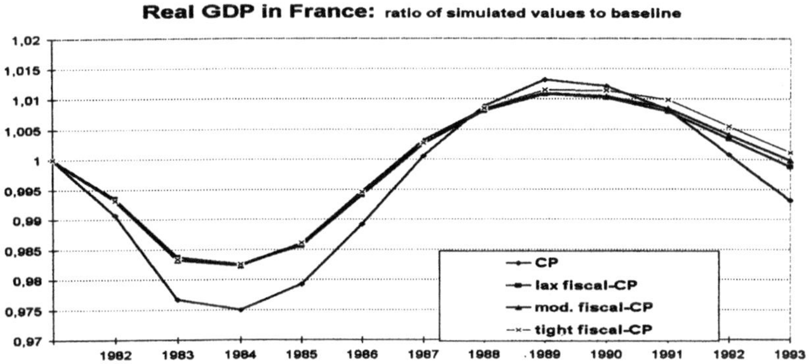

(c)

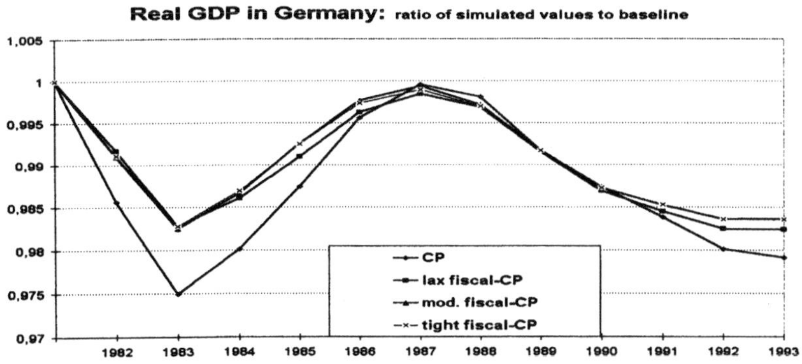

CP scenario. Cycles are dampened and there is an overall loss of about 1 % by 1993 compared to the original CP. (Even thereafter, the magnitude of the relative loss does not change much.) At the same time, inflation is reduced, too. The price level in 1993 is between 3 % to 4 % lower under any fiscal-CP scenario compared to the original CP. Qualitatively, similar results should obtain under fiscal-CUR scenarios as well, because interdependencies between fiscal consolidations in Italy and the hypothetical EMU do not depend on the EMU scenario (CP or CUR) – as seen in the previous subsection.

In France and Germany, the situation is more favorable compared to the original CP scenario. Losses stemming from the hypothetical EMU (under a CP scenario) are reduced in the short run as well as in the longer term due to less appreciative/more depreciative exchange rate impulses. Cycles are dampened in these countries (as in Italy). Over the longer term, losses occurring under the original CP are reduced by more than 0.5 % and 0.3 % in France and Germany, respectively (even beyond 1993). This comes at the cost of higher price levels in each country in 1993 (some 2.5 % higher compared to the original CP). Again, a similar outcome should obtain for fiscal consolidations under CUR.

In all countries, impulses, transmission effects, and the potential interest-exchange trade-off established in section 6 remains the same, qualitatively, under all fiscal-EMU scenarios. However, the trade-off between nominal interest and exchange rate impulses turns more expansionary in all countries[74] under any fiscal-EMU scenario (including fiscal-CUR) due to the more depreciative ex-

---

[74] Under the original CP, there was actually no trade-off in Germany in the first few years of the hypothetical EMU, when both exchange and interest rate impulses are contractionary. But there, too, the overall impact becomes less contractionary under fiscal-CP scenarios.

change rate impulse. Nonetheless, the fiscal contraction does take a toll in Italy under all fiscal-EMU scenarios in terms of reduced aggregate output. (On the other hand, longer term inflation figures improve.)

Observation 10 (Real Effects under Fiscal-EMU Scenarios)
Under any fiscal consolidation program conducted by Italy in the hypothetical EMU, the interest-exchange trade-off observed under original hypothetical EMU scenarios is, qualitatively, retained. Due to interdependencies between fiscal consolidations and the hypothetical EMU, there are, however, additional real effects caused by: a denominator effect (observation 7), and more expansionary exchange rate impulses (observation 8).

Real effects of fiscal consolidations on the hypothetical EMU (observation 10) can now be compared to the impact of fiscal consolidations on the baseline (cf. subsections 8.2 and 8.3). For Italy, a fiscal consolidation plan under hypothetical EMU conditions (fiscal-EMU) produces – as already seen – fairly little output volatility, but results in an overall loss in the longer term (after 10 years) – relative to the corresponding original hypothetical EMU. In contrast, a fiscal retrenchment under baseline conditions (fiscal-baseline) induces considerable output volatility, but may cause both contractionary or expansionary effects in the longer term – relative to the original baseline. (Whereas lax and strict strategies – under baseline conditions otherwise – lead to output losses, the moderate fiscal plan produces increased output of +0.8 % by 1993 at almost no additional inflation.) At the same time, short run contractions in Italy – observed for a fiscal retrenchment plan under baseline conditions otherwise – are reduced under hypothetical EMU conditions (relative to corresponding original EMU scenarios) due to a denominator effect (observation 7) and more expansionary exchange rate impulses (observation 8). (France and Germany enjoy favorable effects if Italy conducts her fiscal consolidation under hypothetical EMU conditions, whereas they are hardly affected under baseline conditions).

These findings – and the analysis in part III – rest on model assumptions (discussed in part I and appendix A), on a specific class of fiscal consolidation programs for Italy (based on a tax rate reaction function; cf. subsection 8.1), and on the application of fiscal strategies to hypothetical EMU scenarios. They are also based on a country that exhibits undervalued exchange rates (relative to purchasing power parity; cf. Hill, 1986), high interest rates and a high level of debt – as captured by the historical baseline as of the 1980s.

Given these conditions, clear policy recommendations can be pronounced for a country such as Italy: (i) it is highly recommendable to join a monetary union (as shown in part II); (ii) if fiscal consolidations are deemed necessary in a situation without monetary union, they may produce favorable results in the longer term depending on the tightness of the fiscal contractions and their supply side effects (as shown in subsection 8.3); (iii) nonetheless, it may be advisable to combine a fiscal retrenchment with the participation in a monetary union (despite minor losses produced by fiscal contractions under fiscal-EMU scenarios relative to corresponding original EMU scenarios), because effects caused by the fiscal retrenchment are clearly outweighed by overall gains from joining a monetary union; and (iv) there may be scope for adjusting the tightness of fiscal contractions (in terms of tax rate responses) – under the conditions of a monetary union – to political circumstances, because results are hardly affected.

Since other member countries of a monetary union gain from contractionary fiscal policies in such a country, they should actually be pushing for fiscal adjustments. This could be taken as an additional argument in favor of the fiscal Maastricht Criteria and the "stability pact".[75] It is based on macroeconomic effects of the adjustment which are expected to be favorable under specific assumptions on monetary policy (critically reviewed in the following subsection though).[76]

9.4 Scope and Limitations of the Fiscal Policy Analysis

In this subsection, scope and limitations of analysis and findings in part III are discussed. As to the first limitation, the analysis, obviously, suffers from the fact that simulation exercises are based on the economic conditions of the 1980s. Interest and exchange rate impulses are overstated (cf. section 7, question 3, page 111), whereas the debt problem in Italy in the 1980s resembles the situation in the wake of the real world EMU. Since effects are largely countervailing, quantitative aspects matter and the qualitative outcome may change under a more realistic scenario. In fact, fiscal effects may dominate the outcome in a real world setting.

Consider the situation for Italy as of 1999. For smaller interest rate differentials in Europe, the expansionary effect through real interest rates is diminished. At the same time, smaller exchange

---

[75] Suggested by the former German Finance Minister, Theo Waigel. Cf. FAZ (1996) as of 13 June 1996.

[76] Typically, the need for fiscal consolidations is justified by fears about overborrowing by member countries of the prospective EMU – as discussed, for instance, in Siebke, 1993, p. 154, or in Kenen, 1995, p. 96.

rate impulses produce a less contractionary effect. Nonetheless, effects induced by fiscal policy are certainly not smaller than the ones discussed in this treatise: they are contractionary in the short run, and expansionary in the medium term. Since various effects and impulses are countervailing, the net effect on Italy caused by the real world EMU cannot be determined a priori. However, the impact of fiscal consolidations on nominal interest and, in particular, on nominal exchange rate impulses and their trade-off is likely not to vanish. This is an argument for pursuing fiscal consolidations in Italy, even if the interest-exchange trade-off were not so favorable, and/or if (contractionary) short term effects of fiscal contractions dominated the overall impact on GDP.

The findings of the analysis can also be used to infer implications – under real world EMU conditions – of fiscal contractions in other countries. Take a more stability-oriented country (without undervalued exchange rates) with relatively low nominal short term interest rates, but with a high level of debt. Belgium may be the country in question. Alternatively, consider an improvement of the fiscal position in a country that is close or under 60 % debt and/or 3 % deficit limits (for instance, Germany or France as of the late 1990s). In the following, it is argued that conditions are also favorable for these countries to correct overexpanionary fiscal policies.

Under real world EMU conditions, it was conjectured in question 5 of section 7 (page 115) that a stability-oriented country with low interest rates would experience a minor or no depreciation and no change in interest rates in the real world EMU without fiscal consolidations (relative to a conceptual scenario without monetary union). If an added fiscal consolidation did, again, produce an additional depreciative effect (due to higher monetary growth and inflation), the expansionary exchange rate impulse would be magnified.[77] Since the overall effect of a fiscal retrenchment is contractionary at first (in the country in question), countervailing effects would prevail in the short run. These are rather favorable conditions for reducing debt or deficit levels (or ratios). Other member countries of the monetary union would also benefit from the depreciative impact on union-wide exchange rates.

The second limitation refers to the overall growth conditions under which a fiscal retrenchment for Italy is analyzed in this treatise. For instance, the underlying growth conditions are more favorable almost everywhere in the 1980s than in the 1990s. It may be argued that a fiscal contraction might have produced more contractionary effects under less favorable conditions. However, given that results are presented relative to the baseline, this should not play a major role.

It is probably more relevant that simulation findings are based on a fiscal retrenchment in one country only. In the historical baseline for the 1980s, Germany and France stayed below prescribed target ratios for debt and deficit. If these two countries had also pursued fiscal contractions, the simulation outcome for Italy and the other hypothetical EMU member countries might have been less favorable due to mutual contractionary spill-overs.

An overall more contractionary outcome is not certain though, because automatic monetary loosening would have been reinforced. We have already seen that the monetary relaxation permitted

[77] Assuming that – in the real world – the expansionary effect on GDP of the country in question were not as large as for Italy under the fiscal-EMU scenario, the denominator effect on debt and deficit reductions would be rather small. Hence, effects of fiscal consolidation policies would now depend on the tightness of responses in the tax rate reaction function.

by the hypothetical ECB under (already discussed) hypothetical EMU scenarios produced considerably stronger expansionary exchange rate impulses for all member countries. If the contraction does not just happen in Italy, but union-wide, the effect of further increased depreciative exchange rate impulses might also outweigh additional contractionary effects.

The third limitation evolves around the justification for these depreciative effects. They were crucial for the reasoning in the last paragraphs as well as for aforementioned simulation results (including observations 8 and 9). A more expansionary (or less contractionary) outcome prevails under fiscal consolidations, because exchange rate impulses in the monetary union are affected by automatic monetary loosening over an extended period of time. This effect depends on the feature of an exogenous nominal monetary target which is embodied in MULTIMOD.[78] (The mechanical response in MULTIMOD of monetary policy to fiscal contractions was discussed in subsection 9.1.) Sensitivities of fiscal policy effects to assumptions on monetary policy were also found by Fair (1994, p. 293).

Automatic monetary loosening (à la MULTIMOD) under contractionary conditions may be considered a desirable property. In fact, exogenous monetary targets come close to monetarist rules which provide for constant growth rates of the money supply. In both cases, discretionary responses in the short term as well as medium term adjustments are not envisaged, but neither of them captures real world central bank behavior.

---

[78] This effect cannot be eliminated unless the target is made endogenous. For instance, it did not help to use exogenous target growth rates over several periods instead of target levels for single periods (cf. question 1 in section 4, and scenarios V.2 on page 213).

To avoid a systematic bias under contractionary conditions, monetary targets would have to be determined endogenously so that the expected change of economic conditions is taken into account in some way. One option is to consider expected actual GDP growth (which corresponds to the actual GDP growth rate in a rational expectations model). This is considered undesirable because output fluctuations are magnified instead of being smoothed out by monetary policy. This is not so under the alternative option, which is the potential-oriented approach of the Bundesbank (Deutsche Bundesbank, 1997 and 1995). It is based on medium term estimates for the growth of potential output to determine monetary target growth. The Bundesbank approach allows for monetary relaxation in recessions and tightening in boom periods. Yet, there is no systematic monetary loosening in the long run, because monetary targets are updated. In contrast, exogenous monetary targets are not changed in MULTIMOD.

If these changes were applied to MULTIMOD, the outcome for fiscal-EMU scenarios would be less expansionary in all EMU countries. The case for conducting fiscal consolidations under conditions of a monetary union would be weaker. Nonetheless, it has been shown that a monetary union offers favorable conditions for a fiscal retrenchment in a country with high interest rates and undervalued exchange rates. At the same time, the analysis illustrates the impact on simulation results of a certain model assumption (concerning the specification of central bank behavior).

10 Conclusion

This treatise emphasizes a potential trade-off between nominal interest and exchange rate impulses in the European Monetary Union. More generally, joining members of any monetary union are likely to experience considerable macroeconomic effects due to lasting changes in interest and exchange rates – relative to a situation without monetary union. These changes are caused by the transiton to the monetary union, because central bank interest rates are equalized and exchange rates are fixed.

Although this is conventional wisdom, the interaction between interest and exchange rate impulses has been largely neglected in the economic (or political) debate on the EMU. The reason may be that the current discussion lacks a sound theoretical underpinning, because the transition to the EMU *and* the period after its actual start are typically not included in the same model. Nonetheless, to avoid adverse economic effects, it is vital that policy makers think about the interest-exchange trade-off when decisions on future EMU candidates or prospective members of any other monetary union are to be taken.

The need to capture joint effects of interest and exchange rate impulses (relative to a situation without monetary union) within the framework of a multi-country model necessitated a number of methodical choices for this treatise: first, to conduct a comparative simulation analysis based on a large econometric model (instead of using a small theoretical model which is analytically tractable); second, to construct counterfactuals in a (historical) ex post analysis (instead of relying on more commonly used ex ante simulations); and third, to make a number of adjustments to the solution algorithm. Given that simulation results refer to a historical time period, interpretations are not straightforward. The analysis in part II and again in part III involved a three stage process: first, obtaining quantitative simulation results; second, extracting qualitative findings (summarized in ten observations); and third, applying them to the real world.

In part II, this approach produced insights in four respects. First, economic (policy) conditions for the real world EMU are qualitatively captured by the simulation analysis (observations 1 to 3) – even though nominal interest and exchange rate impulses are overstated quantitatively. On this basis, the role of transmission mechanisms and the existence of a potential trade-off between nominal impulses derived in the analysis (observations 4 and 5) can be applied to the real world EMU. Second, anticipation effects observed in the run-up to the real world EMU can be substantiated. Third, the knowledge of a potential trade-off between interest and exchange rate impulses can be used to make an "educated guess" of expected macroeconomic effects of the EMU relative to a situation without announcement of a monetary union. Fourth, decisions associated with the EU Summit in Brussels on 2 May 1998 can be critically reviewed in view of the interest-exchange trade-off.

As for the third aspect, the real world EMU is assumed to exhibit a high level of monetary stability and convergence to relatively low interest rates. Under these conditions, it was argued that "core" countries (like Germany, France, Austria, and the Benelux) are likely to experience only minor effects – relative to a situation without monetary union. The opposite applies for the Southern "peripheral" countries Italy, Spain, and Portugal who – historically – have a less unambiguous monetary stability record and high interest rates. These conditions would presumably not have changed completely, if the real world EMU had not been announced. On this basis, model results suggest that there will be permanent (expansionary) interest and (contractionary) exchange rate impulses in the real world EMU *relative* to a situation without monetary union. All in all, Southern EMU members are likely to experience an overall expansionary impact due to (presumably) dominant interest rate reductions.

As for the fourth aspect (referring to the EU Summit), it was argued that the interest-exchange trade-off could have been used as a tool for cushioning short term adjustments in the final transition phase to the EMU (say, in 1998). Interest rate equalization is likely to produce overheating effects in countries with high interest rates. In Ireland, for instance, this was already happening before the start of the EMU (The Economist, 14 November, 1998b). If conversion rates for the Irish punt had been fixed at low (i.e. strong) exchange rates deemed right by the markets (or at even lower rates), overheating effects could have been somewhat alleviated (at least in the short run). Instead, it was decided at the Brussels Summit to use central parities of the ERM as conversion rates, because policy makers wanted to avoid political haggling over conversion rates. As a result, Ireland was stuck with a half-hearted revaluation of central parities (as of March 1998). Since market rates were still lower, depreciations set in and continued until pre-announced conversion rates were matched on 1 January 1999. Hence, Ireland is enjoying a (temporary) competitive advantage in the EMU, but at the cost of parallel interest and exchange rate impulses which are fueling an already hot economy.

In part III, a possible extension to the previous analysis was taken up as a case study. A fiscal retrenchment strategy as required by the Maastricht Treaty was analyzed explicitly for Italy as of the 1980s. It was shown that – under a fiscal retrenchment in Italy (observation 6) – the interest-exchange trade-off revealed in part II is still retained (observation 10). There are, however, interdependencies between fiscal policies and the hypothetical EMU (observations 7, 8, and 9). First, fiscal consolidations in Italy (in terms of improvements of debt-to-GDP or deficit-to-GDP ratios) are supported by an EMU-induced expansionary impact and its effect on the denominator of debt and deficit ratios. Second, if the central bank of the union allows for monetary relaxation in view of the fiscal contraction in a member country, the fiscal retrenchment gives rise to monetary loosening which, in turn, produces more expansionary exchange rate impulses in all member countries. In the short and medium term, the fiscal contraction in Italy *and* contractionary effects in other member countries (caused by the hypothetical EMU) are, therefore, alleviated at the same time.

Results of this treatise also emphasize that effects caused by fiscal consolidations depend on the economic context. If a fiscal retrenchment is conducted in a monetary union, the size and sign of interest and exchange rate impulses are relevant for evaluating the impact on each country. Given a country (like Italy) characterized by depreciating or undervalued exchange rates (in the early 1980s, relative to purchasing power parity; cf. Hill, 1986), high nominal interest rates, and high government debt, joining a monetary union provides ideal conditions for pursuing fiscal consolidations at the same time. This is so, because the fiscal contraction (in the short and medium run) is counterbalanced by expansionary effects caused by a monetary union.

At various stages of this treatise, technical and economic limitations were discussed. For instance, it was remarked that additional effects are likely to coexist in a monetary union besides the potential trade-off between interest and exchange rate impulses established in part II. In particular, the EMU may cause or require changes to the behavior of private agents (especially in money demand and financial markets) or to the conduct of fiscal policies and monetary policies. It was argued (in section 7) that there is, however, no compelling way to model these changes within the framework of a comparative simulation analysis. Furthermore, the case study on fiscal policy (in part III) illustrates that nominal interest and exchange rate impulses and ensuing real effects may be affected by these additional factors, but they remain, nonetheless, relevant in any monetary union.

The trade-off between nominal interest and nominal exchange rate impulses can also be used for making some policy recommendations concerning future enlargements of the real world EMU or any other monetary union. Since at least some prospective member countries will "gain" from lower interest rates, there is one more reason why they can be required to join at appropriate (or even somewhat overvalued, but certainly not devalued or undervalued) exchange rates. This may be particularly relevant for prospective applicants from Eastern Central Europe. In fact, Slovenia and the Visegrád countries Poland, Hungaria, and the Czech Republic as of today resemble Italy as of the 1980s. Their short term nominal interest rates are between 15 % and 20 % and nominal exchange rates are grossly undervalued relative to purchasing power parity (Gemeinschaftsgutachten, 1998).

Therefore, when reflecting on conversion rates for future members of the EMU (or any other monetary union), care must be taken to avoid recession or overheating effects, especially if interest and exchange rate impulses reinforce one another (instead of exhibiting trade-off effects). The right timing for joining a monetary union is crucial, if policy makers want to make sure that conditions are advantageous for all countries involved.

A P P E N D I C E S

A: Economic Model and Solution Algorithm

B: Simulation Results

A.1 Industrial Country Model in MULTIMOD

The most detailed description of MULTIMOD is given in two manuals: Masson, Symansky, and Meredith (1990), and IMF (1991). In this appendix, an overview of the *structure* of the model will be given. Formulae are only used for expositional reasons; implications and interpretations of the model are left to the main text. Likewise, it is not intended to discuss the theoretical background of the model, nor to provide necessary references – as done in the manuals. Moreover, the description is limited to the standard industrial country model because the discussion of a monetary union in Europe does practically not affect developing countries.

The industrial country model (containing 51 equations) is replicated for each of the G 7 countries USA, Japan, Germany, United Kingdom, France, Italy, and Canada, as well as for a so-called small industrial country aggregate (SI) capturing the rest of the OECD. The structure of the industrial country model is identical for each country, but some estimated coefficients vary. Five segments can be distinguished: (i) aggregate demand; (ii) government sector; (iii) money and interest rates; (iv) prices and aggregate supply; and (v) international linkages.

Aggregate demand (the IS curve) is given by

$$GDP \equiv C + I + g + XT - IT. \tag{A.1}$$

Real GDP (expressed in terms of national absorption as of 1980) is determined by real (private) consumption C, real gross investment I, exogenous real public consumption g, total real exports XT, and total real imports IT. Goods are imperfect substitutes internationally. Total imports comprise manufactured goods, commodities, and oil; they depend on various national activity variables and relative prices. Total exports only refer to manufactures (and an exogenous oil component). They depend on foreign absorption and real effective exchange rates.

Investment I and consumption C are derived from intertemporal profit and utility maximization, respectively. Capital accumulation (growth rate of capital) depends on the ratio of the real market value of capital to the (real) reproduction costs (Tobin's q, 1969). Real gross investment I is the change in the capital stock plus reinvestment (depreciations). The consumption function captures a long run fixed proportionality with real wealth, but allows for effects of real disposable income (real net domestic product minus real tax payments) in the short run (Blanchard, 1985). Total real wealth W is given by

$$W \equiv WH + WK + \frac{M}{PA} + \frac{B}{PA} + \frac{NFA * e}{PA}. \tag{A.2}$$

WH is human wealth, and WK is the real market value of domestic capital. Both are present values of capital or labor income, respectively, net of taxes (and minus depreciations in the case of WK). The other terms are stocks of money M, bonds B and net foreign assets NFA (multiplied by the exchange rate to the US-$ to convert to national currency) – all expressed in real terms by dividing with absorption deflator PA.

The government balance sheet is given by

$$B \equiv B_{-1} - (M - M_{-1}) + GE - TAX. \tag{A.3}$$

The change in nominal debt $B - B_{-1}$ (budget deficit) is determined by the change in the money stock $M - M_{-1}$ (seigniorage), the difference between government expenditure GE (nominal government consumption and interest payments on debt) and tax revenue TAX. The latter depends on each country's average tax rate t which is levied on the nominal net national product as well as on interest revenues. To ensure non-explosive debt levels, t is set according to a government reaction function (also called fiscal closure rule). If, for instance, the nominal levels of debt B or deficit $B - B_{-1}$ exceed (exogenous) target values, t is increased, thereby tax revenues TAX go up and the debt level is reduced according to equation A.3 (for a detailed discussion, cf. subsection 8.1).

Central bank behavior is also modeled in a reaction function (monetary closure rule): either they target the money stock or – as members of the ERM (apart from Germany) – the exchange rate to the DM. If, for instance, the money stock surpasses an (exogenous) monetary target, the nominal short term interest rate i is increased, thus causing private agents to reduce their money holdings. Since the money demand is modeled to be accommodated by the central bank at any time, this means that the money supply is brought closer to its target rate (for a detailed discussion of money demand (LM curve) and monetary policy, cf. subsections 3.4 and 3.3). The real short term interest rate r depends on the Fisher parity ($r = i - \pi^e$; π^e is the expected inflation rate). For long rates, the term structure of interest rates is assumed: long rates equal geometric averages of today's interest rate and future expected rates.

The supply side of the model is described by a (constant elasticity of substitution) equation for capacity output $YCAP$ comprising endogenous capital, exogenous labor, and labor-augmenting technical progress. Capacity output enters in a modified (expectations augmented) Phillips curve, which is the main price equation in the model (all other prices are derived from it):

$$\begin{aligned}\widehat{P} = \widehat{P_{-1}} + p_3 * \left(\widehat{P^e_{+1}} - \widehat{P_{-1}}\right) + p_2 * \left(\widehat{PA} - \widehat{P}\right) \\ + p_1 * \left(\frac{GDP}{YCAP} - 1\right).\end{aligned} \tag{A.4}$$

The change in aggregate prices P (GNP deflator) depends on three components: first, capacity utilization ($\frac{GDP}{YCAP}$) captures the Phillips curve relationship; second, $\widehat{PA} - \widehat{P}$ is the difference between absorption price and GNP deflator and accounts for higher import prices which produce higher consumption costs and lead to higher wages, thus pushing up inflation (imported inflation); third, lagged and lead inflation ($\widehat{P^e_{+1}} - \widehat{P_{-1}}$) capture inflation inertia and expected inflation effects caused, for instance, by staggered nominal contract models.

The last segment of the industrial country model comprises external balances and the exchange rate to the US-$. Exchange rates are based on the uncovered (open) interest parity (a detailed discussion is offered in subsection 3.2). International accounts in MULTIMOD can be summarized by

$$NFA \equiv NFA_{-1} + CA. \tag{A.5}$$

$NFA - NFA_{-1}$ is the capital account balance which equals the current account balance (includes trade, services and capital incomes, but no labor incomes or transfers). The balance of foreign-exchange payments could be included in the capital balance, but interventions in the foreign exchange market are not modeled.

All in all, the standard industrial country model is complex in many ways. First, it accounts for numerous international linkages through trade, capital flows, interest and exchange rates. Second, various variables depend on expectations: aggregate inflation, the exchange rate, interest rates, and human and capital wealth. These variables respond immediately to future policy or structural changes announced today. Third, the model comprises numerous non-linearities, in particular in import, export, and aggregate prices, as well as in capital accumulation and consumption functions.

A.2 Fair-Taylor Solution Algorithm

There are two classes of solution algorithms for a system of simultaneous equations. Newton-Raphson procedures are based on the calculation of partial derivatives (Jacobi matrix) which may be complicated, but the iteration process is fast and successful for appropriate start values. Gauss-Seidel procedures (or single-step-methods) are simpler and more reliable, but the iteration process takes longer. In the last twenty years these methods have been applied to nonlinear rational expectations models. Various methods are developed, compared, and/or combined in, for instance, Fair and Taylor (1983), Fisher and Hughes Hallett (1988), Juillard and Laxton (1996), and Hughes Hallett, Ma, and Yin (1996).

In this appendix, the Fair–Taylor procedure employed in this treatise (Fisher, 1990) will be illustrated for the simplest possible case. Analogous to equation 1 in subsection 2.2, suppose a system of equations which contains G=2 endogenous variables (y_1 and y_2), H=1 expectational variable (y_e is to capture expectations on y_1), and K exogenous variable (X) covering T=4 periods (t=0,1,2,3). Moreover, the model is assumed to contain one lag and one lead. The model is solved for periods 1 and 2; period 0 provides the data for the initial values of lagged endogenous variables (Y^{t-1}) in this toy model; period 3 accounts for terminal conditions (cf. question 4, section 4). The system can be described by three equations:

$$
\begin{aligned}
y_1^t &= f_1(y_2^t, y_e^t, Y^{t-1}, X^t, \gamma_1) + u_1, \qquad t = 1,2 && \text{(A.6)} \\
y_2^t &= f_2(y_1^t, y_e^t, Y^{t-1}, X^t, \gamma_2) + u_2, \qquad t = 1,2 && \text{(A.7)} \\
y_e^t &= y_1^{t+1}, \qquad t = 1,2 \qquad \text{(rational expectations)} && \text{(A.8)}
\end{aligned}
$$

The solution algorithm consists of intertwined solution loops for a Gauss–Seidel (inner loop) and for a Fair–Taylor component (outer loop). As to the Gauss-Seidel loop, a partial solution is obtained for each time period (1 and 2) based on equations A.6 and A.7 using an iterative procedure. Consider period 1 first. As to the first iteration, a provisional solution value for y_1^1 is obtained by solving the following equation for any given set of start values of all components of the right hand side:

$$\widetilde{y_1^1} = f_1(y_2^1, y_e^1, Y^0, X^1, \gamma_1) + u_1. \tag{A.9}$$

For the same start values except for $\widetilde{y_1^1}$, a provisional solution value for y_2^1 is obtained:

$$\widetilde{y_2^1} = f_2(\widetilde{y_1^1}, y_e^1, Y^0, X^1, \gamma_2) + u_2 \tag{A.10}$$

This concludes the first iteration. If $\widetilde{y_1^1} - y_1^1$ and $\widetilde{y_2^1} - y_2^1$ are sufficiently small according to some prespecified technical convergence criteria (cf. section 4, question 5), this loop is completed. If not, a second iteration starts (based on the same values except for $\widetilde{y_2^1}$ and $\widetilde{\widetilde{y_1^1}}$, respectively):

$$\widetilde{\widetilde{y_1^1}} = f_1(\widetilde{y_2^1}, y_e^1, Y^0, X^1, \gamma_1) + u_1 \tag{A.11}$$

$$\widetilde{\widetilde{y_2^1}} = f_2(\widetilde{\widetilde{y_1^1}}, y_e^1, Y^0, X^1, \gamma_2) + u_2 \tag{A.12}$$

This process continues until convergence is achieved for both variables in period 1. When the same procedure is also successfully completed for period 2, the first round of the inner solution loop (the Gauss–Seidel component) is finished.

The outer loop (Fair–Taylor component) is simple in this model, because there is only one expectational variable. For period 1, the value for the expectational variable is set to its actually realized value in period 2:

$$\widehat{y_e^1} = y_1^2 \tag{A.13}$$

For y_e^2, this is not necessary, because the corresponding actual value in period 3 does not change; it forms part of the terminal conditions. The first round of the outer solution loop is completed.

If $\widehat{y_e^1} - y_e^1$ satisfies prespecified technical convergence criteria (for the Fair–Taylor component), the algorithm stops, and it is said that an equilibrium solution has been achieved. If not, the second round of the inner loop starts and so forth, until the outer loop convergence criteria are fulfilled (on the basis of satisfied inner loop convergence).

B.1 The Baseline

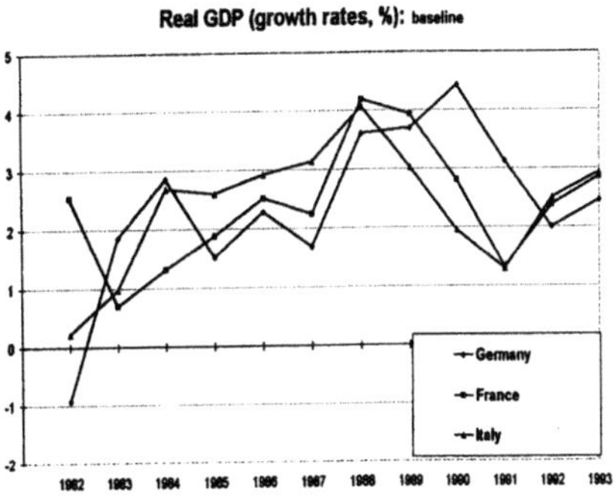

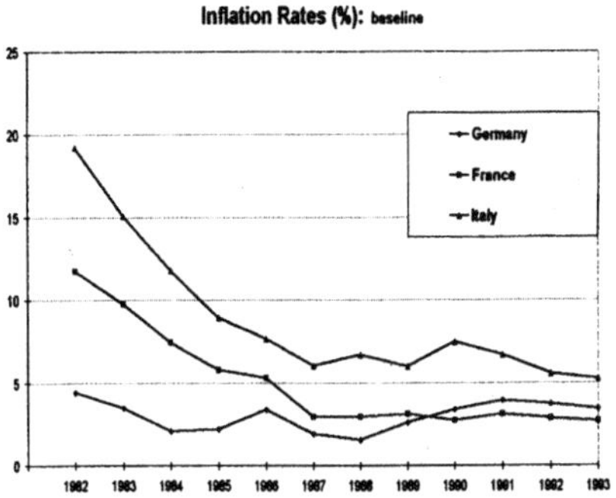

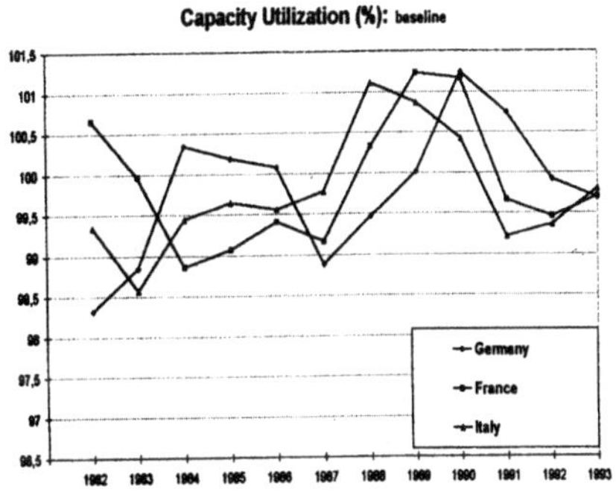

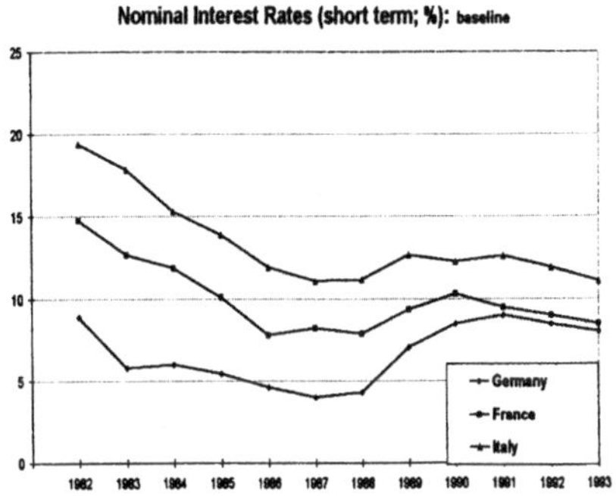

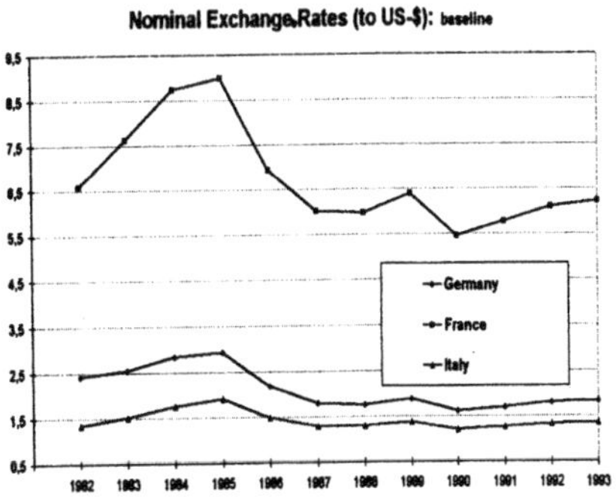

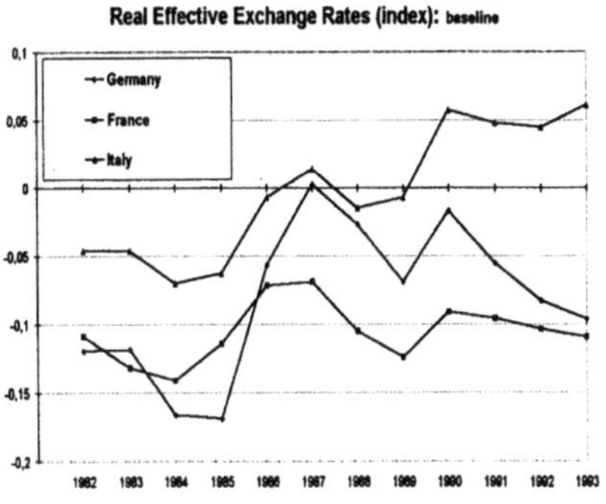

The Baseline – page 2

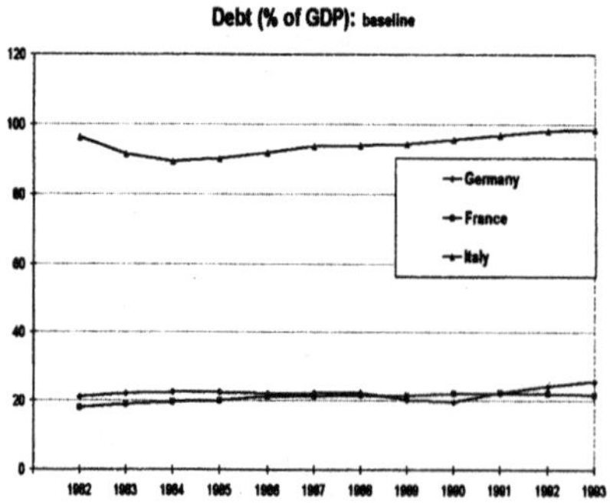

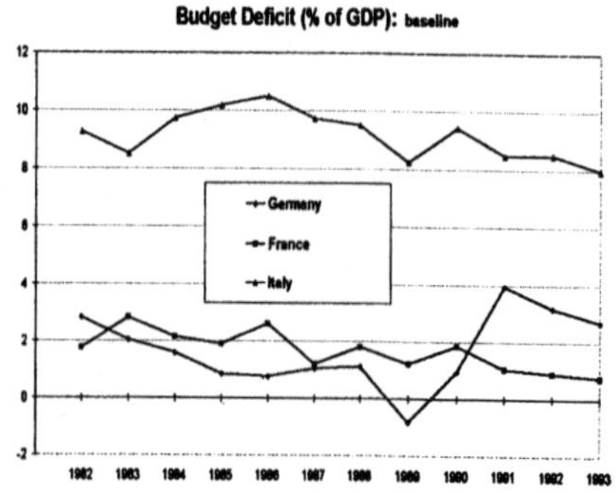

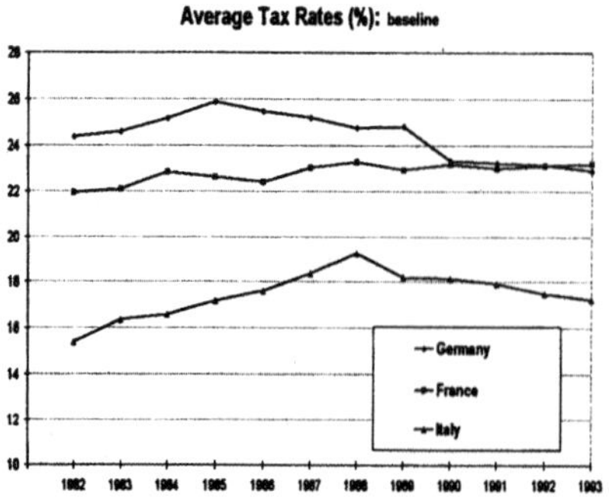

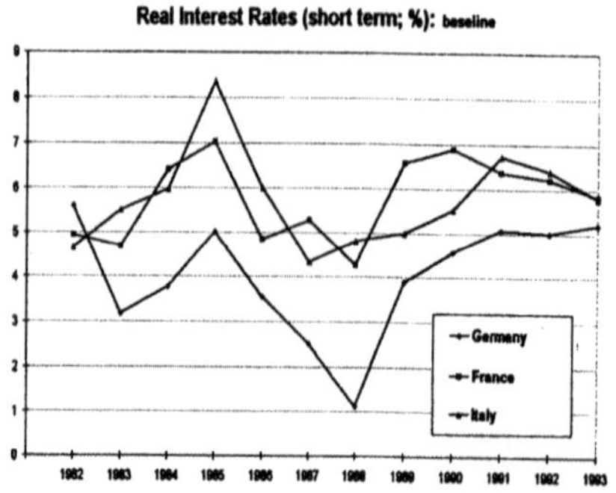

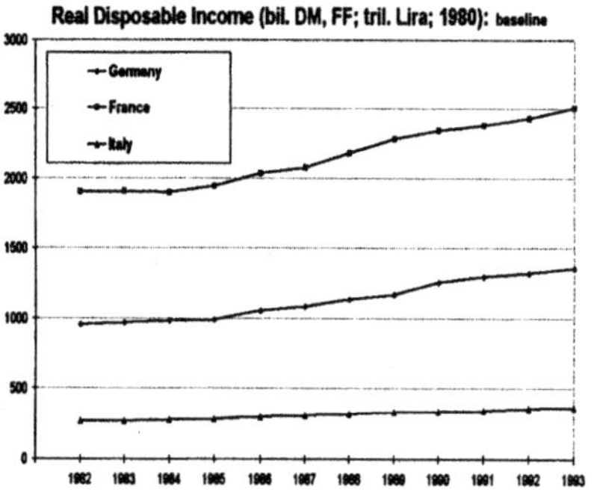

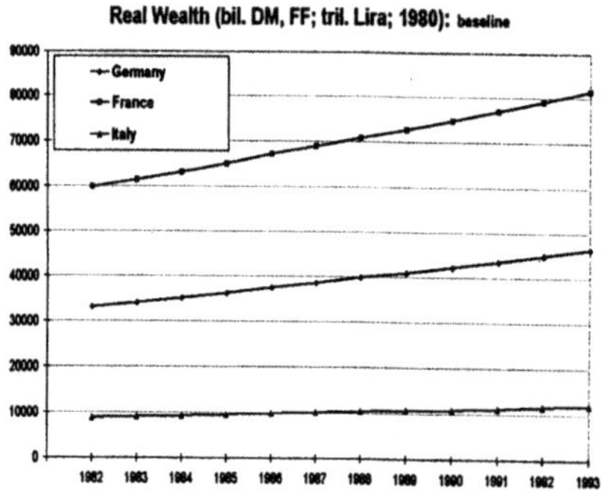

B.2 CUR

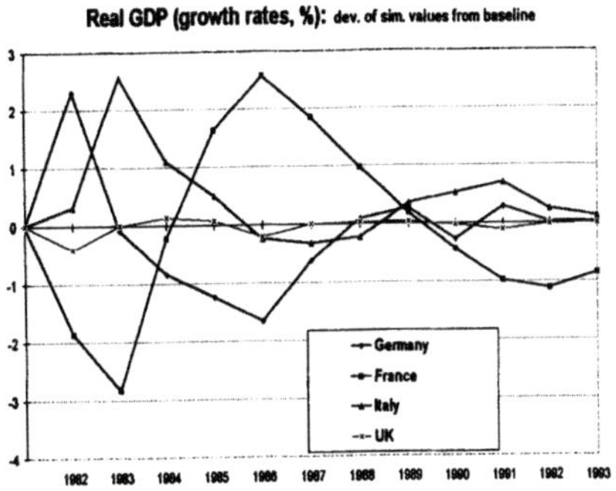
Real GDP (growth rates, %): dev. of sim. values from baseline
Germany
France
Italy
UK

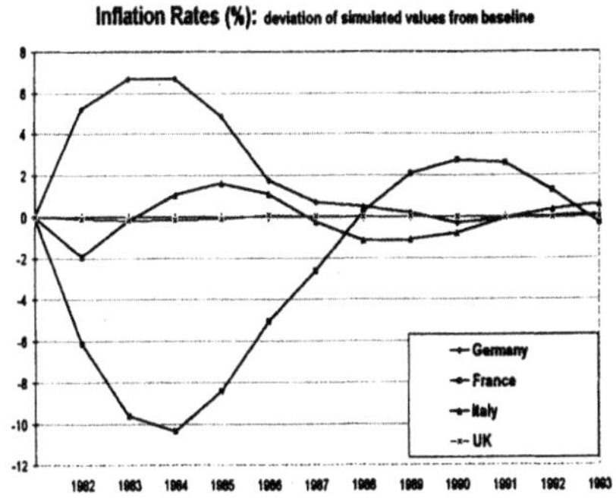
Inflation Rates (%): deviation of simulated values from baseline
Germany
France
Italy
UK

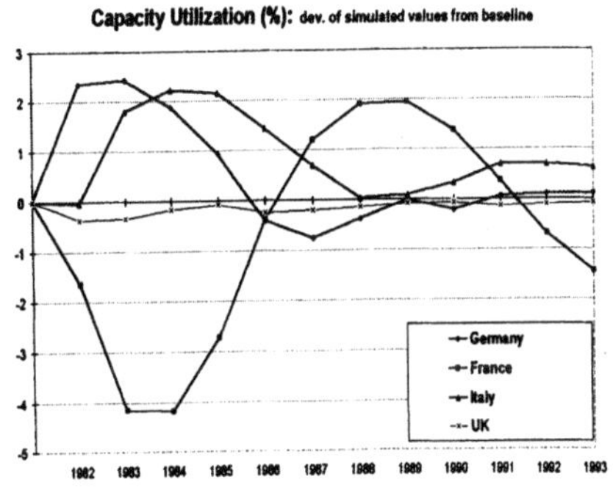
Capacity Utilization (%): dev. of simulated values from baseline
Germany
France
Italy
UK

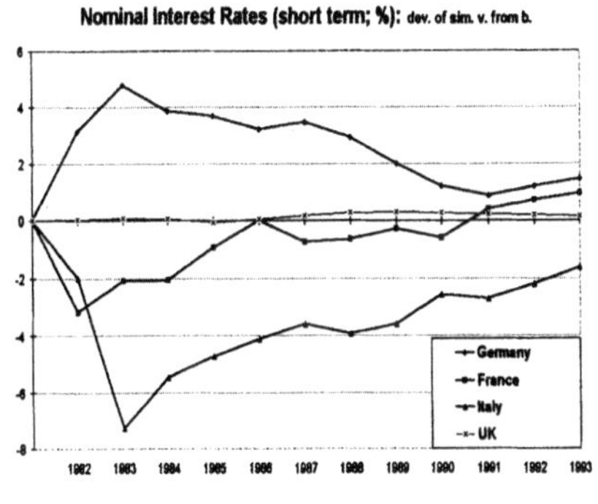
Nominal Interest Rates (short term; %): dev. of sim. v. from b.
Germany
France
Italy
UK

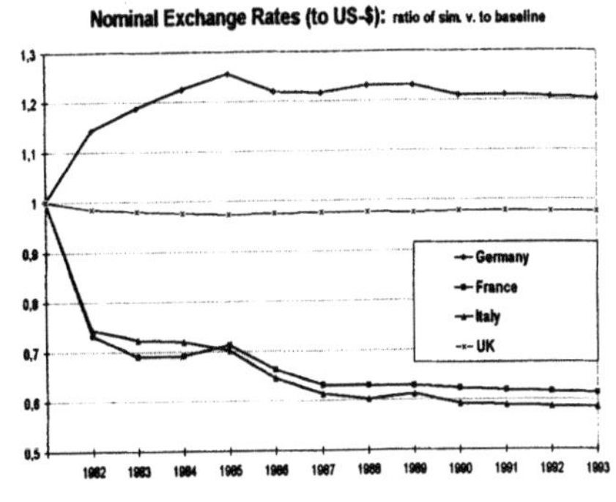
Nominal Exchange Rates (to US-$): ratio of sim. v. to baseline
Germany
France
Italy
UK

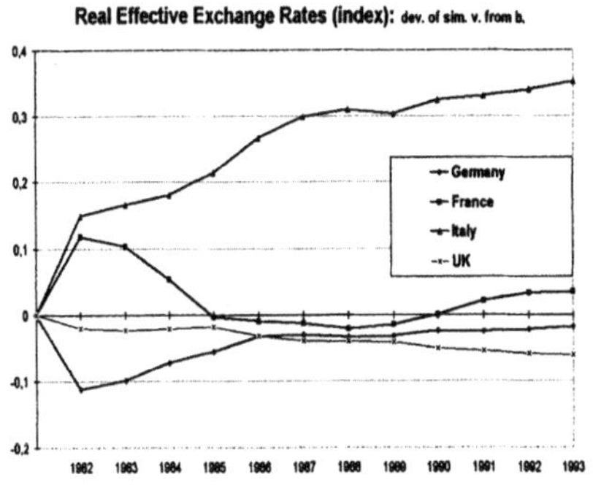
Real Effective Exchange Rates (index): dev. of sim. v. from b.
Germany
France
Italy
UK

CUR – page 2

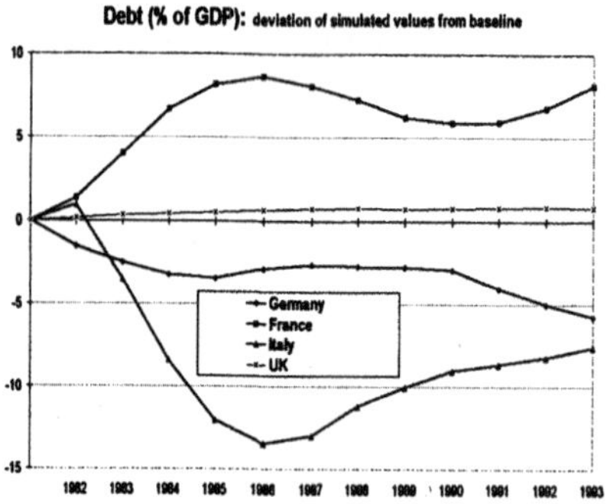
Debt (% of GDP): deviation of simulated values from baseline
Germany
France
Italy
UK

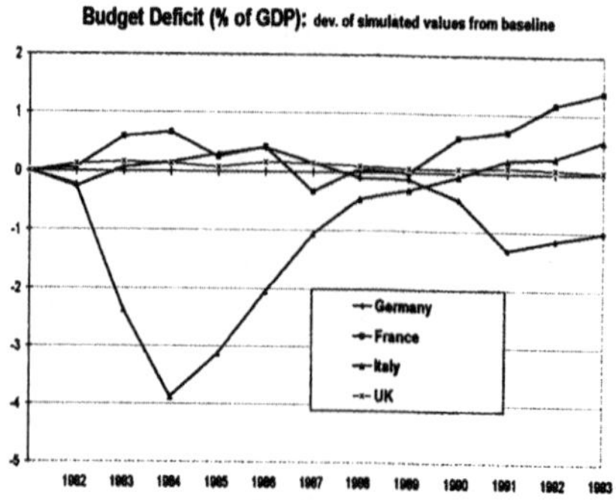
Budget Deficit (% of GDP): dev. of simulated values from baseline
Germany
France
Italy
UK

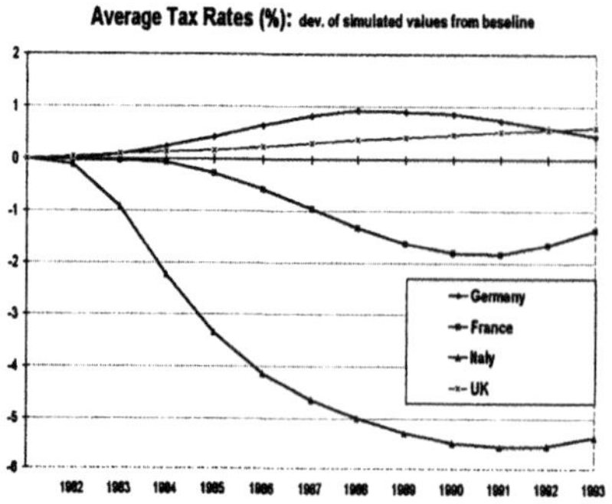
Average Tax Rates (%): dev. of simulated values from baseline
Germany
France
Italy
UK

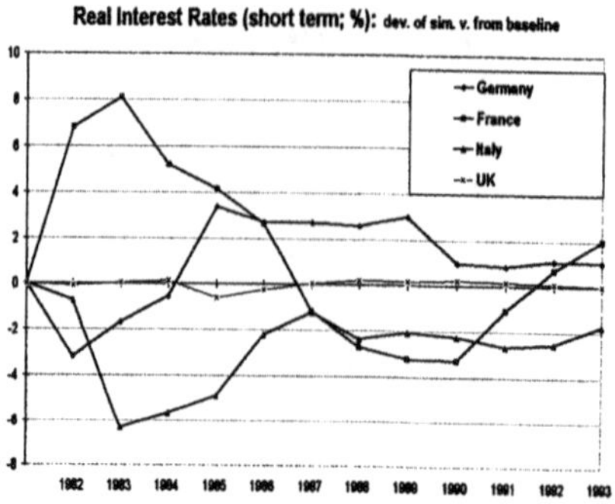
Real Interest Rates (short term; %): dev. of sim. v. from baseline
Germany
France
Italy
UK

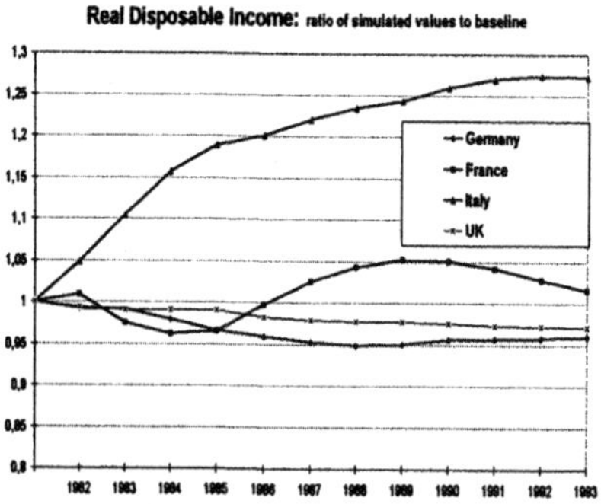
Real Disposable Income: ratio of simulated values to baseline
Germany
France
Italy
UK

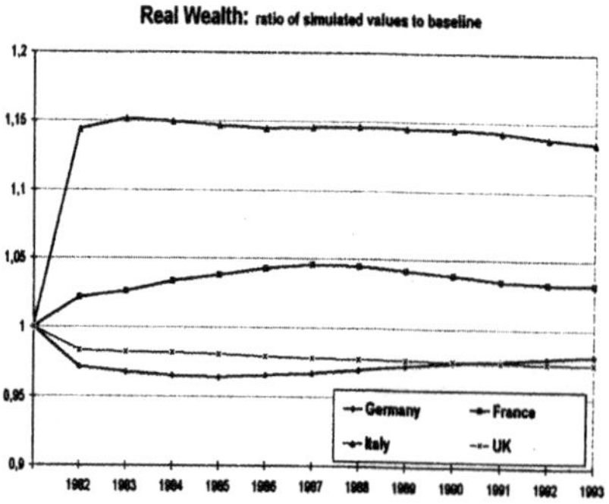
Real Wealth: ratio of simulated values to baseline
Germany
France
Italy
UK

B.3 CP

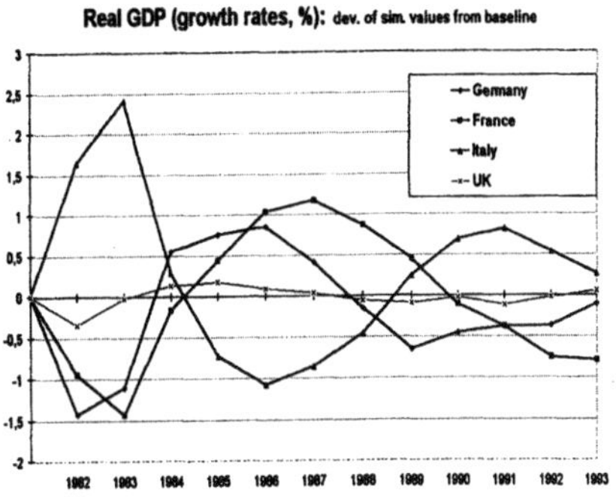
Real GDP (growth rates, %): dev. of sim. values from baseline
Germany
France
Italy
UK

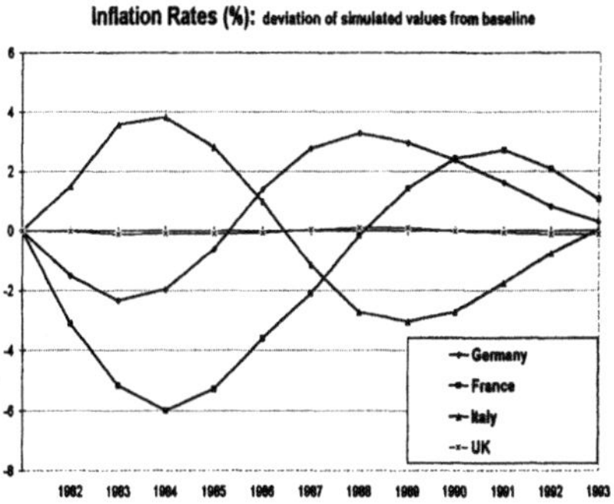
Inflation Rates (%): deviation of simulated values from baseline
Germany
France
Italy
UK

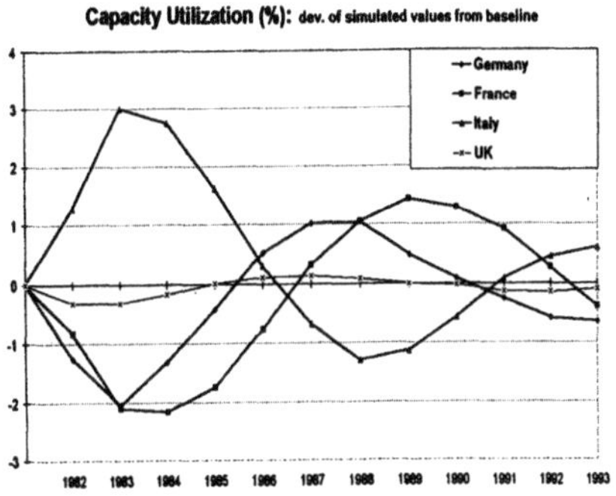
Capacity Utilization (%): dev. of simulated values from baseline
Germany
France
Italy
UK

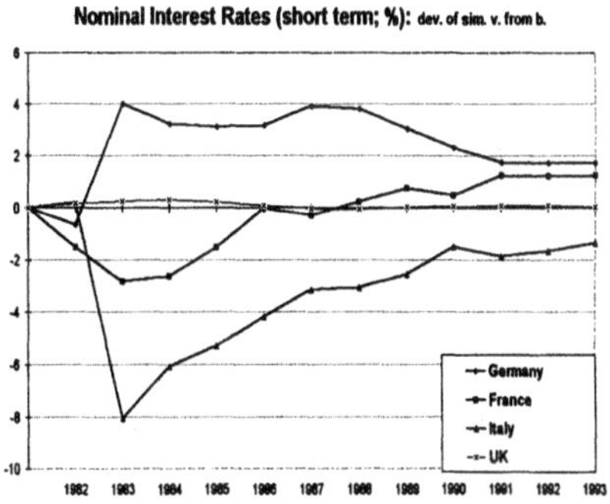
Nominal Interest Rates (short term; %): dev. of sim. v. from b.
Germany
France
Italy
UK

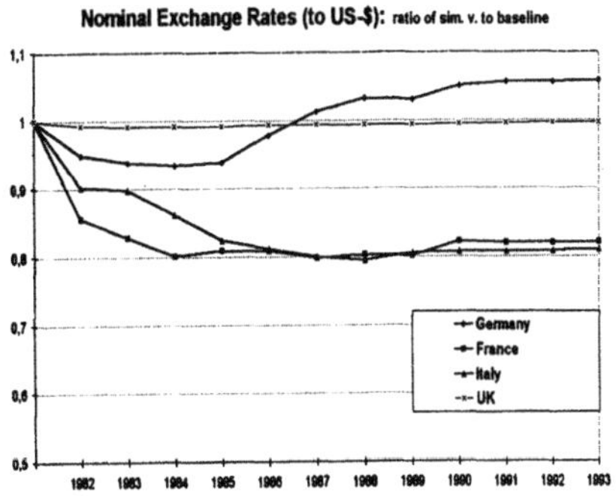
Nominal Exchange Rates (to US-$): ratio of sim. v. to baseline
Germany
France
Italy
UK

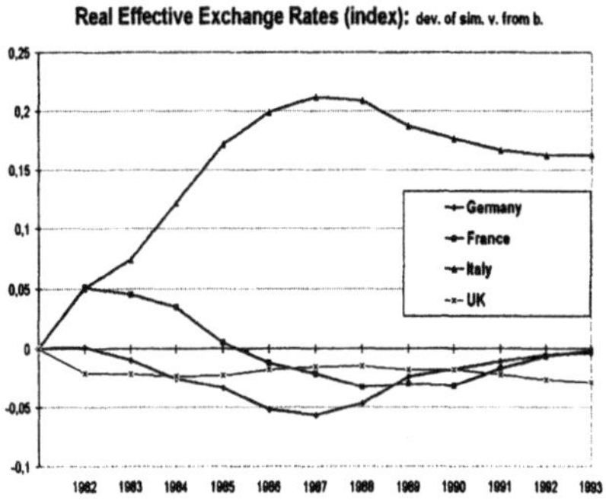
Real Effective Exchange Rates (index): dev. of sim. v. from b.
Germany
France
Italy
UK

CP – page 2

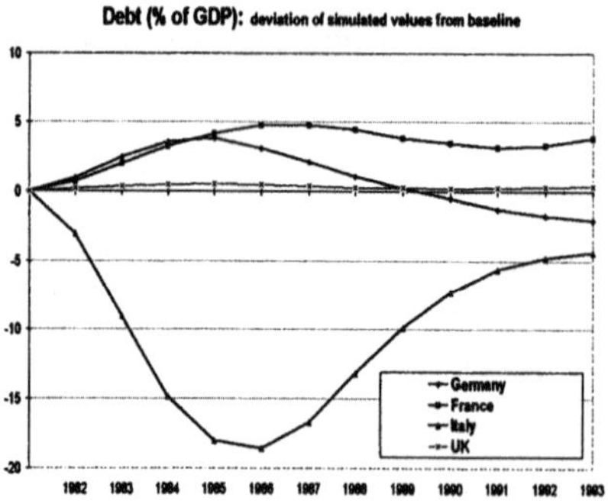
Debt (% of GDP): deviation of simulated values from baseline
10
5
0
-5
-10
-15
-20
1982 1983 1984 1985 1986 1987 1988 1989 1990 1991 1992 1993
Germany
France
Italy
UK

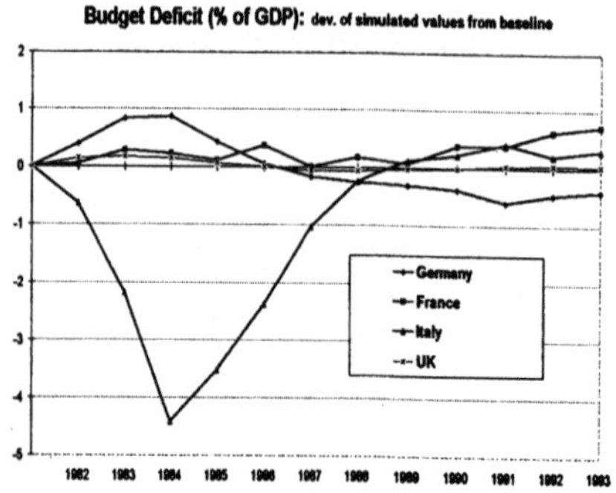
Budget Deficit (% of GDP): dev. of simulated values from baseline
2
1
0
-1
-2
-3
-4
-5
1982 1983 1984 1985 1986 1987 1988 1989 1990 1991 1992 1993
Germany
France
Italy
UK

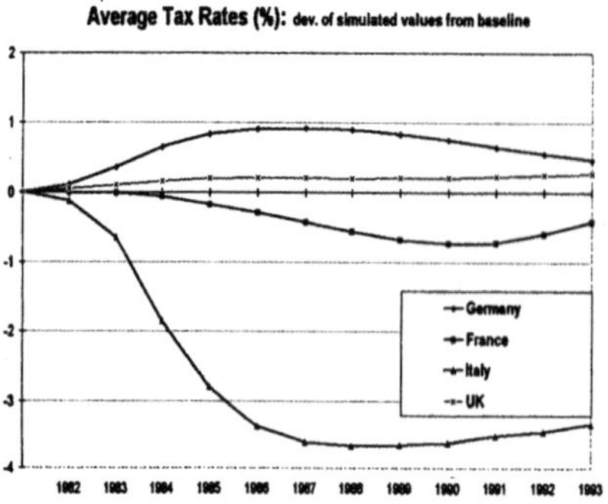
Average Tax Rates (%): dev. of simulated values from baseline
2
1
0
-1
-2
-3
-4
1982 1983 1984 1985 1986 1987 1988 1989 1990 1991 1992 1993
Germany
France
Italy
UK

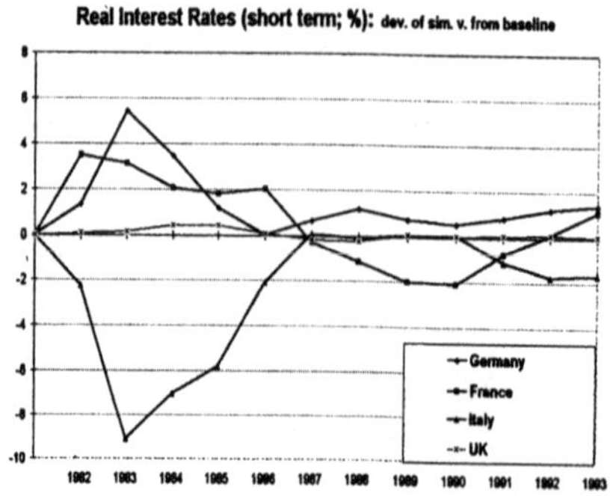
Real Interest Rates (short term; %): dev. of sim. v. from baseline
8
6
4
2
0
-2
-4
-6
-8
-10
1982 1983 1984 1985 1986 1987 1988 1989 1990 1991 1992 1993
Germany
France
Italy
UK

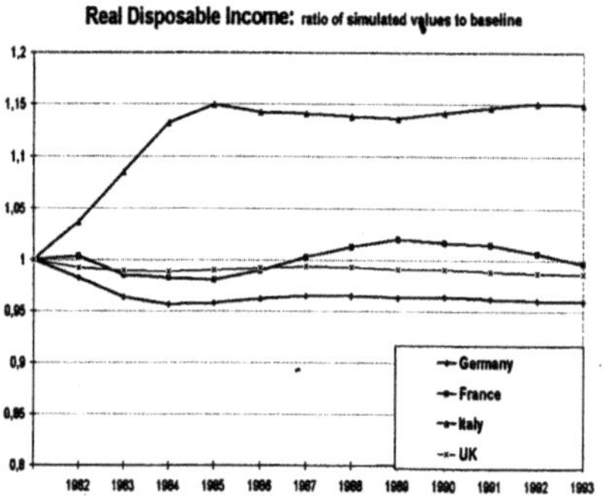
Real Disposable Income: ratio of simulated values to baseline
1,2
1,15
1,1
1,05
1
0,95
0,9
0,85
0,8
1982 1983 1984 1985 1986 1987 1988 1989 1990 1991 1992 1993
Germany
France
Italy
UK

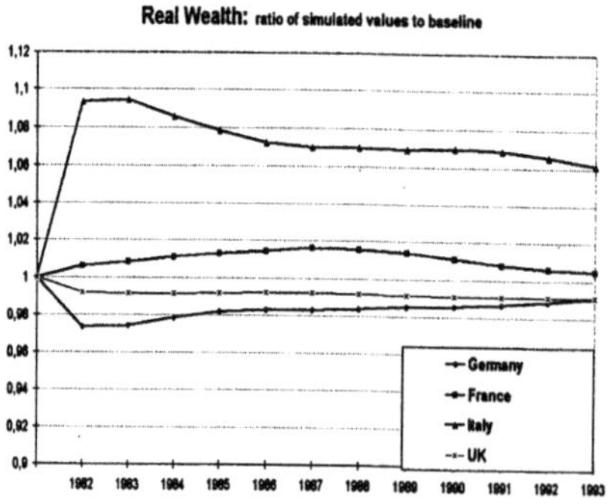
Real Wealth: ratio of simulated values to baseline
1,12
1,1
1,08
1,06
1,04
1,02
1
0,98
0,96
0,94
0,92
0,9
1982 1983 1984 1985 1986 1987 1988 1989 1990 1991 1992 1993
Germany
France
Italy
UK

B.4 PPP

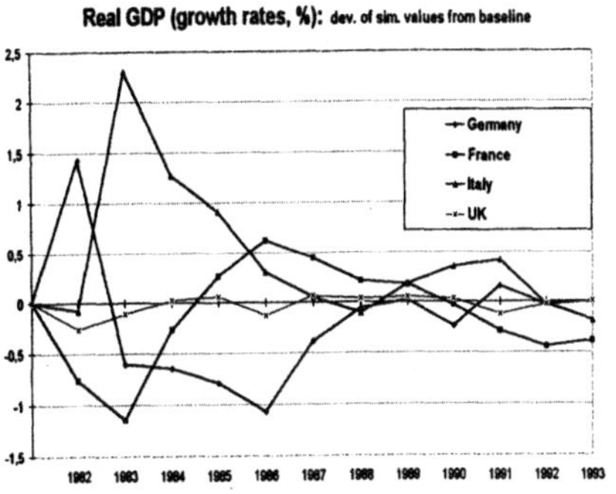
Real GDP (growth rates, %): dev. of sim. values from baseline
Germany
France
Italy
UK
1982 1983 1984 1985 1986 1987 1988 1989 1990 1991 1992 1993

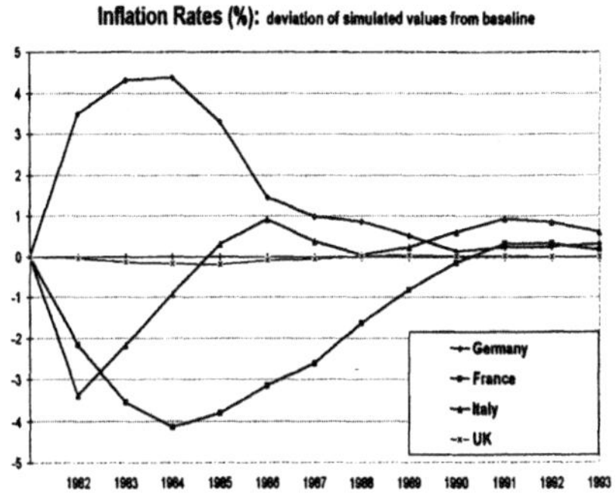
Inflation Rates (%): deviation of simulated values from baseline
Germany
France
Italy
UK
1982 1983 1984 1985 1986 1987 1988 1989 1990 1991 1992 1993

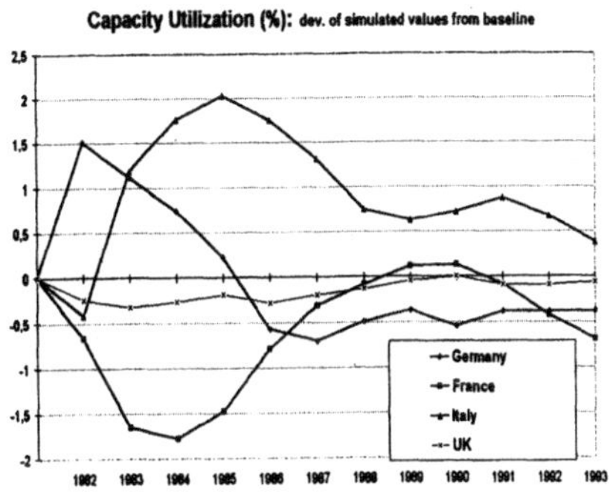
Capacity Utilization (%): dev. of simulated values from baseline
Germany
France
Italy
UK
1982 1983 1984 1985 1986 1987 1988 1989 1990 1991 1992 1993

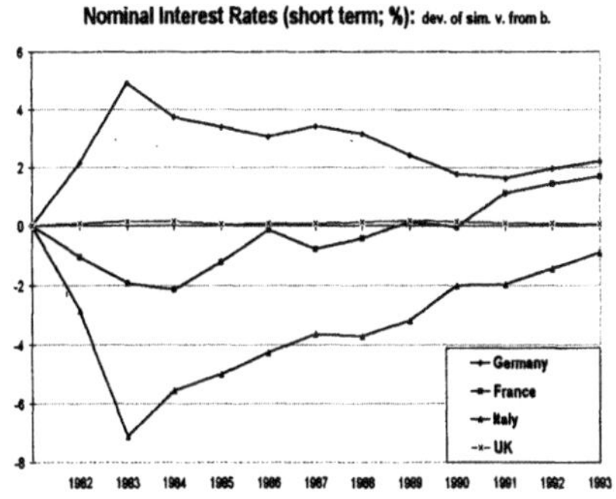
Nominal Interest Rates (short term; %): dev. of sim. v. from b.
Germany
France
Italy
UK
1982 1983 1984 1985 1986 1987 1988 1989 1990 1991 1992 1993

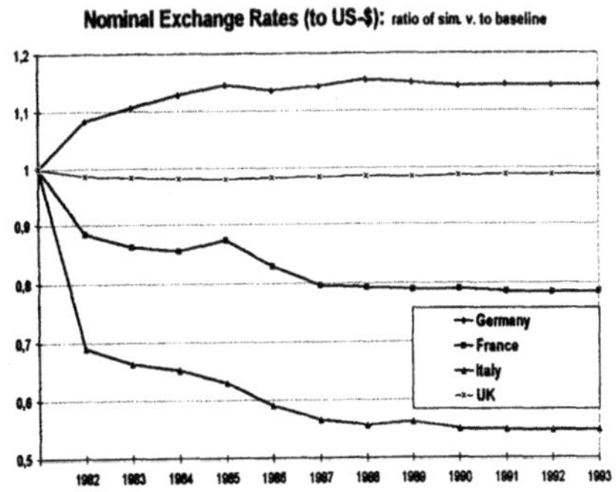
Nominal Exchange Rates (to US-$): ratio of sim. v. to baseline
Germany
France
Italy
UK
1982 1983 1984 1985 1986 1987 1988 1989 1990 1991 1992 1993

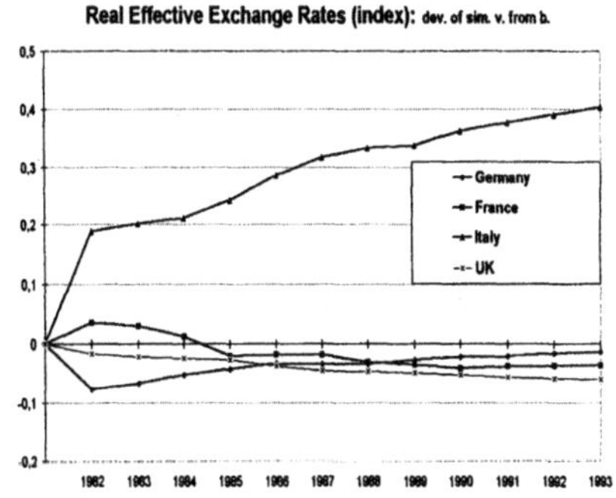
Real Effective Exchange Rates (index): dev. of sim. v. from b.
Germany
France
Italy
UK
1982 1983 1984 1985 1986 1987 1988 1989 1990 1991 1992 1993

PPP – page 2

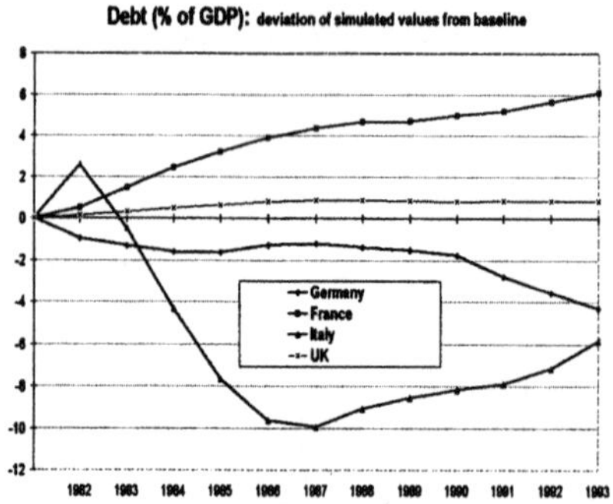
Debt (% of GDP): deviation of simulated values from baseline
Germany
France
Italy
UK

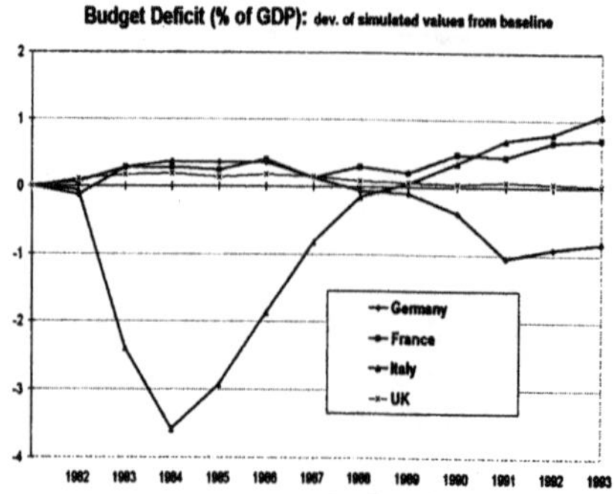
Budget Deficit (% of GDP): dev. of simulated values from baseline
Germany
France
Italy
UK

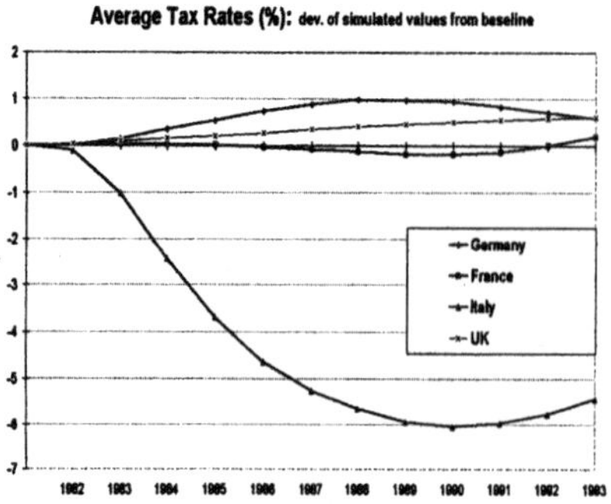
Average Tax Rates (%): dev. of simulated values from baseline
Germany
France
Italy
UK

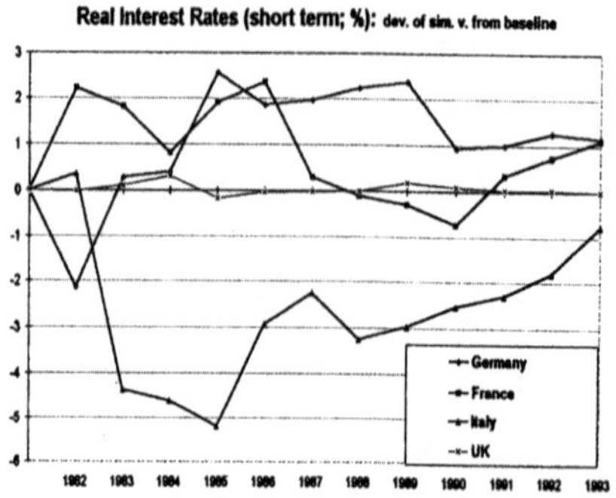
Real Interest Rates (short term; %): dev. of sim. v. from baseline
Germany
France
Italy
UK

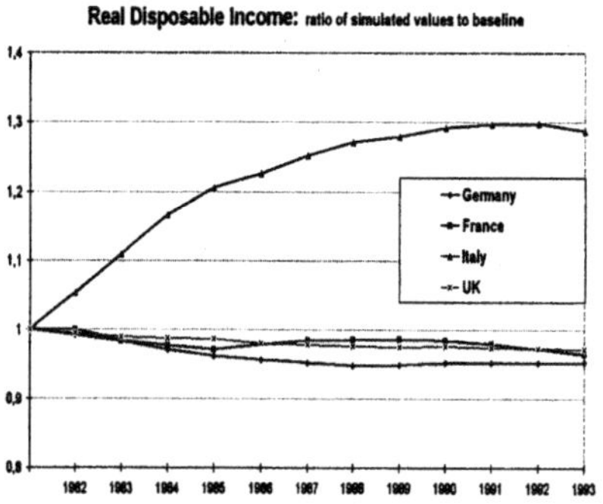
Real Disposable Income: ratio of simulated values to baseline
Germany
France
Italy
UK

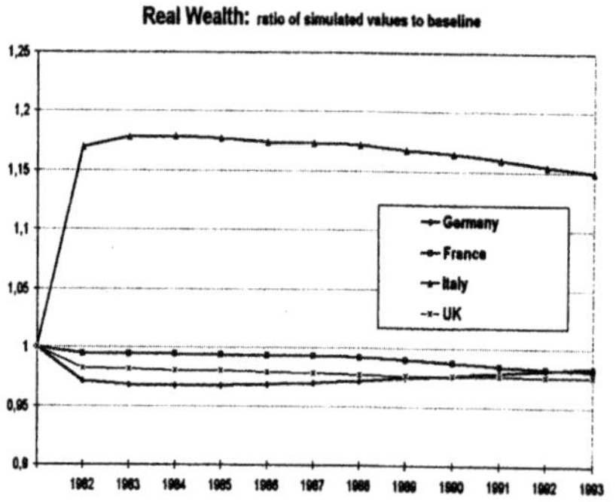
Real Wealth: ratio of simulated values to baseline
Germany
France
Italy
UK

B.5 Lax Fiscal-Baseline

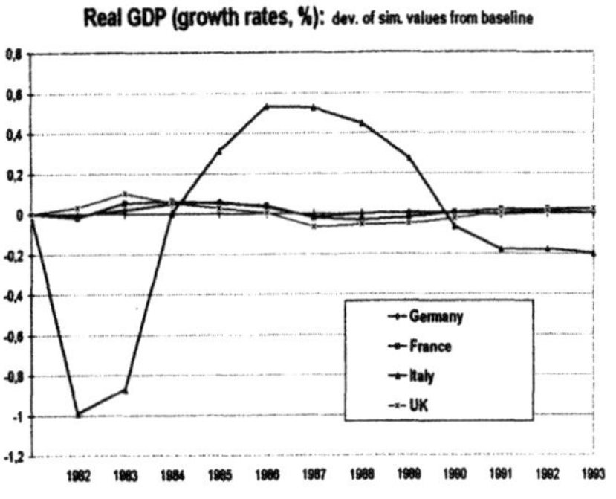

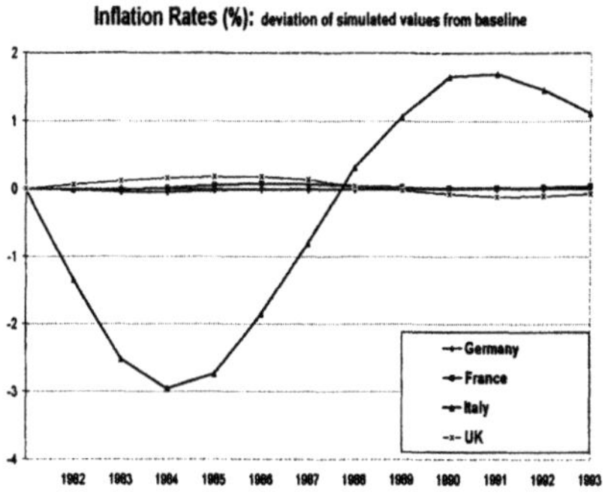

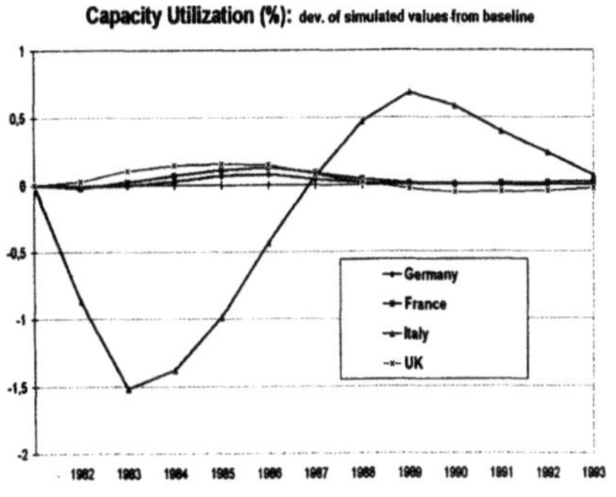

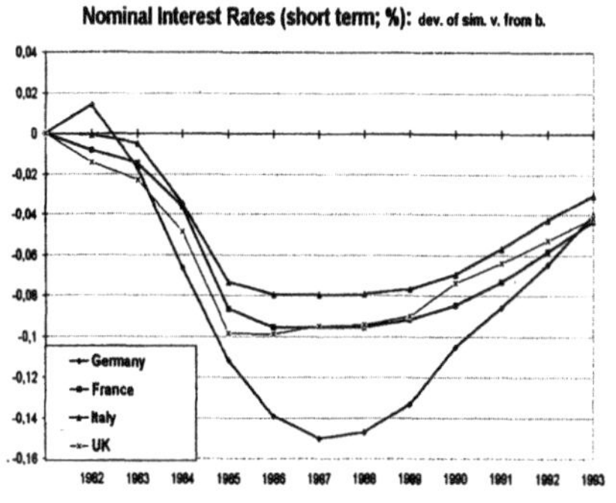

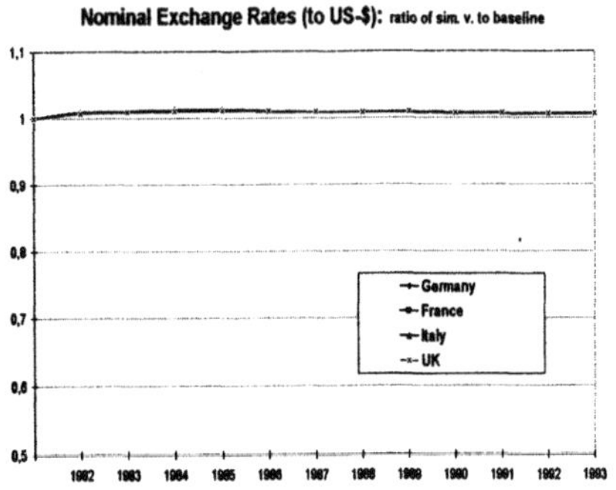

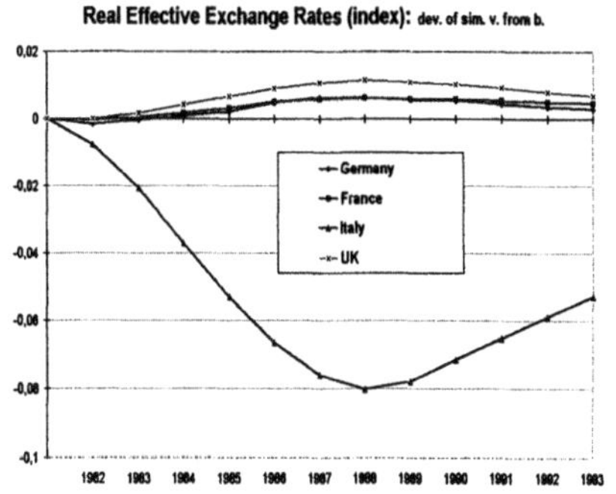

Lax Fiscal-Baseline – page 2

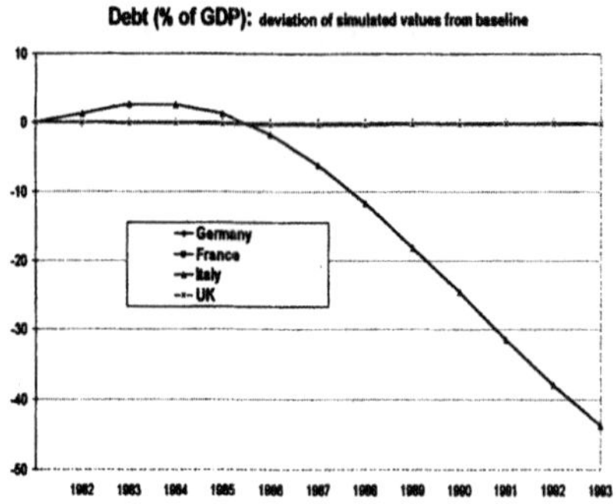

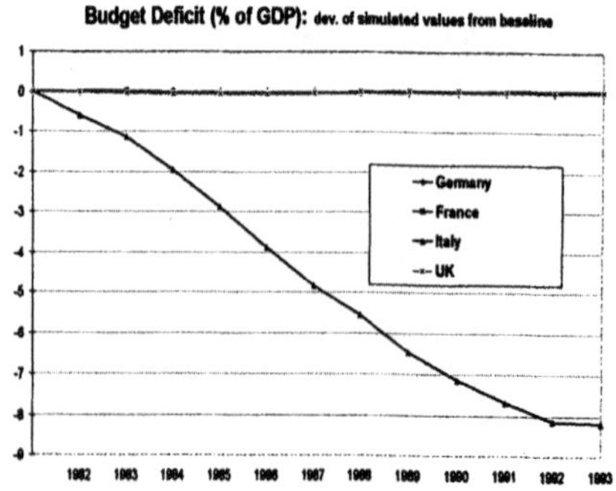

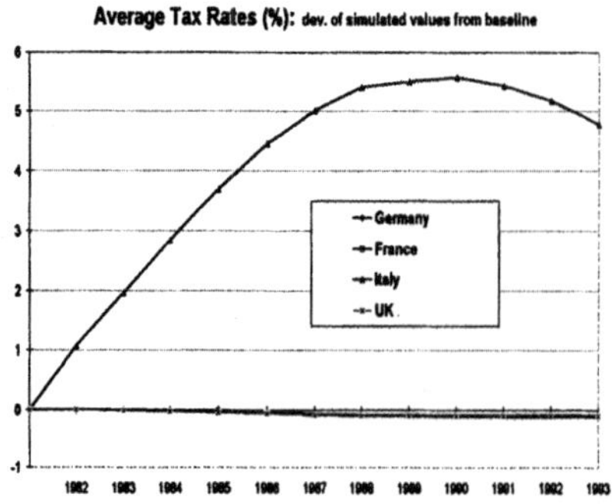

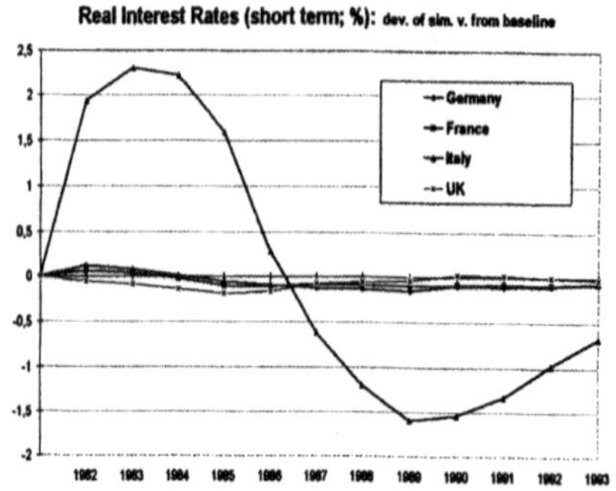

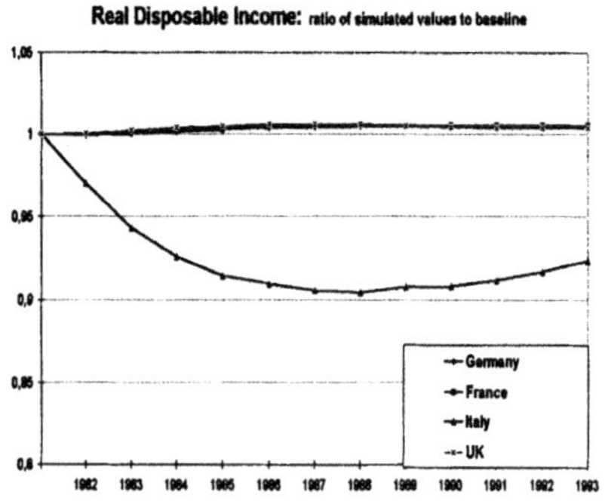

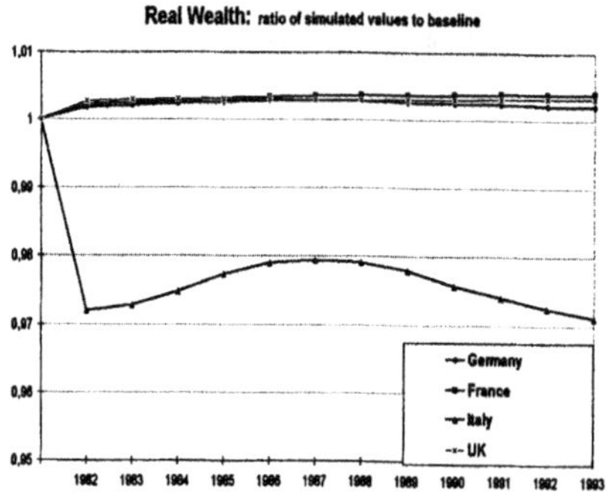

B.6 Strict Fiscal-Baseline

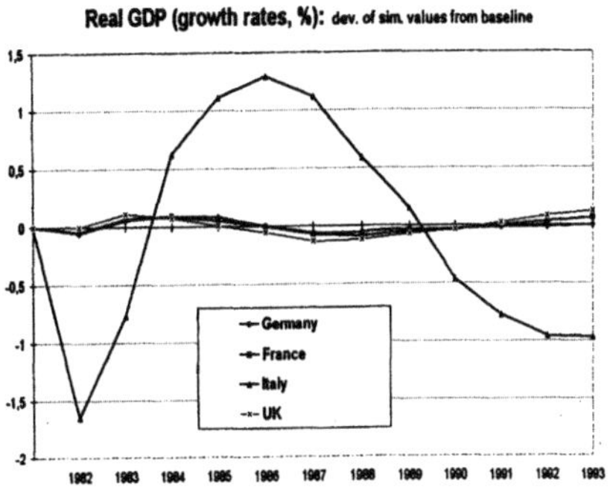

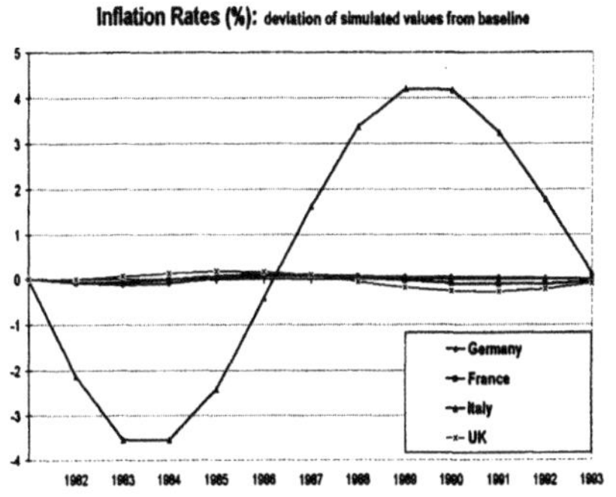

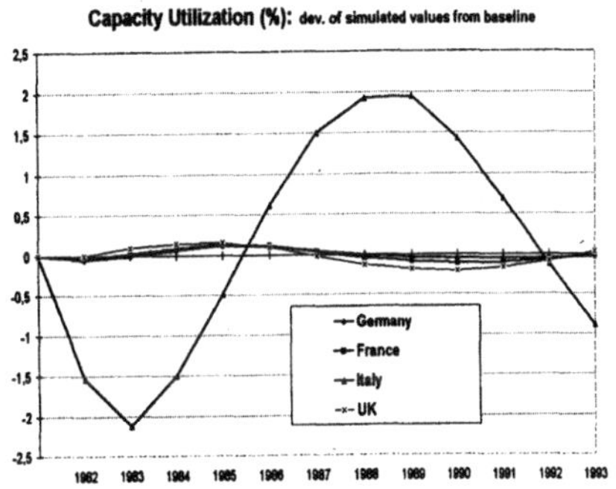

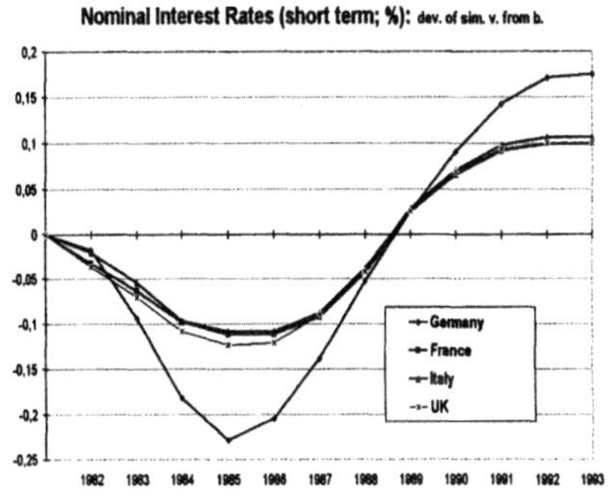

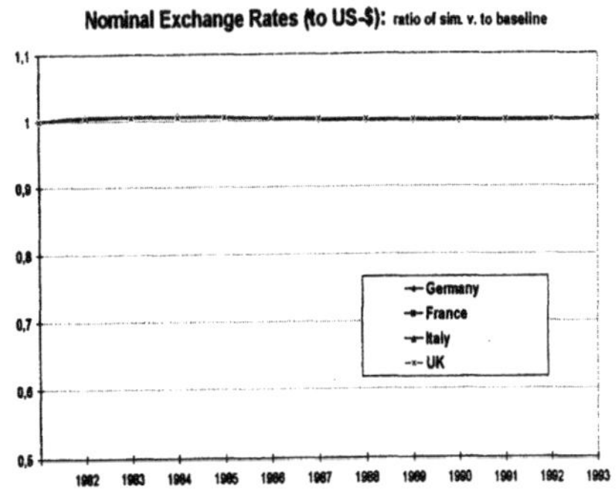

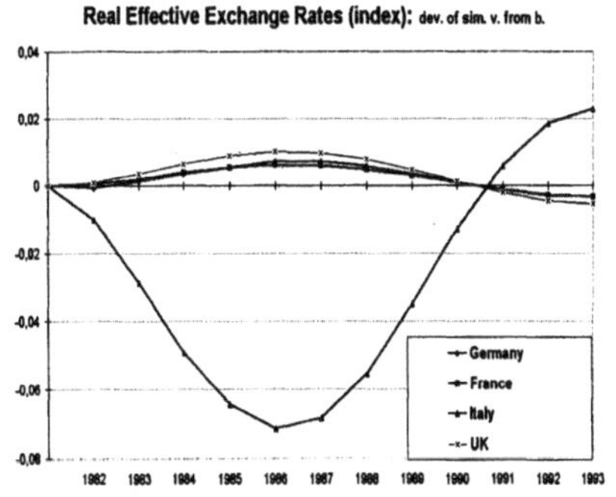

Strict Fiscal-Baseline – page 2

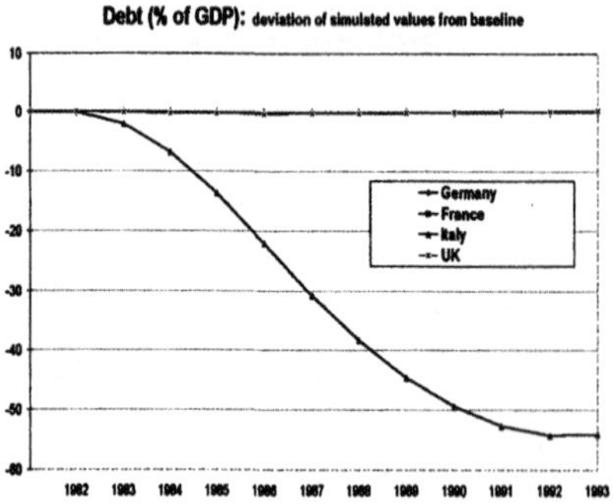

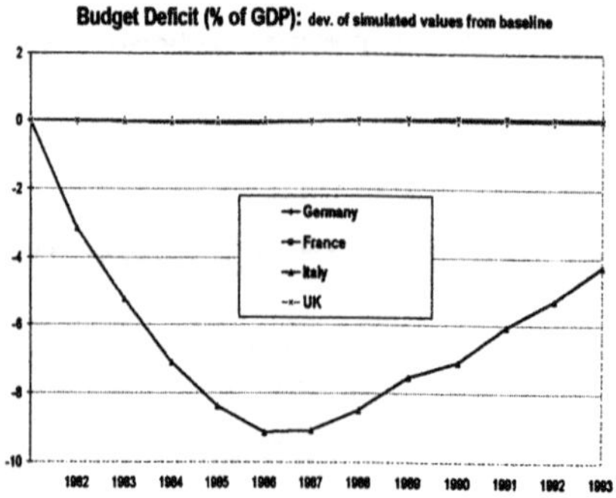

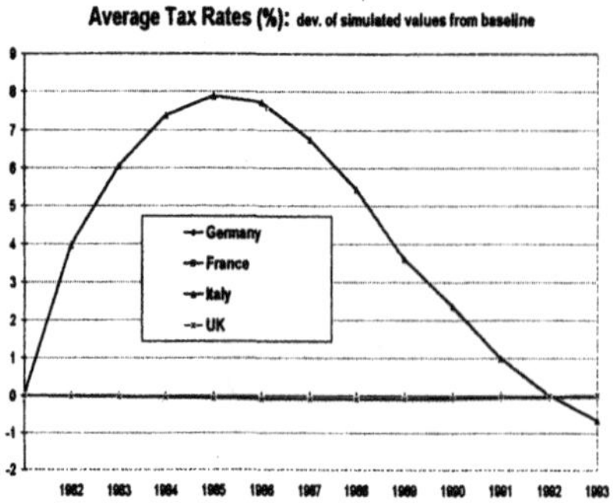

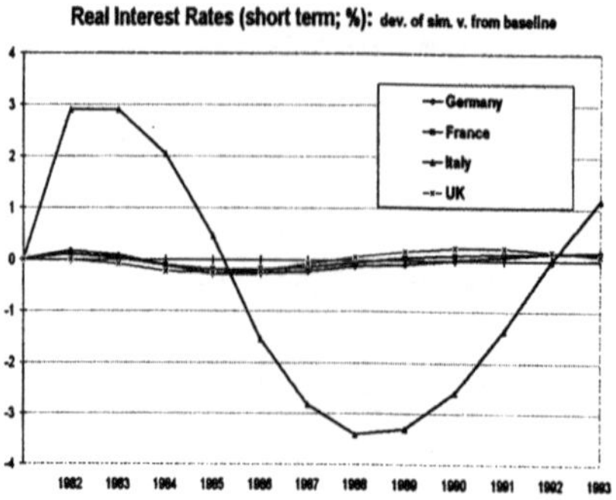

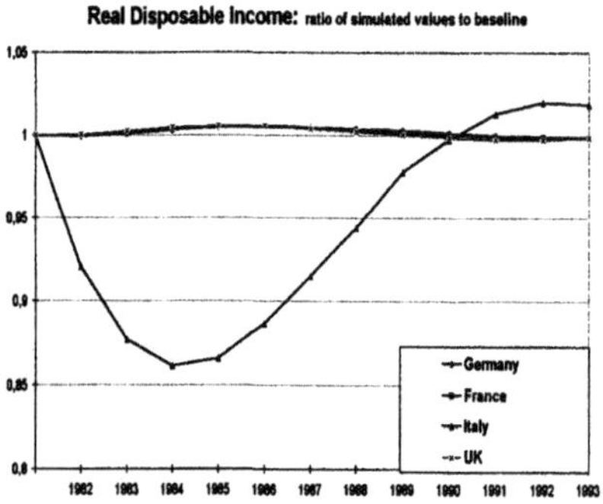

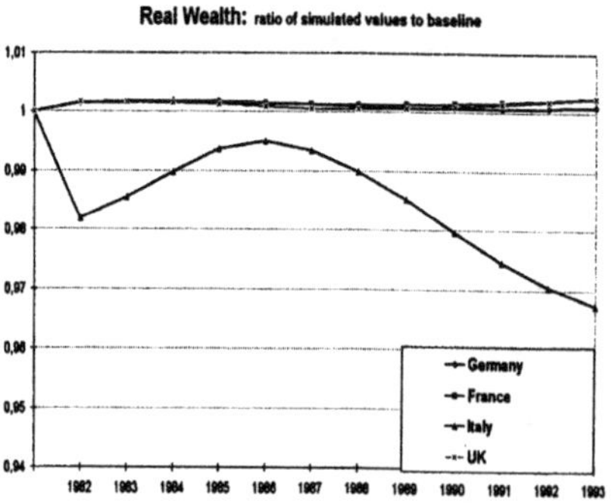

B.7 Lax Fiscal-CP

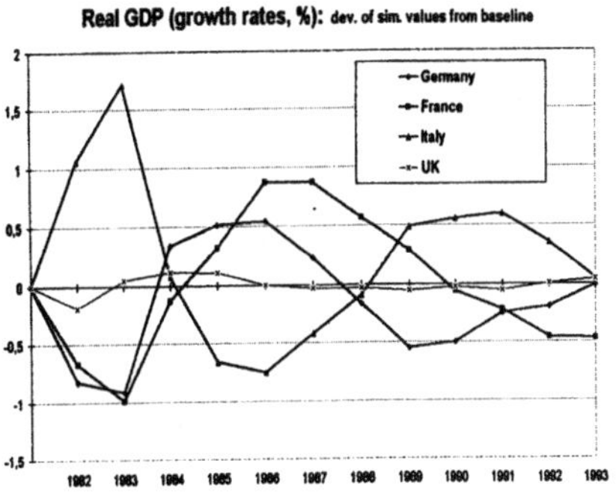

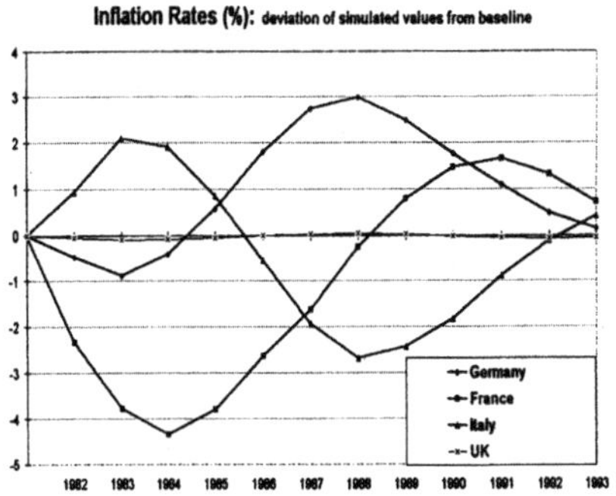

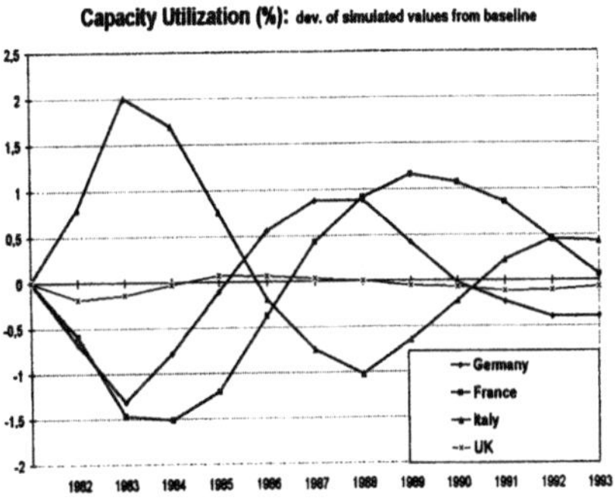

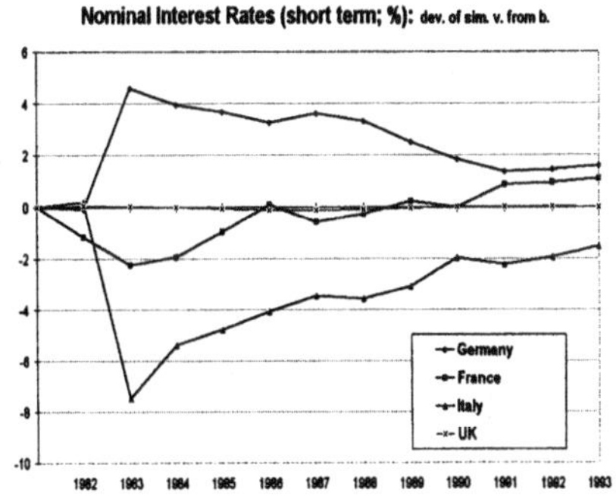

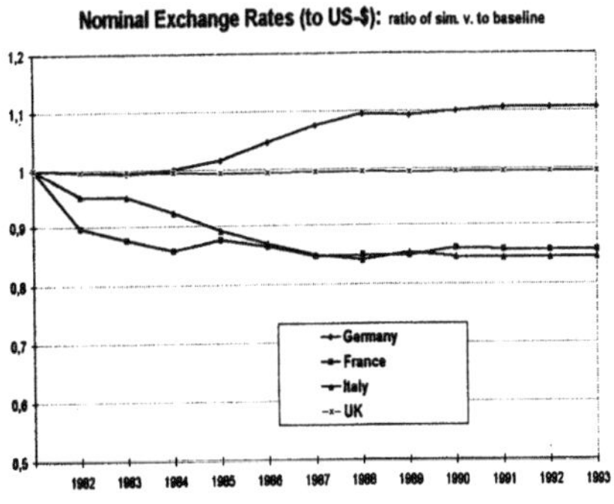

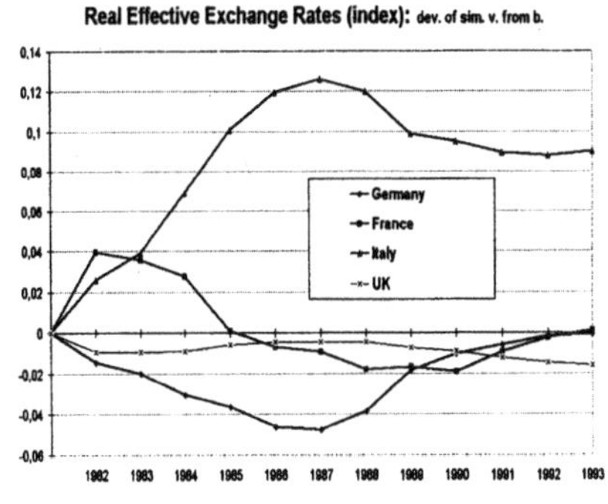

Lax Fiscal-CP – page 2

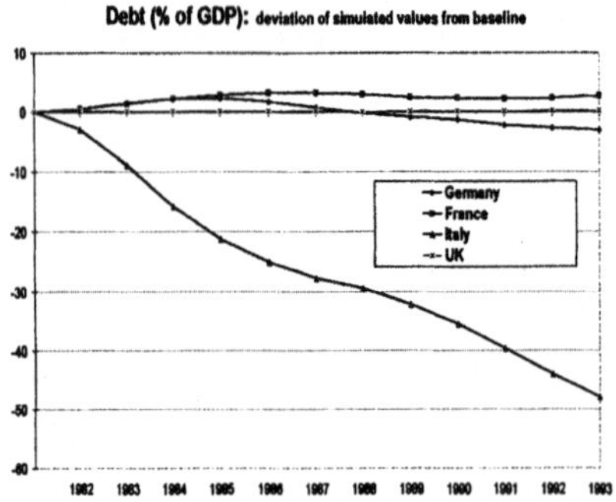

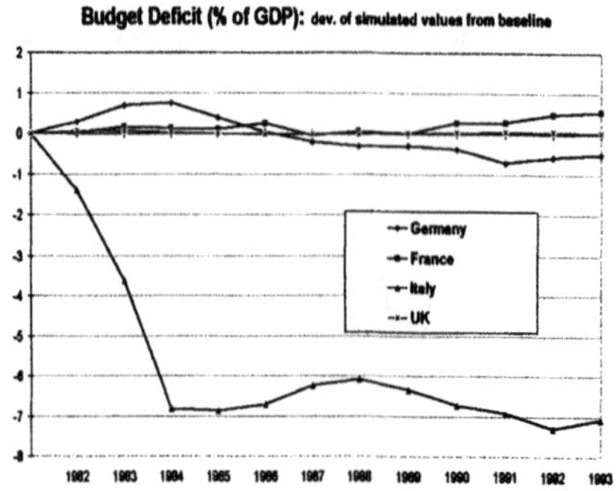

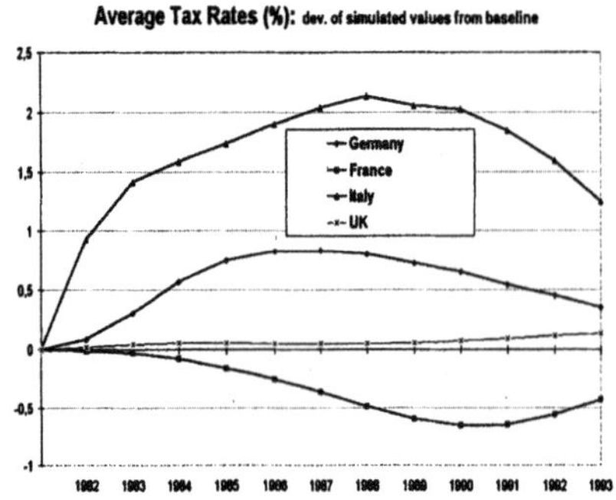

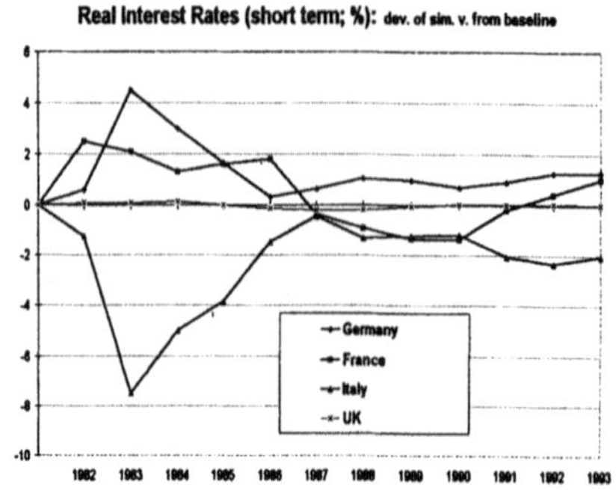

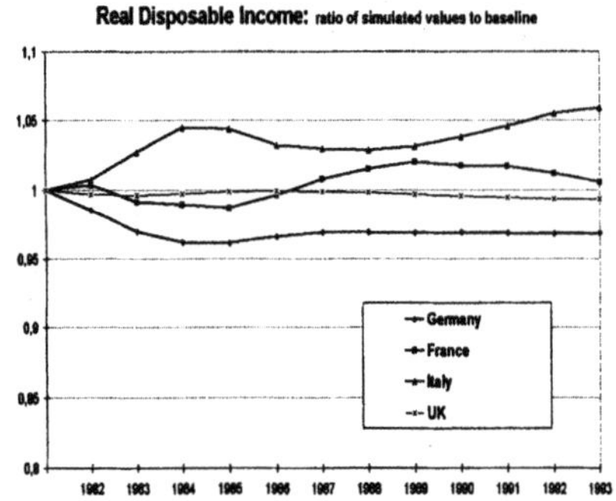

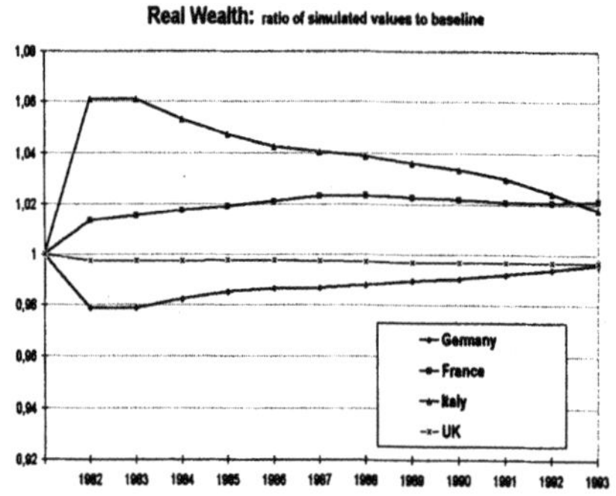

B.8 Strict Fiscal-CP

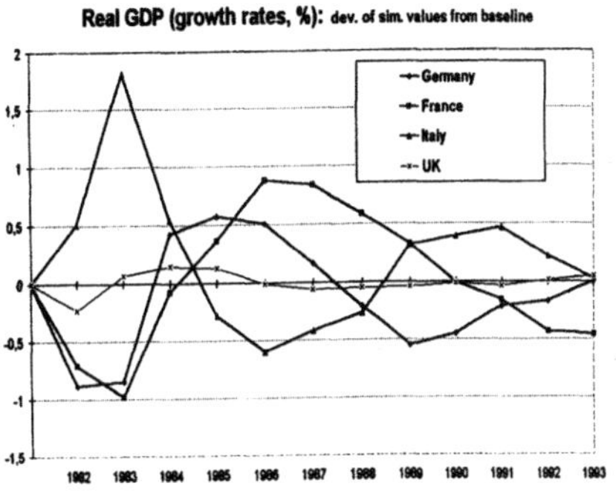

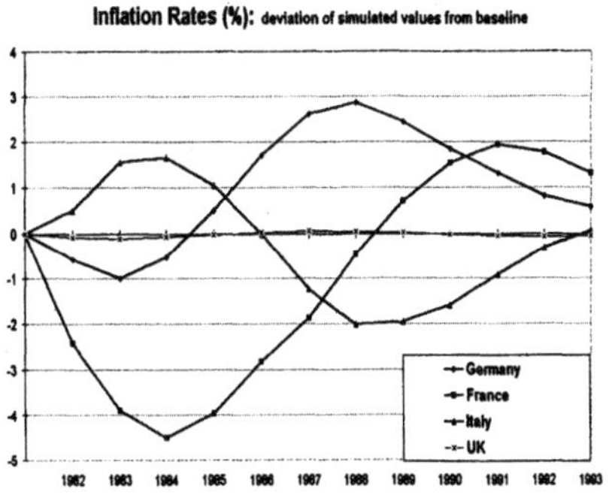

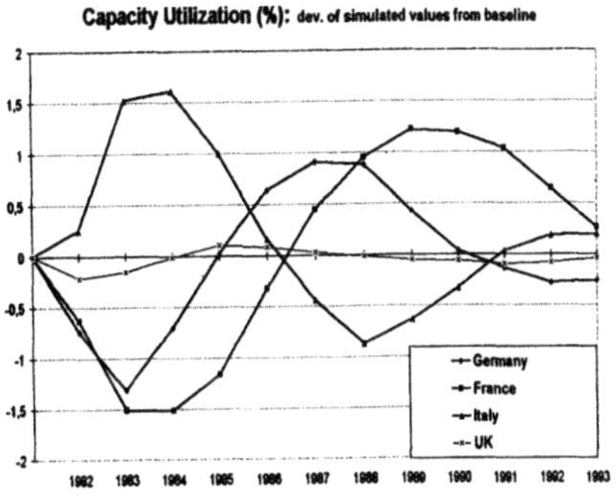

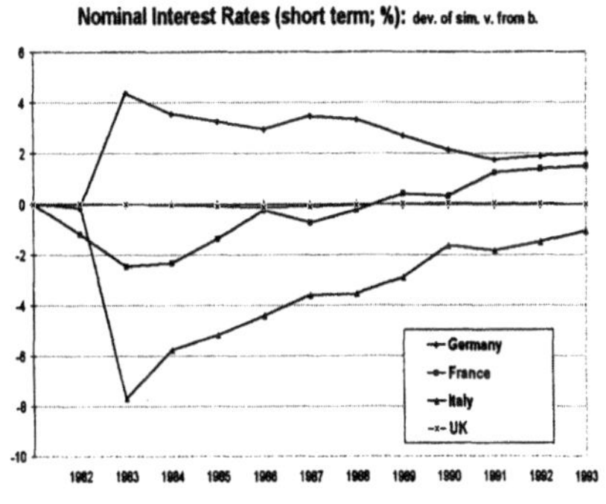

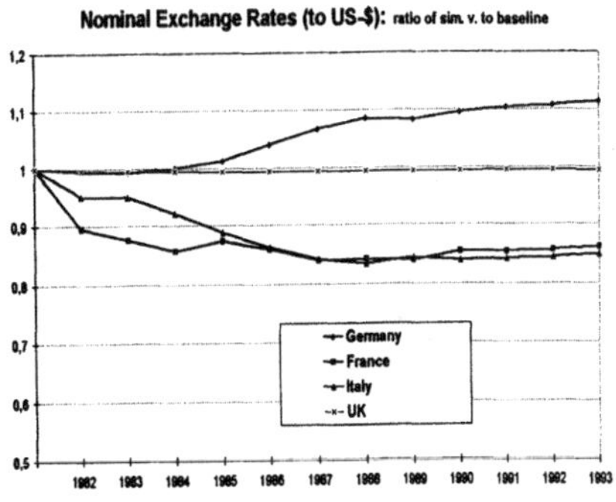

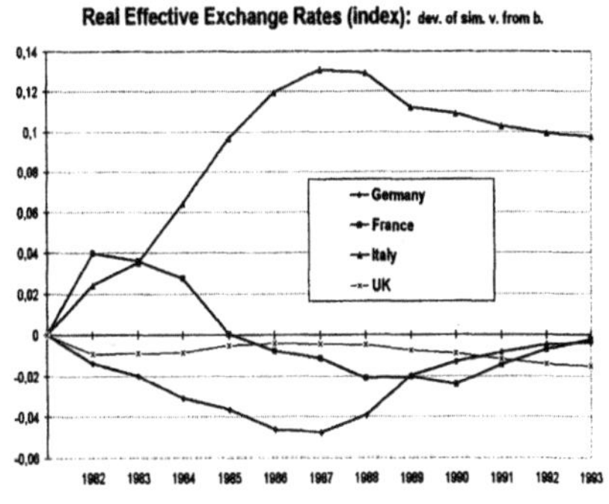

Strict Fiscal-CP – page 2

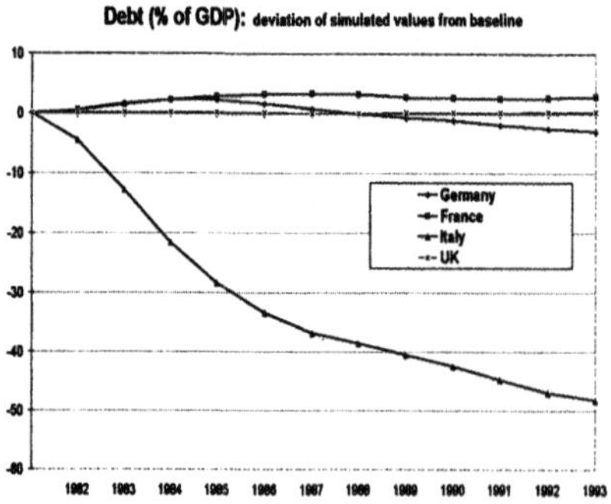

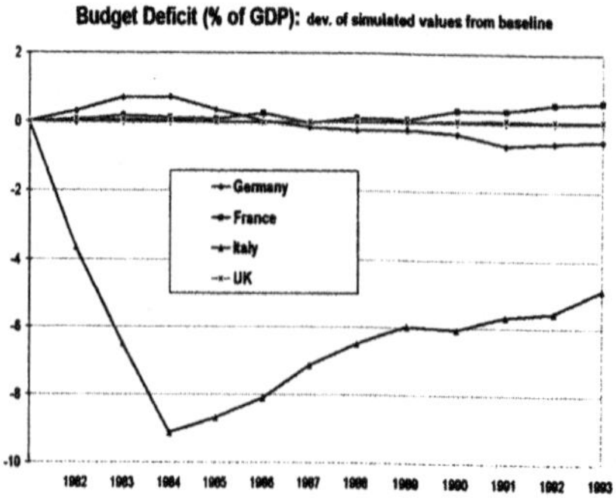

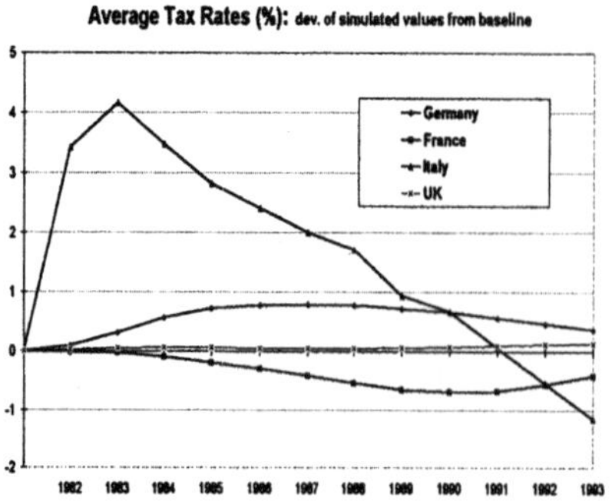

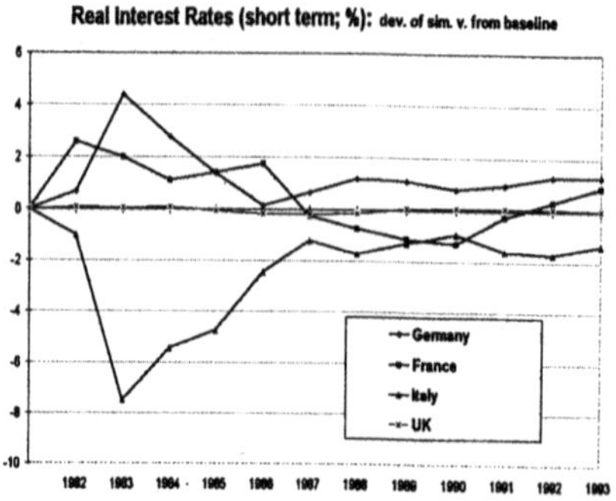

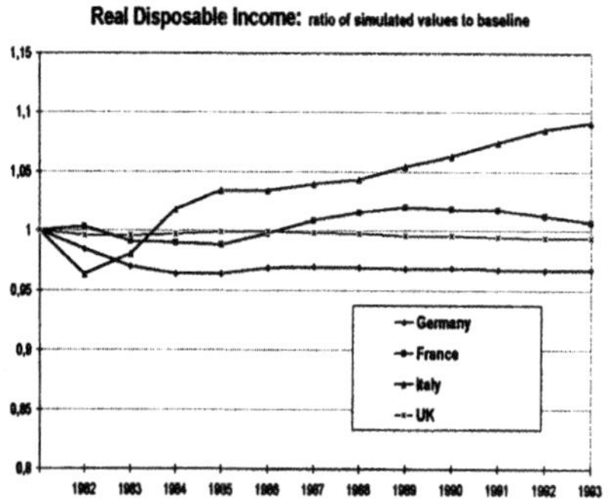

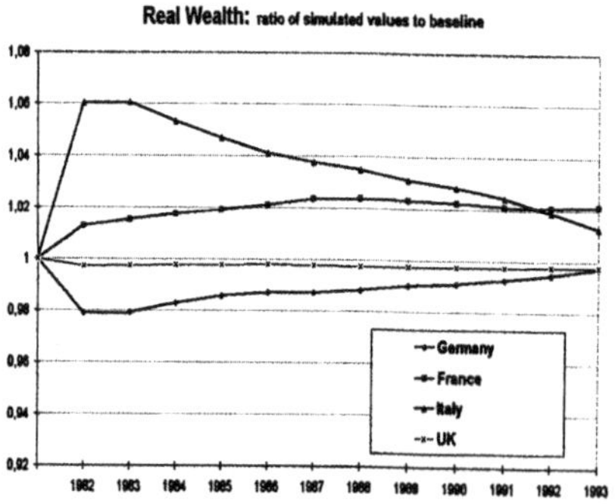

B.9 Lax Fiscal-CUR

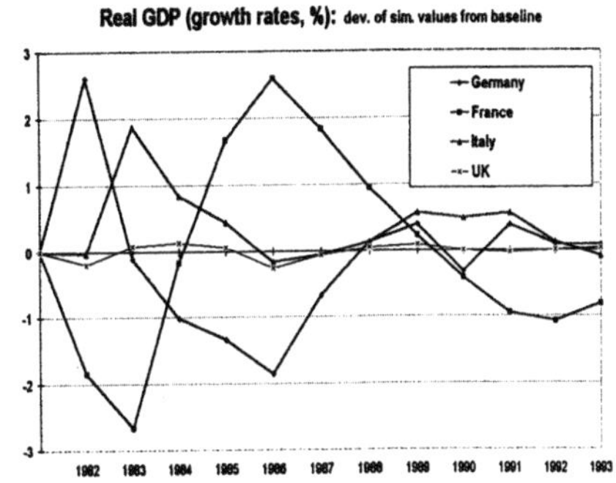

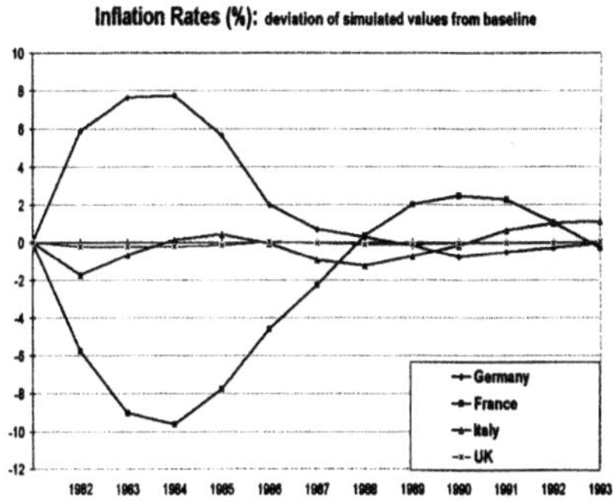

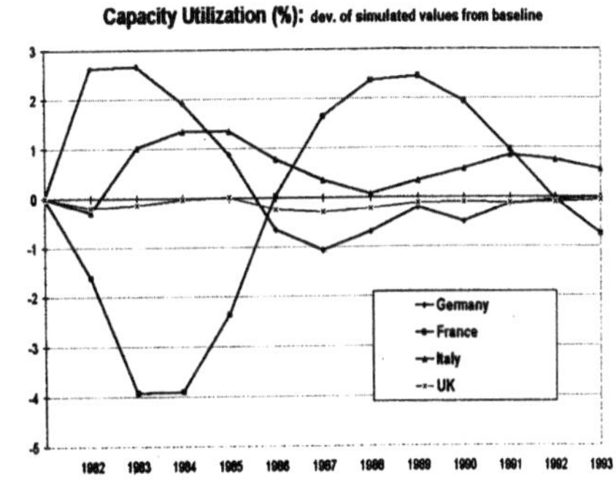

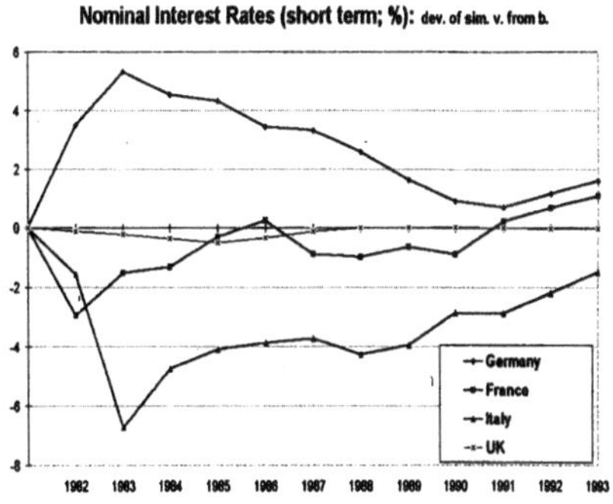

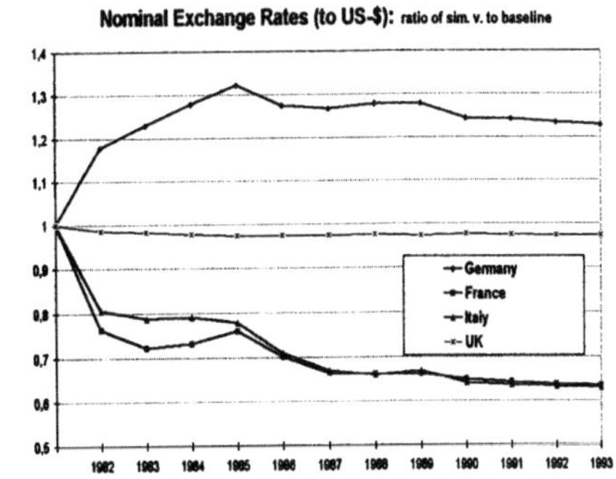

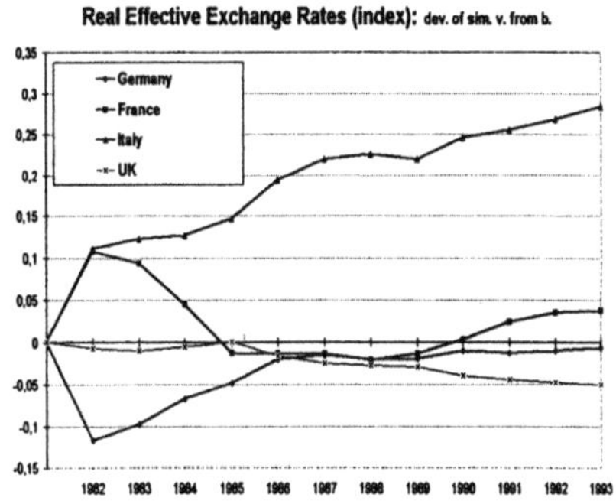

Lax Fiscal-CUR – page 2

Debt (% of GDP): deviation of simulated values from baseline

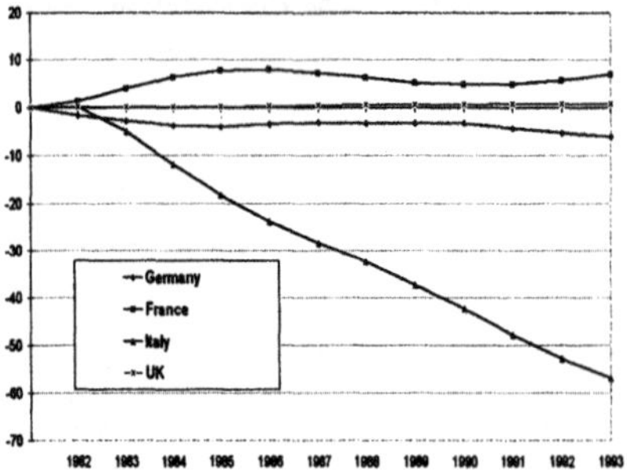

Budget Deficit (% of GDP): dev. of simulated values from baseline

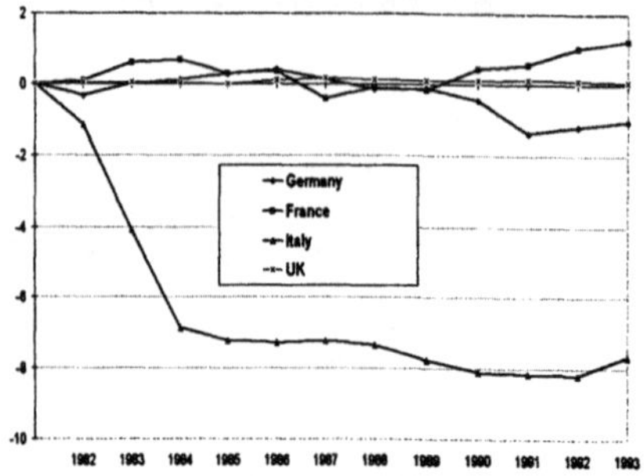

Average Tax Rates (%): dev. of simulated values from baseline

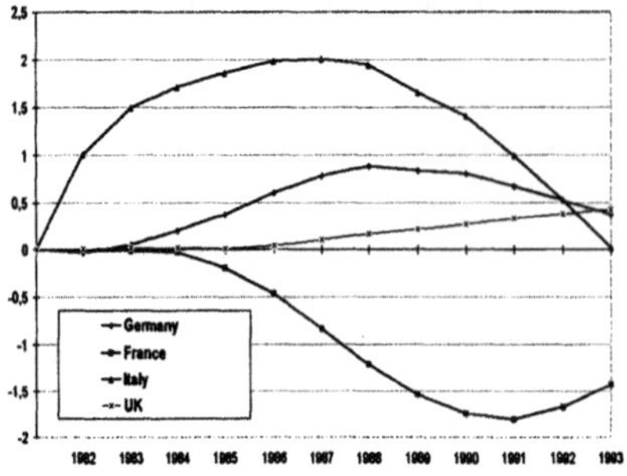

Real Interest Rates (short term; %): dev. of sim. v. from baseline

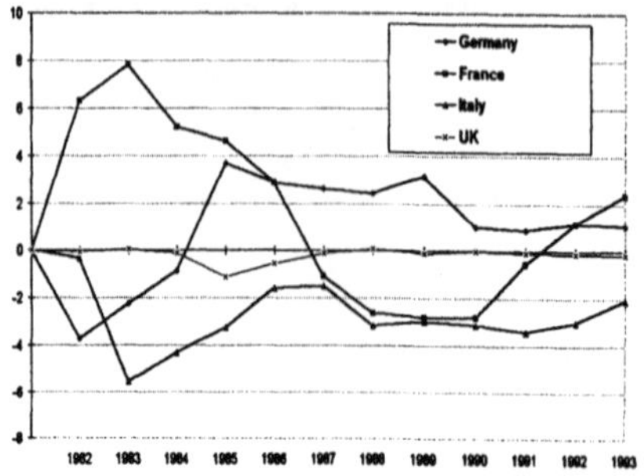

Real Disposable Income: ratio of simulated values to baseline

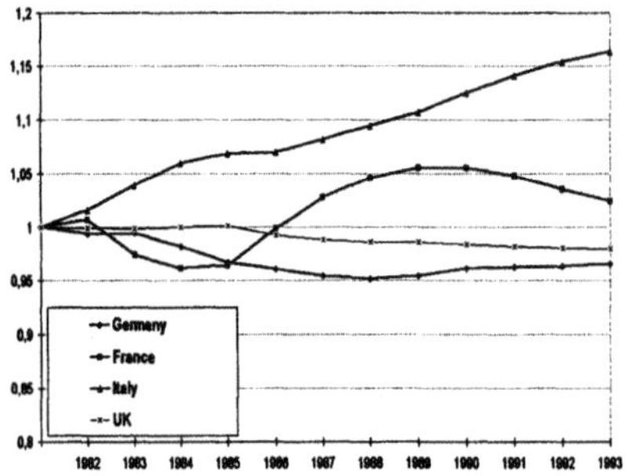

Real Wealth: ratio of simulated values to baseline

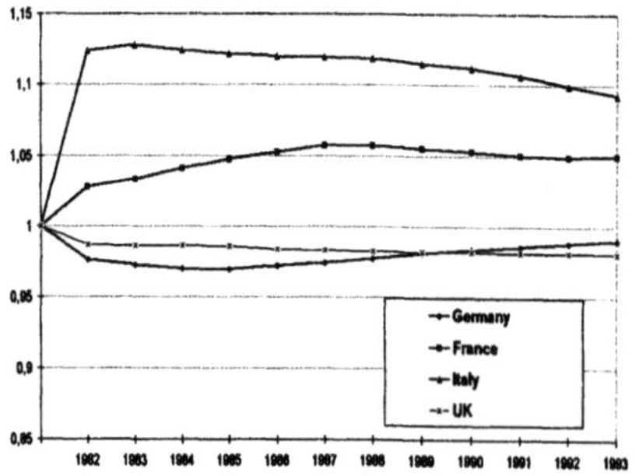

List of Observations

Observations are used to summarize findings of the analysis, mainly simulation results.

List of Boxes

Boxes contain tables, graphs of simulation results, or other figures.

In part III:

Overview: Simulation Exercises and Scenarios

I. The Baseline:

historical benchmark [results in appendix B.1]

II. Hypothetical EMU:

three procedures for fixing intra-EMU conversion rates

CUR (CURrent; model-consistent market rates) [B.2]

CP (Central Parities of the ERM) [B.3]

PPP (Purchasing Power Parity rates) [B.4]

III. Fiscal-Baseline:

fiscal consolidation program in Italy

lax fiscal-baseline (lax on debt & deficit reduction) [B.5]

moderate fiscal-baseline (intermediate on debt & deficit)

strict fiscal-baseline (strong on debt & deficit) [B.6]

mixed fiscal-baseline (lax on debt and strong on deficit)

IV. Fiscal-EMU:

hypothetical EMU and fiscal consolidation program in Italy

lax fiscal-CP [results in appendix B.7]

moderate fiscal-CP

strict fiscal-CP [results in appendix B.8]

mixed fiscal-CP

lax fiscal-CUR [results in appendix B.9]

V. Variations on II (Sensitivity Analyses, cf. section 4):

1. Announcement Period: none or with EMS in place;
2. Monetary Target: growth rates and smoothing over time;
3. Wage Setting: Europ. inflation matters only or partly;
4. Aggregate Exchange Rate Residuals:
   reduced by 10, 20, 30 %;
5. Aggregate Interest Rate Residuals:
   median versus weighted average;
6. Technical Solution Parameters: numerous experiments.

References

[**Alesina**] A. and R. Perotti (1995a): "Fiscal Adjustment: Fiscal Expansions and Adjustments in OECD Countries", *Economic Policy* 21, pp. 207-240;

[**Alesina**] A. and R. Perotti (1995b): "Taxation and Redistribution in an Open Economy", *European Economic Review* 39, pp. 961-979;

[**Allen**] Polly Reynolds, and Peter B. Kenen (1980): *Asset markets, exchange rates, and economic integration – A synopsis* (Cambridge University Press: 1981);

[**Aoki**] Masanao (1981): *Dynamic Analysis of Open Economies* (Academic Press: New York, 1981);

[**Barro**] Robert J. (1974): "Are Government Bonds Net Wealth", *Journal of Political Economy* 82, pp. 1095-1117;

[**Becker**] Otwin (1995): "Wirtschaftswissenschaftliche Systemsimulation", lecture notes (Heidelberg, winter term 1995);

[**Bernheim**] Douglas (1987): "Ricardian Equivalence: an evaluation of theory and evidence", *NBER Macroeconomics Annals* 2, pp. 263-304;

[**Blanchard**] Olivier J. (1985): "Debt, Deficit, and Finite Horizons", *Journal of Political Economy* 93, pp. 223-247;

[**Bohn**] Frank (1997): "Macroeconomic Effects of EMU", in: Christian Hipp, et. al. (eds.): *Geld, Finanzwirtschaft, Banken und Versicherungen 1996* (vvw: Karlsruhe, 1997);

[Bohn] Frank (1998a): "Why Interest Differentials, Monetary Stability, and Conversion Rates Matter – Simulations of the European Monetary Union", *Discussion Paper Series* No. 268 (Department of Economics, Heidelberg University);

[Bohn] Frank (1998b): "Monetary Union and the Interest-Exchange Trade-off", *EIIW Discussion Paper* 49 (Potsdam University);

[Browne] F. X., G. Fagan, and J. Henry (1997): "Money Demand in EU Countries: A Survey", *EMI Staff Paper* 7;

[Bryant] Ralph C., Peter Hooper, and Catherine L. Mann (1993) (eds.): *Evaluating Policy Regimes - New Research in Empirical Macroeconomics* (The Brookings Institution: Washington, 1993);

[Bryant] Ralph C., Catherine L. Mann, and Peter Hooper (1993): "Stochastic Simulations with Simple Policy Regimes", in: Bryant, Ralph C., Peter Hooper, and Catherine L. Mann (1993) (eds.): *Evaluating Policy Regimes - New Research in Empirical Macroeconomics* (The Brookings Institution: Washington, 1993), pp. 373-415;

[Buchanan] James M. (1976): "Barro on the Ricardian Equivalence Theorem", *Journal of Political Economy* 84, pp. 337-342;

[Burda] Michael C., Christoph M. Schmidt, and Heinz-Peter Galler (1997): "Getting Behind the East-West Wage Differential: Theory and Evidence", in: Rüdiger Pohl, and Hilmar Schneider (eds.): *Wandeln oder Weichen – Herausforderungen der wirtschaftlichen Integration in Deutschland* (Institut für Wirtschaftsforschung Halle) Sonderheft 3/1997, pp. 170-201;

[Cassard] Marcel, Timothy Lane, and Paul R. Masson (1994): "ERM Money Supplies and the Transition to EMU", in: *France: financial and real sector issues* (IMF: Washington, 1995), pp. 112-145;

[Clarida] Richard, Jordi Galí, and Mark Gertler (1998): "Monetary policy rules in practice – Some international evidence", *European Economic Review* 42, pp. 1033-1067;

[Clausen] Volker (1998): "Problems in the Transition to European Monetary Union", *Kredit und Kapital* 31:4, pp. 471-493;

[Davies] Simon, and Edward Luce (1997): "UK gilts join convergence bandwagon", *Financial Times*, 29 September 1997;

[Deutsche Bundesbank] (1995): *Die Geldpolitik der Bundesbank* (Frankfurt, 1995);

[Deutsche Bundesbank] (1997): "Strategy of Monetary Targeting", *Monthly Report* January 1997, pp. 17-25;

[Domar] Evsey D. (1944): "The 'Burden of Debt' and the National Income", *American Economic Review* 34, pp. 798 - 827;

[The Economist] (1998a): "EMU – An Awfully Big Adventure", 11 April 1998, pp. 3-5;

[The Economist] (1998b): "Ireland – Interesting dilemma", 14 November 1998, pp. 40-41;

[European Commission] (1990): "One Market, One Money", *European Economy* 42;

[European Union] (EU, 1992): *Vertrag über die Europäische Union* (Luxembourg, 1992);

[European Union] (EU, 1998): *Gemeinsames Kommuniqué zur Festlegung der unwiderruflichen Umrechnungskurse für den Euro* (Brussels, 1998);

[Fagan] G., and J. Henry (1997): "Long Run Money Demand in the EU: Evidence for Area-wide Aggregates" (mimeo, presented at the Econometric Society European Meeting 1997);

[Fair] Ray C. (1984): *Specification, Estimation, and Analysis of Macroeconomic Models* (Harvard University Press: Cambridge, 1984);

[Fair] Ray C. (1994): *Testing Macroeconomic Models* (Harvard University Press: Cambridge, 1994);

[Fair] Ray C., and John B. Taylor (1983): "Solution and maximum likelihood estimation of dynamic nonlinear rational expectations models", *Econometrica* 51, pp. 1169-1186;

[Falk] Martin, and Norbert Funke (1995): "The Stability of Money Demand in Germany and in the EMS: Impact of German Unification", *Weltwirtschaftliches Archiv* 131, pp. 470-488;

[Feuerstein] Switgard, and Jürgen Siebke (1990): "Wechselkursunion und Stabilitätspolitik", *Zeitschrift für Wirtschafts- und Sozialwissenschaften* 110:3, pp. 359-379;

[Fisher] Paul (1990): "SLIM – Reference Manual for version 8.1" (ERSC, Warwick University: mimeo);

[Fisher] P.G. and A.J. Hughes Hallett (1988): "Efficient solution techniques for linear and non-linear rational expectations models", *Journal of Economic Dynamics and Control* 12, pp. 635-657;

[Frankel] Jeffrey A. (1989): "Quantifying International Capital Mobility in the 1980s", *NBER Working Paper* 2856;

[Frankfurter Allgemeine Zeitung] (FAZ, 1996): "Brüssel akzeptiert Waigels Stabilitätspakt", 13 June 1996;

[Frenkel] Jacob A., Morris Goldstein, and Paul R. Masson (1989): "Simulating the Effects of Some Simple Coordinated Versus Uncoordinated Policy Rules", in: Bryant, Ralph C., et al.: *Macroeconomic Policies in an Interdependent World* (The Brookings Institution: Washington, 1989), pp. 203-239;

[Gardner] Edward H., and William R. M. Perraudin (1993): "Asymmetry in the ERM - A Case Study of French and German Interest Rates Before and After German Unification", *IMF Staff Papers* 40:2, pp. 427-450;

[Gemeinschaftsgutachten] der Wirtschaftsforschungsinstitute (1998): *Wirtschaftslage in Mittel- und Osteuropa* (DIW: Berlin, 1998);

[de Grauwe] Paul (1997): "The indeterminacy of the euro conversion rates. Why it matters and how it can be solved", *CEPR Discussion Paper* 1677;

[de Grauwe] Paul, Hans Dewachter, and Dirk Veestraeten (1998): "Stochastic Process Switching and Stage III of EMU", *CEPR Discussion Paper* 1783;

[von Hagen] Jürgen, Stefan Lutz (1996): "Fiscal and Monetary Policy on the Way to EMU", *Open Economies Review* 7, pp. 299-325;

[Hahn] Frank (1994): "An Intellectual Retrospect", *Banca Nazionale Del Lavoro Quarterly Review* September 1994, pp. 245-258;

[Hayo] Bernd (1997): "Estimating a European Demand for Narrow Money", *Volkswirtschaftliche Diskussionsbeiträge* Nr. 78 (Universität Bamberg);

[Helliwell] John F., Guy Meredith, Yves Durand, and Philip Bagnoli (1990): "Intermod 1.1 - A G7 version of the IMF's MULTIMOD", *Economic Modelling* January 1990, pp. 3-62;

[Henry] Jérôme, and Jens Weidmann (1995): "German Unification and Asymmetry in the ERM - Comment on Gardner and Perraudin", *Staff Studies* 42:4, pp. 894-903;

[Hill] Peter (1986): "International Price Levels and Purchasing Power Parities", *OECD Economic Studies* 6, pp. 133-159;

[Hughes Hallett] Andrew J. (1986): "International Policy Design and the Sustainability of Policy Bargains", *Journal of Economic Dynamics and Control* 10, pp. 467-494;

[Hughes Hallett] Andrew J., and Peter McAdam (1998a): "Fiscal Deficit Reductions in Line With the Maastricht Criteria for Monetary Union: .an Empirical Analysis", in: J. Frieder, D. Gros, E. Jones (eds.): *Towards European Monetary Union: Problems and Prospects* (Cambridge University Press: 1997);

[Hughes Hallett] Andrew J., and Peter McAdam (1998b): "Implications of the Growth and Stability Pact: Why the Growth Element is Important", in: A. J. Hughes Hallett, M. Hutchison, and S. E. H. Jensen (eds.): *Fiscal Aspects of European Monetary Union* (Cambridge University Press: 1998);

[Hughes Hallett] Andrew J., and Yue Ma (1994): "Real adjustments in a union of incompletely converged economies:

An example from East and West Germany", *European Economic Review* 38, pp. 1731-1761;

[Hughes Hallett] Andrew J., and Yue Ma (1996): "The Dynamics of Debt Deflation in a Monetary Union", *Journal of Comparative and International Economics* 5:1, pp. 1-29;

[Hughes Hallett] Andrew J., Yue Ma, and Y. P. Yin (1996): "Hybrid Algorithms with Automatic Switching for Solving Nonlinear Equation Systems", *Journal of Economic Dynamics and Control* 20 (6-7), pp. 1051-1071;

[Hughes Hallett] Andrew J., and David Vines (1993): "On The Possible Costs of European Monetary Union", *The Manchester School* LXI: 1, pp. 35-64;

[International Monetary Fund] (IMF, 1990a): *International Financial Statistics* (IMF: Washington, 1990);

[International Monetary Fund] (IMF, 1990b): *World Economic Outlook* December 1990 (IMF: Washington, 1990);

[International Monetary Fund] (IMF, 1991): "Changes to MULTIMOD Since the July 1990 Occasional Paper #71 - Current Model: MULTIAP" (IMF: mimeo);

[International Monetary Fund] (IMF, 1997): *World Economic Outlook* May 1997 (IMF: Washington, 1997);

[International Monetary Fund] (IMF, 1998): *World Economic Outlook* May 1998 (IMF: Washington, 1998);

[Juillard] Michel and Douglas Laxton (1996): "A Robust and Efficient Method for Solving Nonlinear Rational Expectations Models", *IMF Working Paper* 96/106 (IMF: Washington, 1996);

[Kenen] Peter B. (1995): *Economic and monetary union in Europe – Moving beyond Maastricht* (Cambridge University Press: 1995);

[Kreps] David M. (1997): "Economics: The Current Position", *Daedalus* Winter 1997, pp. 59-85;

[Lech] Hagen (1993): "Konvergenzkriterien einer Europäischen Währungsunion: Zur Logik der Bestimmung von Maastricht", *Schriftenreihe* Nr. 317 (Institut Finanzen und Steuern: Bonn, 1993);

[Lucas] Robert G., Jr. (1976): "Econometric Policy Evaluation - A Critique", *Journal of Monetary Economics* (Supplement) 1, pp. 16-46;

[Malinvaud] Edmond (1981): "Econometrics Faced with the Needs of Macroeconomic Policy", *Econometrica* 49:6, pp. 1363-1375;

[Masson] Paul R., and Jacques Melitz (1991): "Fiscal Policy Independence in a European Monetary Union", *Open Economies Review* 2, 1991, pp. 113-136;

[Masson] Paul R., and Steven Symansky (1992): "Evaluating the EMS and EMU using stochastic simulations: some issues", in: Barrell, Ray, and John Whitley: *Macroeconomic Policy Coordination in Europe* (London, 1992), pp. 12-34;

[Masson] Paul R., and Steven Symansky (1993): "Evaluating Policy Regimes under Imperfect Credibility", in: Bryant, Ralph C., Peter Hooper, and Catherine L. Mann (1993) (eds.): *Evaluating Policy Regimes - New Research in Empirical Macroeconomics* (The Brookings Institution: Washington, 1993), pp. 461-475;

[Masson] Paul R., Steven Symansky, Richard Haas, and Michael Dooley (1988): "MULTIMOD - A Multi-Region Econometric Model", in: *Staff Studies for the World Economic Outlook* (IMF: Washington, 1988), pp. 50-104;

[Masson] Paul R., Steven Symansky, and Guy Meredith (1990): "MULTIMOD Mark II: A Rivised and Extended Model", *IMF Occasional Paper* 71 (IMF: Washington, July 1990);

[Mitchell] Peter R., Joanne E. Sault, Peter N. Smith, and Kenneth F. Wallis (1995): "Comparing Global Economic Models", *ESRC Working Paper Series* 7;

[Obstfeld] Maurice (1998): "A strategy for launching the Euro", *European Economic Review* 42, pp. 975-1007;

[OECD] (1983): *Main Economic Indicators* (Paris, July 1983);

[OECD] (1993): *Main Economic Indicators* (Paris, July 1993);

[OECD] (1998a): *Main Economic Indicators* (Paris, April 1998);

[OECD] (1998b): *Main Economic Indicators* (Paris, October 1998);

[Öesterreichische Nationalbank] (ÖNB, 1995): *Kompendium von Texten zur Wirtschafts- und Währungunion* (Vienna, 1995);

[Oldag] Andreas (1998): "Athen kauft das Ticket für's EWS", *Süddeutsche Zeitung*, 17 March 1998;

[Powell] Alan A., and Christopher W. Murphy (1997): *Inside a Modern Macroeconomic Model* (Springer: Heidelberg, 1997);

[**McRae**] Hamish (1998): "Some parts of Europe will be stuck with the wrong interest rates", *The Independent*, 17 March 1998;

[**Rother**] Philipp C. (1997): *Geldnachfragetheoretische Implikationen der Europäischen Währungsunion*, Wirtschaftswissenschaftliche Beiträge 142 (Physica: Heidelberg, 1997);

[**Schulz**] Bettina (1997): "Spekulationen über englischen Beitritt bewegen die Märkte", *Frankfurter Allgemeine Zeitung*, 29 September 1997;

[**Siebke**] Jürgen (1993): "Implications of European Monetary Union for Fiscal Policy", in: *European Monetary Union: Legal Foundations and Economic Implications* (Institut Universitaire International: Luxemburg, 1993), pp. 151-161;

[**Sinn**] Hans-Werner, and Holger Feist (1998): "Eurowinners and Eurolosers: The distribution of seigniorage wealth in EMU", *European Journal of Political Economy* 13, pp. 665-689;

[**Tanzi**] Vito, and Howell H. Zee (1997): "Fiscal Policy and Long Run Growth", *IMF Staff Papers* 44:2, pp. 179-209;

[**Taylor**] John B. (1993a): *Macroeconomic policy in a world economy: From econometric design to practical operation* (Norton: New York, London, 1993);

[**Taylor**] John B. (1993b): "Discretion Versus Policy Rules in Practice", *Carnegie-Rochester Conference Series on Public Policy* 39, pp. 195-214;

[**Tobin**] James (1969): "The Equilibrium Approach to Monetary Theory", *Journal of Money, Credit, and Banking* 1, pp. 15-29;

[Turnovsky] Stephen J. (1995): *Methods of Macroeconomic Dynamics* (MIT Press: Cambridge, 1995);

[Wallis] Kenneth F. (1988): "Empirical Models and Macroeconomic Policy Analysis", in: Bryant, Ralph, D. W. Henderson, G. Holtham, P. Hooper, and S. A. Symansky (eds.): *Empirical Macroeconomics for Interdependent Economies* (The Brookings Institution: Washington, 1988), pp. 225-237;

[Weidmann] Jens (1996): "The Likelihood of European Monetary Union", *Banca Nazionale Del Lavoro Quarterly Review* 49:199, pp. 405-413;

[Welfens] Paul J. J. (1998): "In der EWWU gibt es nur noch einen Konjunkturzyklus", *Handelsblatt*, 14 April 1998;

[Wesche] Katrin (1998): *Die Geldnachfrage in Europa – Aggregationsprobleme und Empirie*, Wirtschaftswissenschaftliche Beiträge 154 (Physica: Heidelberg, 1998);

[Wyplosz] Charles (1997): "How and Why it Might Happen", *Journal of Economic Perspectives* 11:4, pp. 3-22;

[Zurlinden] Mathias (1992): "Stabilitätspolitik in einem Mehrländermodell: Simulationsergebnisse für die Schweiz", *Geld, Währung und Konjunktur, Quartalsheft der Schweizerischen Nationalbank* 3/1992, pp. 269-288.

Contributions to Economics

Sabine Spangenberg
The Institutionalised Transformation of the East German Economy
1998. ISBN 3-7908-1103-3

Hagen Bobzin
Indivisibilities
1998. ISBN 3-7908-1123-8

Helmut Wagner (Ed.)
Current Issues in Monetary Economics
1998. ISBN 3-7908-1127-0

Peter Michaelis/Frank Stähler (Eds.)
Recent Policy Issues in Environmental and Resource Economics
1998. ISBN 3-7908-1137-8

Jessica de Wolff
The Political Economy of Fiscal Decisions
1998. ISBN 3-7908-1130-0

Georg Bol/Gholamreza Nakhaeizadeh/ Karl-Heinz Vollmer (Eds.)
Risk Measurements, Econometrics and Neural Networks
1998. ISBN 3-7908-1152-1

Joachim Winter
Investment and Exit Decisions at the Plant Level
1998. ISBN 3-7908-1154-8

Bernd Meyer
Intertemporal Asset Pricing
1999. ISBN 3-7908-1159-9

Uwe Walz
Dynamics of Regional Integration
1999. ISBN 3-7908-1185-8

Michael Carlberg
European Monetary Union
1999. ISBN 3-7908-1191-2

Giovanni Galizzi/ Luciano Venturini (Eds.)
Vertical Relationships and Coordination in the Food System
1999. ISBN 3-7908-1192-0

Gustav A. Horn/Wolfgang Scheremet/ Rudolf Zwiener
Wages and the Euro
1999. ISBN 3-7908-1199-8

Dirk Willer
The Development of Equity Capital Markets in Transition Economies
1999. ISBN 3-7908-1198-X

Karl Matthias Weber
Innovation Diffusion and Political Control of Energy Technologies
1999. ISBN 3-7908-1205-6

Heike Link et al.
The Costs of Road Infrastructure and Congestion in Europe
1999. ISBN 3-7908-1201-3

Simon Duindam
Military Conscription
1999. ISBN 3-7908-1203-X

Bruno Jeitziner
Political Economy of the Swiss National Bank
1999. ISBN 3-7908-1209-9

Irene Ring et al. (Eds.)
Regional Sustainability
1999. ISBN 3-7908-1233-1

Katharina Müller/Andreas Ryll/ Hans-Jürgen Wagener (Eds.)
Transformation of Social Security: Pensions in Central-Eastern Europe
1999. ISBN 3-7908-1210-2

Stefan Traub
Framing Effects in Taxation
1999. ISBN 3-7908-1240-4

Pablo Coto-Millán
Utility and Production
1999. 3-7908-1153-X

Frank Riedel
Imperfect Information and Investor Heterogeneity in the Bond Market
2000. ISBN 3-7908-1247-1

Kirsten Ralf
Business Cycles
2000. ISBN 3-7908-1245-5

Michele Bagella/Leonardo Becchetti (Eds.)
The Competitive Advantage of Industrial Districts
2000. ISBN 3-7908-1254-4

GPSR Compliance

The European Union's (EU) General Product Safety Regulation (GPSR) is a set of rules that requires consumer products to be safe and our obligations to ensure this.

If you have any concerns about our products, you can contact us on ProductSafety@springernature.com

In case Publisher is established outside the EU, the EU authorized representative is:

Springer Nature Customer Service Center GmbH
Europaplatz 3
69115 Heidelberg, Germany

Batch number: 10725973

Printed by Printforce, the Netherlands